SEER

30 Years of Remote Viewing
...and counting

1983-2013

Angela Thompson Smith PhD.

First Edition: 2016
Second Edition: 2019

ISBN: 9781095787878

PREFACE

"Remote viewing; that 'mind stuff' that was developed for the military," was all debunked years, ago right? Nobody in their right mind would even give it a second look. *"It's all nonsense,"* say the skeptics! *"It's the work of the devil, designed to lead good people away from God,"* chime in the churches! Scientists claim, remote viewing is "not scientific," and there's not "a shred of evidence" or any theories to support it! I've heard all the objections and more! Now put aside your beliefs and skepticism and imagine that all this is real!

Just what is remote viewing or, as it is generally termed, RV? Remote viewing is the trained ability of individuals to perceive other people's activities and locations, objects and events, using something other than the usual five senses. It is a normal human ability that has helped many people in difficult times, particularly during crises. It has humanitarian uses in finding missing people, solving crimes and locating lost or hidden items. Remote viewing has been used by businessmen to buy, run and sell companies, has assisted realtors in locating and selling properties and helped thousands of people to resolve problems.

Did you know that over forty plus years of professional research and development have gone into remote viewing? And that the US government and military have funded and operated remote viewing units for over twenty years? Or that educational groups such as Stanford Research Institute and Princeton University studied RV for over three decades? And did you know of the dozens of remote viewing schools around the US and abroad that have trained thousands of students? Remote Viewing is alive and kicking!

INTRODUCTION

Even before I moved to the States from England in 1981, I knew about remote viewing and the work of researchers Dr. Hal Puthoff and Russell Targ at Stanford Research Institute (SRI) International in Palo Alto, CA. From the late summer of 1978, to the beginning of 1981, I was working as a medical researcher and completing my Master's degree at the Department of Child Health of Manchester University's Medical School, in England. Part of my work involved searching scientific literature sources for interesting neuroscience articles. That was where I came across Puthoff and Targ's classic work, '*A Perceptual Channel for Information Transfer over Kilometer Distances: Historical Perspective and Recent Research.*' The paper was published in the prestigious, *Proceedings of the IEEE*, March 1976. I was more than interested and mailed off to the States for a reprint. Little did I realize where my life would take me in the next 30 plus years and that I would become part of the intriguing world of remote viewing.

My path to becoming a remote viewer began officially when I started volunteering at the Psychophysical Research Laboratory (PRL), a parapsychology laboratory in Princeton, NJ. I was a Spontaneous Remote Viewer, using my natural intuitive skills. Later I volunteered and then worked at the Princeton Engineering Anomalies Research (PEAR) Laboratory at Princeton University, NJ. At Princeton I was familiar with a research methodology called Remote Perception and, later, Extended Remote Viewing (ERV), a stream-of-consciousness method of remote viewing. Many years later, I was trained by two ex-military "Star Gate" remote viewers: Paul H. Smith of RVIS and Lyn Buchanan of PSI, in a method called Controlled Remote Viewing (CRV).

Eventually, in 1994, I set up my own company to carry out remote viewing consulting and to train other remote viewers. Most of my early remote viewing work was unpaid and performed on a humanitarian basis. Later, I was paid by multiple clients for my remote viewing work. The projects in this book range from "blind" (no up-front information) to, partially "front-loaded" (some non-leading up-front operational information), to fully informed. In my opinion all these conditions provide valid RV data when looking for unknown or new information.

After thirty plus years of remote viewing, I have decided to share many of the projects that I have worked on over the decades. Some of the later projects included a team of voluntary, trained and natural remote viewers: The Nevada Remote Viewing Group (NRVG). The members of the NRVG consist of viewers from across the World who are called on as needed and when time and their schedules allow.

Some projects I still cannot talk about due to confidentiality and signed agreements. I was tempted to recount many of my early adventures with OBEs and paranormal experiences, but they can be read about in my book, *'Remote Perceptions: Out-of-Body Experiences, Remote Viewing and other Normal Experiences.'*

The following journal entries and actual cases are taken from my records: journals that span over 30 years. I have limited the content to focus on remote viewing and other consciousness development and excluded material describing my UFO interests and shamanic training and applications. Also not included in this book are the hundreds of smaller projects carried out for private individuals. I have taken out any personal information that might create awkwardness to any individual; it is not my intent to dishonor anyone but to truthfully relate the journey.

Hopefully, these accounts of real-life remote viewing projects and stories will inspire and encourage others to take training and become involved in the exciting world of remote viewing.

Note: The following case entries are taken from my ongoing journals and files. I am not a daily journal writer so the dates on the entries are sometimes days, weeks or even months apart, and sometimes there are several entries for the same date, but they give some idea of what a remote viewer's life is like. The first few years of this document are reviews rather than single journal entries. Also, I have been selective and only included journal entries that have some relevance to remote viewing. Similarly, with the case files, these have been selected from my records as being instructive, useful and interesting. I have not included confidential projects that I have carried out for business clients/customers or groups where I have signed nondisclosures.

Reviews – 1983-1984.

The American Society for Psychical Research (ASPR).

In 1983, I missed an important opportunity to work with Dr. Karlis Osis at the American Society for Psychical Research (ASPR) in New York. Interesting people in the RV world, such as Ingo Swann, had participated in research with Dr. Osis and his staff at the ASPR. In 1983, I had written to Dr. Osis to inquire about their Out-Of-Body-Experience (OBE) research and was invited by to visit the Institute. Unfortunately, at that time, I could not afford the time-off from my job, to take a day or two to visit New York. Who knows, perhaps I would have met Ingo Swann, the "Father of Remote Viewing," and other notables in the OBE and remote viewing world?

Sometimes, when we cannot take a path at a certain time, the path meets up with us again, and I eventually got to meet Ingo Swann and visit the ASPR. Ingo wrote the foreword to my earlier book 'Remote Perceptions,' and I was able to visit with him, many times, when I was in Manhattan, NY.

Each time I visited, Ingo would bring out examples of materials from his students: unclassified remote viewing sessions, clay models, plans, graphs and sketches, and talked at length about his philosophies and ideas. I consider myself fortunate to have received an informal training from Ingo. In 2008, Ingo asked me to carry out a remote viewing session for him. I cannot reveal any personal information, but I

9

did warn him of the coming financial recession that would get worse towards the end of the year. Ingo passed away in 2013 and is sadly missed.

Ingo and RV Trainers: Prudence Calabrese (L) and Angela T. Smith (R).

Somewhere to live.

In the early-1980s, after working my way through years of support jobs; I had finally landed a professional position in medical research. It had taken me four years to get back to the position I had been in when I left England and the job was almost identical. At Manchester University I had conducted research with mothers and babies at St. Mary's Hospital studying infant neurological development and working towards my Master's degree. Now at the University of Medicine and Dentistry of New Jersey (UMDNJ), affiliated with Rutgers University, I would be conducting research at St. Peter's Hospital in New Brunswick, NJ. Once again, I would be part of a team studying the development of neurological behaviors in newborn infants. I was thrilled that I would once again be working in an academic environment, doing work that I knew I could do well.

There was, however, the problem of where I was going to live. I had heard that New Brunswick was a dangerous place to live but, then, I had lived and survived in East Orange, NJ! A few weeks before I was to begin my new job, I dragged a gentleman friend, Mason, down to New Brunswick. Mason was a close friend, a no-nonsense man of incredible intellect and education and someone I trusted to help me find

10

somewhere to live. At the station we bought local newspapers and found a nearby café to scan the apartments for rent. One on Easton Avenue caught my eye, the whole upstairs of a row house on the main street, very close to the hospital and research center.

To my delight I found the apartment very well-suited to what I wanted and within my price range. It was owned by two, aging, Spanish sisters who lived downstairs. My apartment would be upstairs, consisting of a large, sunny, front bedroom, a small living room, another small bedroom that could become an office, a huge light and airy kitchen at the back, and a small bathroom. There was even a private back staircase for the cat. Uh... the cat, that was where the problem began.

The sisters and I had got to the part about the amount of the rent and the deposit and I was preparing to give them the cash when I thought I had better mention my little white cat. The sisters immediately went into a huddle across the room and I heard whispers of, *"No gatitos, Si gatitos, No gatitos!"* I really wanted the apartment and thought it worth fighting for.

In my mind I began a silent, mental litany; *"The cat is fastidious, the cat is very, very quiet, you won't even see the cat, it is very clean and very quiet, the cat will be no bother."* Then, to Mason's and my surprise the sisters turned and with big smiles said "Si, it would be quite OK if I kept the cat in the apartment!" We exchanged money, signed papers, and arranged a move-in date.

Outside, Mason looked at me and asked, *"What just happened in there?"* What was I to say, that I had changed the sisters' minds about the cat? He wouldn't have believed me. And what about the ethics of such a thing? I had used mental influence before, in East Orange, to keep me safe as I walked to work in dangerous neighborhoods. Now, I needed a safe place to live and this justified my action. Remote influence (RI) is a real ability that anyone can develop but needs to be used with wisdom and justification.

"Fetch!"

After I had moved to Easton Avenue in New Brunswick and started my new position as a medical analyst at UMDNJ, my friend Mason and I began exploring the neighborhood. One of our favorite places to stroll was the Buccleuch Mansion Museum Park on Easton Avenue. The mansion was built by a wealthy Englishman for his bride Elizabeth Morris, it was known as White House Farm. His son, Anthony Walton White, went against family tradition and sided with the Revolutionaries, against the British. The house was later occupied during the Revolution by the British, and still shows saber and musket marks on its floors and banisters.

One day while we were walking along the pathways, ahead of us appeared a large tan dog, a German-Shepherd mix. It ran towards us, snarling and barking with obvious aggression. Mason caught my arm and seemed ready to defend me. I made a quick decision to make mental contact with the dog and perceived that it was attacking out of fear: it didn't know us and perceived us as strangers. I realized that he was still a puppy despite his large size, and I decided to invite him to play. I bent down and picked up a couple of short sticks from the path and called out to the dog "Do you want to play? Look, I've got some sticks. Want to play? Fetch!" and I threw one of the sticks beyond the threatening dog. It turned and raced after the stick, bringing it back with tail wagging and, I swear, a smile on its face! Mason was astonished! The dog accompanied us on our walk through the park, retrieving sticks, and even allowed me to pet him.

Animal communication is a debated topic. Scientists say that animal communication is just a reflection onto animals of our own thoughts, wishes and desires but parapsychologists, who have studied animal communication, say that there is a real case for animals who respond to human thoughts and intentions.

The Psychophysical Research Laboratory (PRL).

By the early-1980s, I had been working at the University of Medicine and Dentistry of New Jersey (UMDNJ) in New Brunswick, NJ with the Institute for Child Development for several years. At UMDNJ I was employed as a research analyst, part of the team studying behavioral development in premature infants. I was excited by my research work and yet, I felt I was neglecting metaphysical aspects of my life that had once been so important to me. In the spring of 1984, I read about the Psychophysical Research Laboratory (PRL), located at Princeton Junction, NJ, and learned that they were looking for volunteer subjects to take part in human consciousness experiments. Most of the participants who attended PRL were "first-timers," people who had never taken part in these types of experiments. I was intrigued and wrote to PRL, and they wrote back with reprints about their work.

Some of their previous research has shown that individuals who had prior meditation experience, who had previous Psi (intuitive) experiences, and fell into the ENFP (extraverted, intuitive, feeling, and perceiving) MBTI personality rating, were more likely to do well in human consciousness experiments. I was fortunate to fall into those categories and be accepted into the research.

At the PRL Lab participants were briefed and then placed in a sensory-shielded environment called the Ganzfeld (it was affectionately called "The Meat Locker") where they attempted to mentally pick up information that was being sent to them telepathically from a research participant who was watching a video in another shielded room. In the "Meat Locker" the subject reclined in a lounger, listening to "pink noise" through a headset, with halved ping-pong balls taped over their eyes. The room was bathed in red light to create a homogenous field: the effect was intended to cut out visual and auditory distractions and allow the subject to attend to their inner perceptions.

On my days off, vacation days, and holidays I would catch the local train from New Brunswick, NJ to Princeton Junction. The Laboratory was situated in a modern, business park, surrounded by trees and lawns. I was surprised at the amount of space they had and learned that PRL was funded by a grant from the McDonnell Foundation. John McDonnell, one of the founders of the aerospace firm of McDonnell Douglas, had a long-time interest in metaphysics, and had established a fund to carry out consciousness research.

At PRL, I met the Director, Charles "Chuck" Honorton and his researchers, at that time, Marta Quant, and George Hansen, who taught me a lot about critical thinking and consciousness research. Chuck's later death, from a heart-attack, while he was studying for his Ph.D. at Edinburgh University, Scotland, created a great loss within the parapsychological community.

During the following year and a half, I participated in Ganzfeld sessions as well as taking part in psychokinesis (PK) computer games. PRL made available their extensive library and a computer. When I was not taking part in experiments, I was in the library, eagerly reading everything I could on parapsychology, consciousness, and their relationship to right and left-handedness (laterality).

CASE FILES- 1983-1985

The following case outlines an exploratory project I conducted in 1983. In the past, 'Intuitives' such as Ingo Swann, have attempted to remote view the planet Jupiter, and their perceptions have closely matched the actual, later findings.

The Jupiter Probes.
PROJECT: The Jupiter Probes.
METHOD: Extended Remote Viewing (ERV).
DATE: March 6th and April 3rd, 1983.

CLIENT: Independent/Solo.
TYPE: Exploration.

Many times, in my childhood and teens, I would mentally travel up above the earth to look down on the world using the Out-of-Body-Experience or OBE. It was a wonderful, awe-inspiring experience. In the spring of 1983, I decided to see how far I could go away from the earth. In March and April, I remotely viewed the planet Jupiter to see what I could perceive.

I had read that a NASA space probe called Galileo would evaluate the atmosphere of Jupiter in 1988. There, the probe would encounter intense heat and pressure up to twenty times that of earth and intense cold. Temperatures ranged between -243 to +145 degrees Fahrenheit. The probe would test air pressure, temperature, composition of the atmosphere, cloud density, net radiation and amounts of hydrogen and helium in the Jovian atmosphere. However, the Galileo probe was not launched until October 1989, and did not reach Jupiter until 1990.

So, in March and April of 1983, I decided to do my own view of Jupiter, record my observations and then, eventually, compare my observations with those of the Galileo probe. The viewing took place on two separate occasions between March 6th and April 3rd, 1983:

1. During the first attempt all I could perceive of Jupiter was a mauve-purple haze. Perhaps I didn't get close enough to the surface?

2. I went to the outer atmosphere of Earth and looked at the curve of the Earth, then went out to Jupiter. I went through the purple haze and landed, to my surprise, up to my neck in "water", which I hadn't expected. I looked around and saw a shore composed of quartz. At first, I thought that the shore was made of amethyst but realized that it was the clear quartz reflecting the purple atmosphere. I wondered why the water was not frozen or evaporated away with the extreme changes in temperature reported in the Science Digest. I looked at the "water," it was thick and oily, and I had the insight that it could change its molecular structure to avoid freezing or boiling. There was no sign of human-like life.

3. I decided to go somewhere else on Jupiter and arrived on top of a range of exquisitely beautiful quartz mountains. These were composed of the quartz-like crystal reflecting the purple

14

atmosphere. I tried to estimate their height. They were at least as tall as Mt. Snowdon in North Wales. Although the mountains were made of quartz, they were not transparent.

4. I descended to what I thought were fields of, very tall, purple grass only to find that the grass was again composed of quartz. I don't know if they were "growing." They bent and waved like fields of long grass, yet it was also like looking at a sea of sparkling waves. It was beautiful.

5. Leaving Jupiter, I came back to Earth and saw the west coastline of Europe very clearly. I traveled north to see the south coast of England and flew in close over the patchwork quilt of little fields. I flew east until I came to the United States and back to my own body.

Unfortunately, delays set the timetable back for Galileo to reach Jupiter and the probe only recently entered Jupiter's atmosphere, thirteen years after my initial remote viewing. Although all the data has not yet been analyzed, it is interesting that one of its findings is that Jupiter has more water in its atmosphere than originally estimated. It has also been suggested that there are mountains on Jupiter. The most interesting, recent, feedback has been regarding the "water."

Feedback: An online NASA article, 2015, revealed the existence of a form of "water," described as an "ocean." Atmospheric pressure and temperatures have compressed the Jovian atmosphere; mostly hydrogen and helium, into a liquid. This gives Jupiter the largest ocean in the solar system, an ocean made of hydrogen instead of water.

PRL- Laterality Project.
PROJECT: Handedness (Laterality).
METHOD: Research.
DATE: 1985.
CLIENT: PRL.
TYPE: Research.

After a few sessions at PRL, (where I was successful at perceiving information in the Ganzfeld experiments) I was invited to become a regular, volunteer participant and took time during my days off and holidays from UMDNJ to study in their library and even conducted a laterality pilot study.

15

"Chuck" Honorton set up the study where postcards were mailed to "first-timer" Ganzfeld participants inviting them to send details of their hand-preference (laterality). This data was correlated with their Ganzfeld results and some interesting results were found. Participants who rated themselves as strongly right-handed did about average on the Ganzfeld study, but, participants who did not consider themselves strongly right or left-handed (mixed handers) did remarkably well and their results were statistically significant.

That is, individuals who considered themselves mixed-handed or ambidextrous had more "hits" on the Ganzfeld than the right or left-handers. This led me to review what we know about mixed-handedness and how this relates to human consciousness. In the literature I found that PRL's research bore out some previous findings: mixed handers do better on tests studying intuition.

1986

JOURNALS

Following are extracts from my personal journals that share some of my experiences during the times I was preparing to work at PRL, while I was volunteering there and my move to work at the Princeton Engineering Anomalies Research (PEAR) Laboratory at Princeton University.

Journal: September 7, 1986 - *The Omega Factor.*
Since coming back from my vacation in England, I have been watching a series on New Jersey TV called, *The Omega Factor.* The series focuses on adventures of the paranormal by a psychic and other people involved in his discoveries. Apart from enjoying the series for its content, I have become aware that my basic knowledge of parapsychology is rather sketchy. So, I plan to do some serious study on the subject. (Later I was to learn about the parapsychology work being done at Edinburgh University and within the States. Years later I watched the DVD series again and recognized key researchers and their research!)

The two books, that I am planning to start my studies with, are from my own library entitled, *'Parapsychology and The Nature of Life'* by John L. Randall and *'Parapsychology and Extrasensory Perception'* by Raymond Van Over.

Randall's book first deals with the increase in the "development of those sciences which have contributed most directly to the mechanistic

16

theory of life" and then goes on to talk about the problems, failures and successes of parapsychology, followed by a third part that speculates about the future of parapsychology. (Not a very positive book to start with, but it's at least a start.)

Both books seem to state that there is a rift in Human Nature. Randall sees it between mechanism and humanism; Van Over sees it as between our animal and human aspects. It could be these schisms have biological counterpoints. Van Over's rift may be the lower and upper parts of the brain: our ancient and modern brain, while Randall's could relate to the left and right sides of the brain.

This week my good friend Mason brought over a book of poems by W. B. Yeats, 'Yeats Selected Poems.' As I read them, I felt as if I had read them before, long ago. Some of the poems touched my soul: The Lake at Innisfree; The White Birds; The Cat and the Moon, Crazy Jane on God; and A Meditation on Time of War. The last poem, I believe, was written by Yeats after experiencing the Oneness of the Universe, a psychic experience that is perceived in a flash of intuitive insight.

I learned that Yeats was interested in mystical literature and the supernatural. He became a Rosicrucian and belonged to the order of the Golden Dawn. The rose in his poems sometimes denoted spiritual matters. He wrote his poems based on the legends and myths of ancient Ireland. Yeats held the belief that there would be a revolution when an order of Celtic mysteries had been established. His poem, The Secret Rose, reflected this belief. He also belonged to a group that believed that truth cannot be discovered but is revealed.

Journal - September 7, 1986 - Rune Work.

It has been several years since I started working with the Runes again and I feel that my interpretive abilities have improved. (I first began reading the Runes: an ancient language and divination tool in England in 1980.)

Back at the beginning of the year I read the Rune stones for M, a secretary at the Medical School in New Brunswick. The three-stone reading indicated marital problems, separation, and new beginnings related to work and study. She said that this was, indeed, the case; she was working on separating from her husband and going back to school to get better qualified.

Two weekends ago I went over to Seaside Park, NJ, to stay the weekend with several friends. We were up until the early hours reading the Runes and talking. I read the stones for P and they indicated a change in job. She reported that everything the stones said was very accurate. Another friend, D, wanted her stones read. They indicated that she was concerned about fertility and indeed she was! She was planning on getting pregnant.

In the past, there have been other successes with the runes. Shortly after I began studying the stones in 1981, a friend came to dinner and we got to talking about the Runes. He didn't want a reading but just drew out a stone from the bag, the fertility stone! He dropped it back in the bag when I told him the interpretation. Then he told me about a problem he had, his girlfriend was pregnant!

Journal: Fall, 1986 - *The Koestler Chair of Parapsychology.*

One of the magazines that I enjoy reading is *Omni Magazine* (sadly now out of print) that publishes great stories and news from the paranormal world. I recently read a news story there by Daniel Cohen about the writer and researcher Arthur Koestler leaving 700,000 English pounds to endow a Chair of Parapsychology at Edinburgh University in Scotland. There was an initial outcry from the skeptics but, eventually, researcher Robert Morris took over the post as lead investigator. In the article he says that he is "about eighty percent convinced that what is generally called Psi (ESP) represents something new." But he is skeptical of people who claim to be 100% correct.

Another news story in *Omni Magazine* by Sherry Baker relates to research that a hormone related to water retention may somehow trigger extrasensory abilities. William Roll, then director of the Psychical Research Foundation in Chapel Hill, N. Carolina, heard the idea from a French endocrinologist, Alan Assailly, who was studying mediums during the 1950s. He discovered that most of them suffered from water retention! Roll wrote that the water-retaining hormone vasopressin "might play a role in psychic abilities." Research found that psychically talented women have been found to have unusually high levels of progesterone, a hormonal precursor to vasopressin.

Journal - September 13, 1986 - *Runes Again.*

About six weeks ago, a friend E Mc called me to read the Rune stones for her. Her parents had been having "bad vibes" about a trip they were planning on taking. The reading indicated sickness as a possibility. Today, E called me to tell me that during her parent's trip, her mother developed severe abdominal pains while on a mountain lift.

Journal - September 20, 1986 - *Lucky Matches.*

Today I received a package of sales material from the *Reader's Digest* including a sweepstake promotion in the form of a rub-off card: the goal being to rub-off three identical squares in the minimum number of tries. I didn't plan on sending in the card or buying anything but wanted to see if this could be done.

I sat and looked at the card and decided that the three identical pictures (stars) would be in a diagonal setting rather than down vertically or across horizontally. So, I scraped off the center box and got one star. Then, I had to decide whether the three stars were from left to right or right to left diagonally. I decided to scrape off the bottom right square and got a second star. To complete the line, I scraped off the top left to reveal the third star, to complete the line!

It occurred to me that all the squares might contain stars, so I quickly rubbed off the remaining squares. This confirmed that the first three squares that I rubbed off were the only ones to contain the stars! About six years ago in England, a group of friends and I conducted a similar psi experiment. We used a card with about 16-20 rub-off squares. The card depicted a soccer game and the objective was to find the square that showed the ball.

We used a ring on a thread as a pendulum and we each took turns, starting at the first square, to ask for a "yes/no" response. Each person received a "no" until about the eighth square when it said "yes." We confirmed the response, through the next person, who also got a "yes." Then we rubbed off that square and found the ball underneath! We also, then, rubbed off the other squares to see if there were any more hidden balls, there were none. The ball was under the first square where we got a "yes" response!

Journal - September 23, 1986 - *PRL.*

Today I received a packet of material from the Psychophysical Research Laboratory (PRL) at Princeton Junction, regarding their parapsychology research. I filled out their questionnaire and will mail it off tomorrow. The packet contained some interesting literature on ESP and Charles Honorton's Lab.

Journal - September 27, 1986 - *Coincidences.*

One of the questions asked by PRL was about meaningful coincidences, otherwise known as synchronicities. I could not think of any current examples, but I decided to keep a record of any that happened since or any that I remembered, here are two.

Last year, I spent Thanksgiving with friends in the Poconos, PA. During a break, we noticed an orange salamander among some logs, under the house deck, and we stood around talking about it for a short period. Then I went back into the cabin to continue reading my book (I think it was *Supernature* by Lyall Watson). I turned the page to read a section about salamanders!

Today, I was catching up on my reading of the week's newspapers. I had got to the Tuesday section and, there, saw a photograph of a woman wearing a *Hill Street Blue's* T shirt. I also noticed that, while I was looking at the photograph, the theme music from *Hill Street Blues* was playing on the radio.

I don't believe that coincidences are random occurrences. I believe that life is a series of coincidences, only some of which are recognized, or we pay attention to them. This recognition is based on our life experiences and our openness to accepting a pattern in life. For example, how many times have you heard a new word, then, within a day or two have heard it several times? We may have heard the word before but not paid attention to it.

Journal - October 10, 1986 - *More Lucky Numbers.*

Still on the theme of coincidences, I have noticed that certain numbers seem to crop up more often than others. I haven't studied numerology, but I have read that certain numbers have special significance. I have always felt that "8" was "my" number, it was well-rounded and stood for infinity. Lately "7" and series of sevens have been very prominent.

Journal - October 15, 1986 - *PRL.*

A colleague, A, and I were planning to visit PRL, following an invitation in response to my returning their questionnaire. I decided to call PRL to let them know about the colleague, so they could set up for two subjects. It seems that they were trying to call me, to let me know that their computer was off-line. I will still be going down to look at the facility and see a film about the work at PRL.

Journal - October 18, 1986 - *Introduction to PRL.*

Yesterday I went down to Princeton Junction to take part in an Introductory Session and want to record my perceptions of PRL. The Ganzfeld research computers were down so I couldn't take part in any Ganzfeld experiments. However, I did play with some of their PK computer games.

My initial reaction was that PRL was a modern research facility and the staff went out of their way to be friendly and helpful, even picking me up at the Princeton Junction train station.

I had an initial interview with MQ and then I and another subject were shown around the lab and watched a video film about the work at PRL. Next, we observed some PK computer games and worked with them, but I didn't do too well, neither did the other subject. I think we were both too nervous.

We then completed a personality profile on another computer: the Myers-Briggs Type Indicator. (I (15), N (43), F (35), P (13)) I think it well summed up my personality and showed I had strong intuitive and feeling scores.

Lastly, MQ showed me around their library and their stock of reprints (which interested me a lot). Finally, I played some more PK games on MQ's computer and I had more success, scoring several hits.

Journal - October 24, 1986 - *OBEs.*

Talked to MQ of PRL yesterday and I have made an appointment to visit the lab on the morning of November 7, to take part in their Ganzfeld experiment. MQ is interested in getting together to do some OBE exploration using *The Christos Technique*, that I had told her about, to look at Past Lives. (*The Christos Technique* was developed by Glaskin an Australian journalist, taking the most successful parts of eastern and western spirituality in order to have Out-of-Body Experiences into his past lives).

Since my discussion with her and looking through old journals, I found my old dream diary from 1979-1982. Looking through this record I found various instances where my dreams were precognitive (for example, telling of the death of a friend, J, my marriage to R, and other situations: J's death was unexpected due to a car accident and there were no plans to marry R when I had the dream).

I also found, in the dream journal a reference to a dream of a neighbor who I later learned had died. "Night of the 21st July 1975 dreamed of an old neighbor getting on a bus. Someone said, 'Look there's Mrs. L.'" She looked young, plump and cheerful. I knew her 20 years ago. I learned the next day by a notice in the paper that she had died suddenly the previous day.

Journal - October 25, 1986 - *Reprints.*

I sent off for scientific reprints from: Keith Harary (Remote Viewing Project); Dr. Steven LaBerge (Lucid Dream Project); Ichinose Wellness Research Foundation (Subtle Energy-Homeopathy Project); Dr. Herbert Benson (Tibetan and Chinese Projects); and Dr. John Zimmerman (Bio-Electromagnetic Project).

Journal - October 26th, 1986 - *Rune Play Workshop.*

Today, I attended a Rune Play Workshop held at Wayne Library, NJ and given by Dr. P. M. H. Atwater. The group hosting the event was the Metaphysical Center of New Jersey. Here I learned a new method of reading the Rune stones. These were the Norwegian method (also called the Goddess Runes), consisting of fourteen symbol stones and two question stones (male and female). We learned the symbols and practiced throwing.

Journal - November 7, 1986 - *First Ganzfeld.*
I visited PRL at Princeton Junction to take part in their Ganzfeld Psi study. The Researcher MQ picked me up at the train station and we arrived at PRL at about 9:30 a.m. After getting wired up for the session, in the electrically and acoustically shielded research lab there were electrical problems with the communications system but that got sorted out by their engineer.

The session began with a relaxation tape over headphones and was followed by a 30-minute session where LM, the Sender, tried to convey an image to me. She was sat in another shielded room, watching a randomly selected picture on a TV monitor. She could hear what I was saying but I could not hear her. The Researcher MQ was out at the control desk and could hear what both of us were saying.

During the half hour session, I talked out what was going through my visual imagery. MQ reported that my perceptions that related to the key target picture were: woman with hair standing on end, a calico cat, lady in a crinoline with a parasol; storm, thunder and lightning; a dog shaking his fur; shooting star; blue velvet background; planets in space; eclipse of the moon; shooting up into the sky; a witch on a broomstick; sun flares; solar flares; sunspots, hearing solar wind; an explosion; lots of yellows and reds; dark/light contrast; intense activity and energy. I also perceived a lesser amount of images that related to the three decoy targets.

When I was given the opportunity to look at the four target pictures (the real target and three decoys), I got a very strong feeling that the woman with her hair standing on end was the "right one." I cast my vote for the woman and was right, I had scored a hit! I was also able to correctly assess the time that I had been in the experimental room - 30 minutes.

Journal - December 8, 1986 - *Being at One.*
This has been quite a positive time in terms of psychic development and synchronicities, I had talked with a colleague at work and was telling her how excited I was that I was going to meet up with my friend F After three and a half years. (F and I had met when our US-bound plane bumped us off our flight back in 1983 and we had to spend time in London.) I had spoken to him back in August and he said he would

try and come out east around Christmas time and would be in touch. When I got home from work there was a letter from F saying he would be in the area on the 19th and wanted to get together!

Over the past couple of weeks, I have had several instances of "enlightenment" of being "at one" with the Universe and understanding what life is all about. It is like the feeling you get when you find the missing piece to a jigsaw or see the connection between two things, but more intense.

Yesterday, I took part in a telephone study conducted by *Omni Magazine* on Interspecies Communication. The study consisted of calling an 800 number and listening to animal sounds, then completing a questionnaire included in this month's *Omni Magazine*. (I imagine it was trying to assess what the animal sounds meant). It was very interesting, and I mailed off my response yesterday.

Journal - December 8, 1986 - *Intuitive Knowledge* 1.

As my meditation for today I am going to test an assumption that I read about, which is that we already have knowledge inside of us to discover, we don't discover it out in the external world. (I don't know who suggested this). I have already experienced something like this when I was thinking about the oddness of coincidences. I had the realization that life is a series of coincidences, but we only recognize them when we are in the correct state or mind-set.

Sorry Einstein!

I relaxed in a warm bath and read a book on parapsychology to set my thoughts on the right path to seeking new information. While I relaxed, I listened to the waste water gurgling down the pipes and my free-association thoughts took me to pipes, rats, sewers, cockroaches, people in sewers, flashlights, and eventually to the nature of light. This mode of inquiry is often called contemplation and is thought to have originated with the Christian religious orders, but I think it is much older than that.

I thought about the light from a candle and flashlight and compared it to the light traveling to us from a star, at presumably the speed of light. The candle or flashlight can be seen, if there are no obstacles in the way, for up to a mile or maybe more. As the distance increases, the intensity of the light decreases. If you shine a flashlight up into the night sky, could it be seen from the Moon, from the Milky Way? If light travels so fast why not? Several answers came to mind.

To travel at the speed of light, light must reach a certain mass. That is why we can see the light from a star but someone in space could not see a flashlight from Earth. And, as light travels, it loses energy in the form of electrons and there is a proportional loss, according to the distance traveled. So, if light from a star has lost half its energy by the time it reaches Earth, say, it means that the distance to the star may be different to what we had originally measured. (We measure light-years distance on the fixed or agreed-upon speed of light).

For example, we measure a certain star as ten light years away but because the light has altered its composition or mass, the star-system may really be nearer than we thought, say five light years away.

As we increase space-travel, this knowledge can be tested. For example, within the solar system, the slow-down of light-mass will not make an appreciable difference but the further we go into deep-space, the more we will understand the phenomenon.

Journal - December 8, 1986 - *Intuitive Knowledge* 2.

I tried to look within myself for knowledge, again and did the usual pre-relaxation. The Pineal, Light Perception and Hair or Why We Go Grey! The pineal gland situated in the center of the brain has been demonstrated to be able to detect light and controls our diurnal/nocturnal cycles, provokes melatonin to darken and protect the skin, and probably many other functions. Light and dark cycles are important to our well-being. During the dark we sleep, and dream and more natural births occur at night. All this knowledge I already knew from my nursing and medical research experience. However, my free association musing asked the following questions regarding the pineal and light.

If the argument goes that people tan in sunlight and remain pale in areas where there isn't much sunlight, couldn't the same argument be made for the hair? People from the southern hemispheres generally have darker hair than people of the more northerly countries. The general idea being that the skin darkens to protect it from too much light. The paler hair and skin of northern people allows them to absorb more light.

But, why should the body need to absorb light and why protect it against too much? The generally accepted answer is that sunlight promotes the production of vitamin D in the body. However, I believe that to be only one function. I feel that melatonin production and vitamin D formation act as signalers to the pineal to inform it of the presence or absence of light.

For many cultures' hair has an important symbolic role. Some cultures and religions forbid the cutting of hair. In the Bible Samson lost his strength when his hair was cut. Women, with their individual cycles; menstrual, maternal, etc. are expected to take greater care of their hair. It is possible that hair is as much a sense organ, in terms of light perception, as the skin.

It would be interesting to see if bald men have disturbed sleep/wake cycles. It is possible that as we get older, the pineal gland needs more light to function and the hair lightens or grays to allow this to happen. Sounds wacky but who knows?

Feedback: Modern scientists are now speculating that this is the case, that animal and human hair can function like a fiber-optic cable and convey light through its core, deep into the layers of the skin.

Shuttle Glitches.
PROJECT: Shuttle Glitches.
METHOD: ERV.
DATE: August 30th, 1984 and January 1986.
CLIENT: Independent.
TYPE: Exploratory.

On August 30, 1984 the news media announced that the shuttle Discovery was unable to be launched because of "glitches." I decided to have a "mental look" at what could be causing the problem but had no feedback on my attempts.

In January 1986, the shuttle, Voyager, launch was delayed for about 5 or 6 days. I decided to look to see what the problem was. I perceived a small screw blocking the F15 fuel line that could not be seen from visual inspection. I tried, unsuccessfully, to convey this information to the personnel at the site.

Feedback: The following day the media announced that a "bolt" was found blocking a "fuel valve."

1987

Princeton Engineering Anomalies Research (PEAR).

From 1987 through 1992 I worked as a member of staff at the Princeton Engineering Anomalies Research (PEAR) Laboratory. PEAR was one component in an interdisciplinary research and educational enterprise at Princeton University, called the Human Information Processing (HIP) Group. The Group brought together "Faculty, staff, and students in engineering, computer science, psychology, and philosophy for collaborative study of the role of human cognition, perception, and creativity in a number of contemporary human/machine technologies."

During the year and a half that I was visiting PRL I was aware that the Lab's time was ending. The funding was drying up and going to more conventional study centers such as the Cognitive Research Laboratories at Princeton University. The PRL staff suggested that, as I was still interested in psi research, that I should contact the Princeton Engineering Anomalies Research (PEAR) Laboratory at Princeton University, where I could continue to be involved.

I had already heard and read about PEAR. In 1983, Professor Robert Jahn, Brenda Dunne and Roger Nelson had published 'Precognitive Remote Perception,' a Technical Report in which they evaluated 227 formal precognitive remote perception trials. The results of this impressive body of data indicated that their efforts were highly significant. The PEAR document concluded that "Precognitive remote perception techniques can acquire significant amounts of compounded information about spatially and temporarily remote target locations, by means currently inexplicable by known physical mechanisms."

My first visit to PEAR almost did not occur. I had written to the Lab and when Brenda Dunne called back to ask if I was interested in visiting, she gave me directions to the Lab, that was in the basement of the School of Engineering and Applied Science of Princeton University. (The Lab has since closed after almost 30 years of research work). I had no problem until I got to the basement and took a wrong turn. It seemed, the Lab kept such a low profile that even the students did not know that PEAR existed or even where it was located! Finally, I found the narrow orange door, simply labeled C131 that led to the Lab and, let me tell you, this door was deceptive, it gave no indication of the wonders inside!

Visitors to the Lab, particularly from overseas or from conventional laboratories, would often ask, "Where is the Lab?" when they are standing right in the middle of it. Apart from the six computers, and arrays of other technology, the Lab could have been someone's home, complete with carpeting and sectional orange couch. However, it is not every home that can boast a ten-foot tall pinball machine used to test macro-psychokinesis. Other attractive, but very seriously scientific devices, were a pendulum, complete with crystal ball, and a water fountain bathed in colored lights.

After a few months volunteer participation at PEAR, my funding at the Institute for Child Development at UMDNJ in New Brunswick, ended, and I had to decide what I wanted to do. Brenda Dunne, the PEAR Lab Manager, approached me with an offer to work at the Lab and I jumped at the chance! Brenda warned me that this would not be regarded by the scientific community as a good career move but what I was not prepared for was the scalding criticism that was poured upon me by my scientific colleagues. Scientists, who I had admired for their openness and capacity for fairness, publicly berated me for daring to move to such a "suspect" area of research. Where was their commitment to freedom of inquiry? Being raised British and determined (some call it stubborn) I decided to put aside my plans and move to Princeton. I am glad that I did.

From January of 1987 to the fall of 1992 my life became a kaleidoscopic inside view of the parapsychology field. The "world and her brother" came through the narrow orange door marked C131, into the often-bizarre world of the PEAR Lab.

PEAR was, originally, the concept of rocket scientist Robert Jahn, Professor Emeritus and past Dean of the School of Engineering. He was a respected, classical Princeton aerospace scientist and scholar. Over thirty years ago one of his students approached him to ask if he would be her adviser for her undergraduate thesis. The topic she had picked, however, was highly controversial. She wanted to build a microelectronic random-number-generator (RNG) to replicate some of the psychokinesis experiments that had been carried out by Helmut Schmidt at the Mind-Science Foundation in Texas.

Jahn's response was to discourage her but she reminded him of his commitment to free inquiry. He conceded on the terms that they would conduct site visits to the various parapsychological research laboratories around the country and she would prepare a report to convince him of the need for such a project. They did this and, a year later, the student had completed her project and succeeded in obtaining significant scientific results.

Jahn had kept his personal beliefs quite separate from his scientific research and teaching but he realized that if there could indeed be a subtle connection between the human mind and a device, like an RNG, then this was something that should be scientifically examined. We have entered an increasingly technical world, where even the slightest disturbance of an electrical signal can cause significant deviation from the normal operation of a device. For example, if the device was a control system for a rocket that slight deviation could have devastating consequences. So, the PEAR Laboratory was born.

The Lab's first experiment included a replication of the RNG experiments and Jahn brought on board Brenda Dunne, who had been working on remote viewing experiments at the University of Chicago, and Roger Nelson, an experimental psychologist. Later, he added John Bradish, an electrical engineer, and York Dobyns, a theoretical physicist to complement the interdisciplinary team.

Brenda had conducted successful remote viewing experiments with Prof. Bisaha at Chicago University and met Jahn when she was giving a presentation of her work at a Parapsychological Association (PA) annual meeting. Setting up the Lab was not easy, however, and Jahn and Dunne met a great deal of initial skepticism and resistance from the Princeton University authorities. Jahn, who had reached the top of his field in aerospace engineering, now became suspect for even daring to think about such topics as psychokinesis and remote perception, let alone set up a laboratory to study these topics!

In his capacity as Dean of the School of Engineering, Jahn was able to remodel part of the School's basement area into a laboratory, and, with the help of a private grant, furnished it, and added the equipment needed to set up the first experiments. The walls were paneled, the floor was carpeted, and the famous orange couch was installed. Later, he was successful in winning grant monies from several major funders including the McDonnell and the Rockefeller Foundations.

Psychokinesis (PK) Research.

Prior to my being hired at PEAR, I had volunteered as an "operator." PEAR did not have "subjects" as the lab was studying the overall effect of human intention on micro-electronics and other systems. They did not study the human aspect of the interaction, just the outcome. As an engineering laboratory, they were concerned about the small but cumulative effect of human intention (micro-PK) on systems such as Random Number Generators (RNG) also called Random Event Generators (REG).

Over five years as a member of staff I was able to complete sixty-six sessions with the diode random event generator local sessions, sitting in front of the device and "intending" it to deviate from its normal random path. There were other experimental protocols too; a random water fountain, a free-swinging crystal pendulum and a drum but I really enjoyed working with the RNG. The intentions of the operator were to make three attempts: to create a Baseline by doing nothing to affect the device, to cause the device to put out more positive signals and go High, or to generate more negative signals and to get a Low result.

The attempts were randomized, and the operator could see their progress by colored parabolic curves on the computer screen: green for Baseline, red for High and blue for Low. I found that I got my best results by using an unfocused state of consciousness. A decade later I was able to contribute some of my observations on micro-PK towards

Dr. Pamela Heath's book '*The PK Zone*,' which was later republished as '*Mind-Matter Interaction.*'

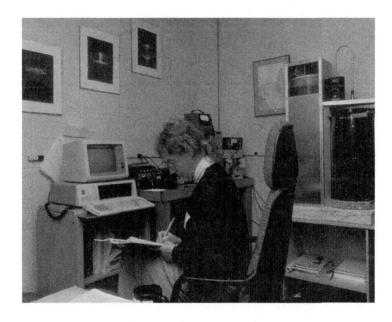

Angela Entering Data at the PEAR Lab.

Not all my attempts at micro-PK attempts were successful but there were enough successes to create a statistically significant database. My Baseline stayed at a non-significant Z score of 0.638, while my Low intention ran significantly low with a Z of 1.927 (P = .027 for the statisticians) and my High attempts ran high at a nicely significant Z of 2.919 (P = .002).

One of PEAR's in-house research publications talks about how their extremely large micro-PK database was divided by gender. It was found that females provided most of the data and had the most significant results. Included in the database were three female "prolific operators" who provided the bulk of the significant results. I feel that this finding was lost in the general statistics published by the Lab, which was unfortunate.

Precognitive Remote Perception (PRP).

During April and May of 1992, I was slated to partner with a Lab Visitor as he travelled in Asia. The PEAR Precognitive Remote Perception Program (PRP) was set up so that pairs of individuals could mentally share information about their location and activities, even when there were thousands of miles between them. This method was based on the ASPR and SRI Out-Bounder research. Back in Princeton, I was scheduled to make five attempts, at set dates and times, to describe where this individual would be, what he was seeing and doing, his surroundings and any other interesting data. During his travels, he would do the same, at set dates and times he would make five attempts to perceive my surroundings, activities etc. Both of us would also complete scoring questionnaires that would be independently submitted to PEAR and computer coded. I enjoyed this aspect of the work, as well as the psychokinesis research, as it gave me a chance to use my natural psi abilities in a practical way.

Even though each traveling partner (the agent) had to be at a location on the designated date and time, the viewing partner (the percipient) could carry out their perceptions beforehand, that's the Precognitive part of PRP. PEAR had discovered that even if the viewing was carried out hours, days or even weeks before the individual visited the target site, the viewing effect was not weakened. When the Lab Partner and I received our results, we found something interesting had happened. Each of our first four attempts showed that we perceived significant amounts of information about the other person's location, but our fifth attempts were way off, in interesting ways.

During the fifth attempt at my colleague "sending" information and me "receiving," he was busy checking out of his hotel and what I described was the exterior of the hotel, rather than his activity. When he attempted to view my activity around that time, he somehow "shot forward" 40 days to a conference that was being arranged by PEAR and held at Princeton University. While he was in Asia, he had not known about the conference and only decided to attend once he returned. What he described in his last session was an exact layout of the conference room, the participants and even named individuals! My five sessions were significant with a Z score of 1.767, beyond chance expectation!

While I was at PEAR, I was able to travel abroad, on vacation, to conferences and on visits to other labs, and was able to act as both Agent and Percipient from England and the States, and from such exotic places as Russia and Kenya.

Journal - March 15, 1987 - *Three Research Labs.*

I continue to live in New Brunswick, and I am working as a Research Analyst at the University of Medicine and Dentistry of New Jersey (UMDNJ). My main research activities are working with Moms and their newborn babies at the local hospital studying laterality (handedness etc.).

I have been going down to the Psychophysical Research Laboratories (PRL) to participate in Ganzfeld (telepathy, remote viewing) and PK (Psychokinesis) studies as a volunteer. I heard about the PRL PK studies through a small article in *Omni Magazine* about their Psi Invaders research:

"Video game junkies who would like to improve their odds might want to try their hand (and head) at Psi Invaders at the Psychophysical Research Laboratories (PRL) at Princeton, NJ. In this parapsychological version of Space Invaders, the player's laser shoots down the 'bad guys.' Just as in the original, only the laser is programmed to misfire frequently. At these times players must make their laser fire through psychokinetic 'will' or through ESP, unconsciously timing their responses to bring about a hit." *Omni Magazine* also noted that another Psi research group, Science Unlimited Research Foundation, was also offering Psi Invaders as well as other PK research games at their lab in San Antonio, Texas.

I was already participating in PRL's Ganzfeld research, so I also volunteered for their PK computer studies, too. On my days off, during vacation time and holidays I traveled down to Princeton Junction from New Brunswick, NJ and usually spent the day at the Lab. The Mind Science Foundation, another lab studying psychokinesis and located in San Antonio, TX had a small article in Omni Magazine, too:

"Helmut Schmidt of the Mind-Science Foundation in San Antonio is conducting a nationwide study of psychokinesis. He mails volunteers cassette tapes of recorded random tones, along with instructions to spend fifteen minutes a day ('like meditation') trying to alter the tones, to change their position on the scale. After a couple of weeks, subjects send the tapes back to Schmidt, who compares them with the originals. He reports that volunteers have indeed made changes! (I participated in all three studies at the three labs but, sadly, all three have since closed).

In addition to my regular research position in New Brunswick and participating at psi-labs, I am also continuing my own study of the runes, the I-Ching and the Tarot, although the Runes have always remained my favorite.

Journal - 1987, Journal - *Psychokinesis.*

I continue to have pennies materialize in my apartment in the weirdest places: such as on a recently washed kitchen floor and this reminded me of a watch that went missing from one apartment and turned up at another! A small watch, that had been a gift from my mother, went missing while I was living at a small attic apartment in West Orange, NJ around 1984. I remembered putting it on top of the microwave oven in the kitchen. I later remembered and looked for it, but it was nowhere around. I thought that maybe someone I was dating, at that time, had stolen it, or it may have slipped off onto the floor or behind furniture. I even searched in my jewelry box drawers, but it wasn't there.

When I moved to another apartment in 1985, in Orange, NJ, I made a note to look for the watch as I packed, and I even looked under the edges of the carpets when all the furniture was packed.

About six months later, I was looking for something else in my jewelry box and there was the watch! My questions were where did the watch go and how did it come back to the right owner in a place where I would look even though I had moved about three miles away?

My current thinking is that this phenomenon may be linked to extradimensional shifts that move in and out of our dimension moving objects as they pass through and relocating them as they return.

Journal - 1987 - *Cardiff University.*

Exploring my psi abilities reminded me of a study in which I had participated in the late 1970s at Cardiff University, Wales, where I did my undergraduate degree. A colleague Brian Sharratt was carrying out An Investigation of Strategies used in a Computer Controlled Concept Attainment Experiment:

"The present study is an extension of the work by Brunner, Goodman and Austin on strategies used in concept attainment tasks with the experiment being set up and controlled by computer. By using a light pen sensitive C.R.T. display subjects were able to control their approach to the tasks in choosing whether to draw examples of the concept or state specific hypotheses. This flexible approach was used to produce descriptive analysis of the development of the subjects' strategies."

Basically, the subject was given mixed examples of categories and had to decide which of several alternatives the computer was using to generate the examples. At first the study was confusing but there was an "Aha!" moment when I knew how it worked. The remaining sessions were all correct, to the amazement of the research student, even though he had no control over the computer's choices. Later, he gave a scientific talk and mentioned my results showing the steep peak in my graph when I started giving correct responses and pointed it (and me, awkward) out to the audience. Was this anomalous (psi) or just a fluke?

Journal - March 18, 1987 - *The Key.*

I was thinking today about the various ways that are available for accessing "hidden knowledge." This hidden knowledge is sometimes referred to as the Akashic Record, The Matrix, The Source, or The Library. There are many ways of obtaining the information contained within the Source of the hidden knowledge. Also, there are two possible sources of this knowledge: (a) the Source lies within our own minds and, although we are not consciously aware of it, we can access it through various means or (b) the Source is external to our minds. Some people think the Source is God, others that the knowledge exists on another plane or dimension, or, in some way, free-floating. The knowledge can be accessed through a multitude of practices such as: meditation, the IChing, Tarot, Runes, and Channeling. There are sects that believe knowledge comes to them through prayer and other groups read chicken entrails! In ancient times, in China, a turtle shell was baked, and the cracked remains read to reveal knowledge!

The thought has occurred to me that underlying all these methods is a "Key"; a principle or main concept. It seems that whatever the type of practice, the results appear similar. For example, an I-Ching, Tarot and Rune reading for a situation will, very often, reveal very similar answers.

I believe it could be possible to use any form of medium and you could get the same sort of reading. For instance, at Christmas I forgot my rune stones when I visited friends, so I improvised with a set made from Hershey Kisses. The reading that I did for my friend was as accurate as any I have done with the rune stones. Similarly, any type of two-sided coin can be used for the I-Ching casting. So, what is the "Key" or concept that underlies all these practices? I intend to find out. (2016 – I'm still looking!)

Journal - February 23, 1987 - *Institute of Psychophysical Research.*

Today I received a letter that was forwarded onto me from Manchester University, from the Institute of Psychophysical Research. It included a questionnaire that requested information on Out-of-Body Experiences (OBEs).

The Institute is now being funded by the Strutt Research Fund, part of the British Medical Association, and the questionnaire is part of a pilot program. Charles McCreery must have remembered me from several years ago when I wrote to him about my OBEs and I did some "fly-ins" to the Institute. (I wrote about these in my book Remote Perceptions). I completed the questionnaire and sent off a note to Charles McCreery letting him know that I am now living and working in America.

Journal - April 27, 1987 - *The National ESP Laboratory.*

Read a short blurb in a British magazine for a series of ESP tests that are being carried out by Russell Targ's National ESP Laboratory. It read:

"Can your ESP beat Wall Street? Russell Targ, the physicist who tested Uri Geller and was recently featured on the PBS science show NOVA, has developed a new ESP test for psychic talent."

For years, the U.S. government has quietly funded research in 'remote viewing,' a way of using psychic abilities to investigate the future. This investigation carried out since 1972 by Targ and others at SRI International was recently applied to the ultimate test of precognition; predicting what will happen to the stock market. Targ and his colleague, psychologist Dr. Keith Harary, used remote viewing to predict how the price of silver options would change over 9 consecutive weeks. Each week, the prediction was correct. The odds of achieving such a success by mere chance or guessing is one in 50,000. Targ's funders earned $120,000 from the predictions and a new and exciting application of ESP was born.

Although some subsequent predictions were not successful, other laboratories quickly picked up on this new direction in psychic research. Four have repeated Targ's experiment and each has found a similar pattern of success.

The remote viewing ability is widespread. The SRI studies have shown that almost anyone can learn to harness and apply these latent talents. "Ordinarily, people never get the feedback they need to sharpen these skills," Targ says. "Too often psychic abilities are simply dismissed as 'lucky hunches' or intuition."

Now, Targ has developed a way for members of the public to learn more about remote viewing and have their own abilities measured scientifically. In the ESP test, people are shown how to develop and use their remote viewing skills, as was done at SRI. The test measures these abilities against the silver market, just as in Targ's original experiments. It also shows participants how they might learn to apply ESP to areas, such as business, sports, politics, and personal decision making.

"The test is easy and fun to take" says Targ. It is administered at home via the mail over a three-month period. Targ has established a telephone hotline so that test takers can enjoy checking how well the market follows their predictions.

Targ's non-profit organization, the National ESP Laboratory, is hoping to find gifted individuals for its own research in remote viewing. "We believe that it is time that ESP abilities get used, not just talked about," Targ explains. "Everybody has some remote viewing ability and can improve it with practice. And somewhere out there are the ESP geniuses - we hope to find them."

Journal - May 1, 1987 - *The National ESP Laboratory Research.*

I received a letter from Russell Targ's research group that included instructions on the parts of the study and included a write-up by the Wall Street Journal of Targ's work. I plan to participate.

Journal - May 6, 1987 – *Mind Science Foundation – PK.*

I got the results of the PK experiments that I did for the Mind Science Foundation, trying to affect tones on pre-recorded tapes. Overall, I did well, according to the Foundation, especially when I was trying for a High Aim Score and Low Aim Score. When the scores were broken down in categories of sounds, I did better on Organ on High and Low Aim, Slow Piano for Low Aim, Slow Whistle for Low Aim, and Fast Whistle for High Aim. According to their letter they are working on another series and will send the next tapes when they are ready.

Journal - September 25, 1987 – *Introduction to PEAR.*

Today I went down to Princeton, NJ to attend an introductory session at the Princeton Engineering Anomalies Research (PEAR) Laboratory at Princeton University. I had written to them over a year ago but only just got a visit granted! I met the Lab Manager, Brenda Dunne, this morning at PEAR and she gave me some background on the Lab and the people who work there.

The Lab is situated in the School of Engineering and the aim of the Lab is mainly understanding human/computer-machine interaction. They have a variety of research games to investigate this interaction and I took part in some of them today including Murphy the wall-size pinball machine, and the Pendulum, a free-standing crystal bob pendulum enclosed in a Perspex case.

The Random Mechanical Cascade - Murphy:

Murphy, officially named; the Random Mechanical Cascade, measures macro (or large scale) psychokinesis (PK). On a wall, just inside the Lab was an impressive game which took up the whole wall. It consisted of a giant "pinball" machine in which balls fell over pegs into nineteen bins. The collected balls formed a Gaussian curve with the most balls in the center and least at the ends. The game consisted of two tasks and a baseline run. The two runs were to either influence more balls to go into the right bins, then to try and get more balls into the left bins. The balls are counted by computer and a Polaroid picture is taken to show how the balls fell. I was able to get a decent right shift that the Lab staff said indicated some PK activity. I don't think my results were significant, but it was fun, and I can do them again when I next visit.

Another Lab member was working on a PK machine to measure the effects of human thought on the movement of a free-swinging, crystal bob pendulum. The machine was still in the experimental stage, but I managed to get some marginally positive results.

Journal - August-September 1987 – *OMNI article; Psychic Waves.*

An article for Omni Magazine's Antimatter section by D. Scott Rogo covered the topic of Psychic Waves; brain waves and ESP. The article asked:

"Does anything unusual occur within the brain when a person receives an ESP message?" Two researchers affiliated with the University of Illinois think it does. Cognitive neuroscientists Charles A. Warren and Norman S. Don conducted their research with a single subject whose brain activity was monitored by an electroencephalograph. His job was to guess the geometric symbols printed on a series of standard Zenner (ESP) cards. (Each card is printed with a cross, circle, square, star or wavy lines).

When the subject finished carrying out this task, the researchers looked at the brain signals, also known as event-related potentials or ERPs. These consist of tiny electrical fluctuations that occur milliseconds before or after the reception of any given stimulus. The two researchers looked specifically at the ERPs for predetermined millisecond periods before and after the subject made their guesses.

As it turned out, the researchers said, their subject guessed correctly close to 50 percent of the time. (A scoring rate of 20 percent would be experienced as a result of chance.) When the researchers checked their EEG data, they discovered that the ERPs often accompanied the correct guesses at a rate of 72.7 percent. "We have several hopes for future work in this area" Warren says. "One is that studies using such ERP monitoring will be able to yield even more accurate indications of psi."

<u>Journal - October 22, 1987 – *American Society for Psychical Research – ASPR.*</u>

Today, I was invited by George Hansen of PRL to go with him to a meeting at the American Society for Psychical Research (ASPR) in Manhattan, NY. The ASPR is housed in a huge old Victorian building, next door to the Dakota Hotel. The interior of the ASPR is very Victorian in character and almost like a museum. Jim Matlock, the librarian and archivist, showed me around including Dr. Karlis Osis' office and experimental rooms. Dr. Osis is currently working with a psychic trying to establish OBE trips with some sensitive equipment. The library was impressive, and I got to have a look at Michaeleen Maher's Ph.D. Thesis and other interesting journal articles. I also met Patrice Keen and I will try and come into NY sometime to have lunch with her. Another interesting "meet" was with Jasper, the ASPR cat (named after the JSPR, the ASPR Journal)!

<u>Journal - October 23, 1987 - *Michael Lewis Recommendation.*</u>

For the past few years I have been working as a medical researcher at the University of Medicine and Dentistry of New Jersey located in New Brunswick, NJ, specifically in the Department of Child Health with Prof. Michael Lewis's group. I have been thinking about long-term research prospects and the idea of working towards my Ph.D. One of my options would be Edinburgh University in Scotland. I asked Prof. Lewis for a recommendation to send to Prof. Robert Morris at Edinburgh University, Dr. Lewis wrote:

"Ms. Thompson has spent the past three years working in my Institute on a project involving high-risk children and their families. Ms. Thompson has been an active and valuable member of our staff. She has participated in the design of our experiments and in the execution of many of its features. She has interviewed parents and tested children. In general, she has involved herself with the subjects and families. In this regard she has shown herself to be professionally competent, interpersonally sensitive and highly competent. From an interpersonal point of view, Ms. Thompson is a pleasure to have on the staff. She brings cheer, goodwill, intelligence, and common sense to her work and to her relationships with others. Besides her intellectually curious mind, she is a pleasure to interact with and we shall be very sorry to see her go."

(I include this Letter of Recommendation, not to praise myself but to contrast with a later event when I told the Head of the Department that I had been offered a job at the PEAR Lab at Princeton University. He went "ballistic," telling me that I was making the worst decision of my career! This shows how deep the antagonism is towards anything unconventional in the conventional research world.)

CASE FILES - 1987

The Exodus.
PROJECT: The Exodus.
METHOD: Natural RV.
DATE: 1987.
CLIENT: PRL.
TYPE: Exploratory.

While I was volunteering at PRL, I met a researcher who was very skilled in hypnosis and we had regular sessions to try and break past the limits of the Out-of-Body (OBE) state. The following remote viewing/OBE entitled The Exodus was initiated during this time of exploration, in February of 1987, when I wanted to find out whether I could remote view the future, as well as the past and present. What I viewed troubled me greatly and I realized that I had a responsibility to share this information.

The Exodus commences in the year 2030 and covers a time period of about fifty years. In this scenario it appears that the Earth's atmosphere, particularly around the northern hemispheres, undergoes a rapid, unexpected, and devastating deterioration, necessitating the evacuation of the people of the northern hemispheres to the lands around the Mediterranean. Many will die on the journey and assimilation into the new cultures is difficult. Eventually the northern atmosphere resolves and people start returning to their ancestral lands to begin a new life. I chose the name Exodus to denote the mass moving of entire nations under conditions of duress and distress.

1988

JOURNALS

Journal - February 1, 1988 - *Job Offer.*
The past three months have seen some interesting personal changes and more changes are in the offing. My participation at PRL

has dwindled to a halt and, due to their lack of funding, they will probably close. I told the Research Associate that I would come down for one last visit, but I don't really think I will have the time.

My volunteer participation at the PEAR Lab has increased and at Christmas Brenda Dunne brought up the possibility of working at the Lab. This possibility culminated in a definite job offer which began today. My position is described as technical assistant at the Lab. I will also be moving down to Princeton by the end of February.

I have continued corresponding with the Mind Science Foundation (Dr. Helmut Schmidt) and the National ESP Laboratory (Russell Targ) and will continue to take part in Remote PK and Associative Remote Viewing (ARV) experiments. All in all, this is an exciting time of life with the promise of more exciting times ahead.

Journal - February 1, 1988 - *First Day at PEAR.*

This was my first full-time day at PEAR and even though I have been going down part-time, the day was quite stressful. I suppose every first day is like that. I had some time today to do some runs on the Random Mechanical Cascade (RMC: also called Murphy) and the REG. When I got home to New Brunswick, I found another PK tape from the Mind Science Foundation which I will do at the weekend.

Journal - February 4, 1988 - *First Week at PEAR.*

This has been my first week, full-time at PEAR and it has been both a tense and exciting week as I undertake new activities and duties.

Journal - February 7, 1988 - *Retro-PK Studies with Sound.*

Worked on PK5, another experimental tape from the Mind Science Foundation and got some interesting results. The effort was to try and affect the recorded tones, the originals of which were stored in Texas. I concentrated on three thoughts: "Keep the tone pure," Keep noise low," and "Switch off noise." I visualized a mental switch to turn off or turn down the noise level and visualized this switch being capable of extending back in time to the noise level source.

Journal - February 10, 1988 - *REG Participation.*

I had a good day at the Lab. I felt in a "high energy phase" and decided to complete my tenth REG series. I was able to get the high up to 100.62, the highest yet but I couldn't keep it at the high level, and it came down to 100.46 (still significant at the 0.5 level). Brenda then tried to graph all my series, but the graph went off the screen, the screen turned blue and the computer shut down! These results were great because I didn't think that I could generate micro-PK but here it is freaking out the computer!

Journal - February 13, 1988 - *National ESP Lab.*

Still working with the National ESP Laboratory, receiving and sending my perceptions. I got my results from the third prediction and it was correct. I perceived a cookie jar and the target was a coffee pot with the same shape and lid. My descriptors matched sufficiently for it to be a hit. Similarly, the previous one, the Eifel Tower target was also a hit, but I have also had two misses.

Journal - March 6, 1988 - *Jupiter Prediction to NASA.*

It has now been a month since I started working full-time at PEAR and it has been an interesting four weeks. There have been new people to meet and lots of new things to learn. PEAR expressed some interest in my OBE adventures and asked if they could place my Jupiter Probe prediction on record with JPL/NASA. I agreed.

Journal - March 26, 1988 – *Quit While Ahead.*

I received the fifth results from the National ESP Lab (I missed some at the beginning of the series). Unfortunately, my last effort was not successful, but my overall results worked correctly with odds of one in thirty-four. These results are very encouraging and comparable to other psi tests I have completed. The ESP Lab offered five more trials but I decided not to participate further for several reasons: a possible conflict of interest with working at PEAR and the feeling that I should have a professional commitment to one lab; to quit while I'm ahead; it seems a waste of time and energy to repeat what I have already done.

Journal - June 26, 1988 – *SSE.*

I received news this week, that my position at PEAR has been made permanent; I started work at PEAR and moved down to Princeton five months ago. In early June, most of us from the Lab went up to Ithaca, New York for the 7th Annual Meeting of the Society for Scientific Exploration (SSE). I was recently made a member and helped get the program together this year. I gave a short talk on the anomalous recovery of the Colombian orphans (where I worked in the 1970s), which went well and I met people that I had read about: Hal Puthoff, Carl Sagan, Jessica Utts, Rick Berger etc.

Journal - July 3, 1988 – *Cloud Busting.*
Today was a good day to try cloud busting. It was a hot, sunny day with light fluffy clouds. Brenda had told me awhile back that she and her son were able to do this PK activity. First, you select a cloud and concentrate energy on the cloud to disperse it. The first one that I concentrated on disappeared in about a minute and a half. Then, to see if it was really "mind power," I tried another one with a similar-shaped cloud as a control. The cloud that I was focusing on faded and disappeared, but the control cloud kept its shape. Later, I chose a bigger, bulkier cloud and had the same effect! Each time I noticed that, for a while, nothing seemed to happen, then fuzzy patches appeared, then the cloud disappeared quite quickly after that.

Journal - August 8, 1988 – *Stopping Clocks.*
On Saturday I went into New York with a lady friend to visit a writer/colleague J. At J's apartment I think I made a clock stop! When we arrived on the quarter hour, a mantle clock started chiming very loudly and very discordantly. I thought to myself, "Do we have to put up with that every fifteen minutes, all afternoon?" Then I forgot about the clock as we talked, and I didn't realize that it hadn't chimed all afternoon. Several hours later, J commented that the clock had stopped and tapped it to get it going again.

Journal - September 5, 1988 - *The African Chest.*
In the spring my housemate agreed to look after a large carved wooden African chest for a friend. The chest from Mozambique was beautifully carved and was about 6' long by 3' wide and tall. It contained African fabrics and tribal masks, was locked with a small padlock, and sat in the living room.

Back earlier in the year, we had experienced a psychokinetic (PK) effect when a metal ashtray had jumped in the air and fell back onto the chest where it had originally been sitting. It wobbled a bit, then came to a stop.

Today, we experienced another anomaly. The friend came to collect some fabrics from the chest but had forgotten to bring the key for the padlock. I mentioned that my brother and I used to open locks in our childhood home, with hair pins. We joked around a bit about opening the chest with a hairpin and so, my housemate produced a hair pin to try. I delved inside the padlock with the pin but remarked that

41

something had to "turn over" but I couldn't find anything inside to catch the pin onto. I stopped probing around and the padlock opened with a loud click amazing us all. The friend was able to retrieve her fabrics and was very grateful for the assistance.

Journal - September 7, 1988 - *Meeting Dr. Wayne Carr.*

A few months ago, I came across an ad in the local paper calling for pilot subjects for a biofeedback study. I eventually took part in the experimenter's Electro-encephalograph (EEG) pilot study. Dr. Wayne Carr was looking at brain synchronization, trying out some new EEG equipment and needed some pilot data. I did some visualizations and meditation during the EEG runs trying to get some feedback. (I met Warne Carr again in the 1990s when I audited a weekend remote viewing class he was holding in Las Vegas.)

Journal - September 9, 1988 – *Retroactive PK – By-Mail.*

Back in the winter and spring I took part in retro-PK experiments run by the Mind Science Foundation in San Antonio, TX. Called "PK-By-Mail," the study was run by Dr. Helmut Schmidt and Dr. Marilyn Schlitz and he sent an update on the results of the study. I discovered I fall into a Myers-Briggs personality group that Schmidt calls "the meditators" and in the "feeling/perceptive" group.

Schmidt describes psychokinesis (PK) as "the influence of mind over matter" and most PK happens "in the moment." But Schmidt has an idea that PK occurs at the moment an event is observed and there seemed to be a retro-active effect!

Hundreds of volunteers, from all over the country, participated in Schmidt's and Schlitz's study. The volunteers were mailed cassette tapes with instructions to try to obtain either high or low tones, according to instructions. The originals of the tapes were sequestered in the San Antonio labs.

The volunteers were the first individuals to hear ("observe") the taped sounds and the returned tapes were then compared to the original taped sounds.

According to Mind-Science, there were three interesting results: there was evidence for an overall PK effect; that participants who had studied meditation did better on the tests, and subjects who fell on the "feeling" and "perceptive" scales of the Myers-Briggs personality inventory scored better than the "thinking" and "judging" types.

42

Journal - September 11, 1988 – *PEAR Update.*

It has now been over eight months since I started full-time work at PEAR and a whole year since my first visit. It has been and exciting and productive year and I feel that I am at the right place at the right time in my life.

Several of us at the Lab have noticed that the Epson Apex computers that we are using for lab work seem to be susceptible to emotional states. For example, when we play the computer game Rogue, there seem to be PK effects with other anomalies happening. On one occasion, I was working on the computer while I was waiting for a date to arrive, a date that I was feeling nervous about, and was trying to decide how to cancel. The computer screen began displaying a whole series of weird graphics and Rogue characters in the middle of text and data analysis.

Journal - September 11, 1988 - *Brain and Mind.*

While not directly related to remote viewing - the following are some interesting scientific findings about the brain and the mind. I found an interesting paper by Volkmar Weiss (Leipzig) regarding memory, intelligence, the brain and the mind. (1986): "Nine is about the maximum number for memory retention, strongly related to intelligence; there are measured correlates between the speed of evoked electro-magnetic brain waves and IQ replicated in thirty independent studies; an IQ above 130 (about 5% of the population) is related to possession of a double autosomal-recessive Mendelian allele, and mental power, short-term memory capacity and Spearman's G (IQ score) turn out to be correlated."

Weiss says that the message of all this can be "nothing else than information eliciting particles/waves because they obey Bose-Einstein statistics" and behave as bosons in the sense of quantum physics. He adds that the brain must be understood as a "macroscopic quantum oscillator." I am not a physicist, so I leave the physics to them.

Journal - September 25, 1988 – PK Games.

Recently, a colleague mailed the lab some computer games, many of which are based on random systems. These games seem to be particularly susceptible to psi. (ESP & PK). One game, Battleship, consists of placing battleship shapes on the screen and then the computer drops "hits" on them. You also must guess where the computer has placed its ships and drop "hits" on them. This game is not much fun anymore as four times out of five I can guess where the computer has placed its ships and hit them before the computer hits mine!

The computer game Rogue is also very psi prone and I have learned to make "demands" of the program. For example, I will only play if the computer will provide "food, identify scrolls, and good armor." Usually it complies! The game also used to lock me into rooms without doors in the game and "starve" me, but it doesn't do that anymore!

Journal - October 16, 1988 - *Computer Games Update.*
During the past few weeks, I have experienced an increase in my psi abilities. It could be a practice effect as I have been playing the computer games that our colleague sent. For example, in the game Battleship, I can guess 8 out of 10 times where the computer has placed its ships, at the same time avoiding the computer's shots at my ships. In another game I use the same strategy to find where submarines are below my boat (Sea Battle) and deflect the computer's shots at my boat. However, both these games are now defective and will not allow me to play: Battleship won't let me position my boats and Sea Battle aborts when I score a good hit!

Journal - October 16, 1988 - *Space Shuttle.*
The world was so relieved when the latest space shuttle successfully launched a few weeks ago. It was with horror that we all watched the Challenger explosion and held our breath as the current shuttle made its ascent and descent. I was looking back through some older journals and remembered an event where I located a problem in a prior shuttle which was later discovered and reported in the media.

I think this earlier version was called Voyager. In early January 1986, this shuttle was delayed for five or six days and I decided to do an OBE to see what the problem was. I found a small screw had blocked the "F15" fuel line. This could not be seen from visual inspection. I tried to convey this information to personnel, but they were unable to see me.

The following day, the radio and TV announced that a "bolt" was found blocking a "fuel valve." I am sure that this was the same piece of hardware that I saw! I had no such pre-knowledge of the Challenger disaster and, even if I had, there would have been little I could have done, the problem was too big and didn't occur until after the launch. I am pleased that the shuttle program is back online again.

Retrocausal Psychokinesis (PK) – Recap.
PROJECT: Retrocausal Psychokinesis (RPK).
METHOD: ERV.
DATE: 1986 – 1988.
CLIENT: Rhine Research Center.
TYPE: Research.

In 1986, the Rhine Research Center, at Durham, NC, along with the Mind-Science Foundation in Texas, was soliciting participants to take part in studies of "retrocausal psychokinesis." While many psi researchers were studying psychokinesis (PK); the effect of mind on matter, the group was suggesting that the effect could go back in time as well as forward! They were sending out pre-recorded audio tapes and asking participants to listen to the tones and try to psychokinetically affect them. The tapes were then returned and compared to master tapes at either the Mind Science Lab in San Antonio or the Rhine Research Center at Duke University.

Over a period of months, I received audio tapes, listened to them, tried to affect them with my mind, and then mailed them back to the Rhine Research Center. Dr. Helmut Schmidt was the lead researcher on the project at the time. I didn't seem to have much effect until I received a tape containing piano and organ tones. When my results came back for this tape, I found that I had been able to significantly shift some of the tones to a lower frequency and my statistical Z score was 1.87, that was significant! I used to play the cello in High School and have always loved low frequency sound so perhaps this helped me alter the tone, who knows?

RNG Data Signatures.

Researchers Dean Radin and Joseph Lubin at Princeton University, in 1988, conducted a neural networks study using four RNG databases from the PEAR Laboratory. (After the fact, I was informed that my dataset was that labeled as belonging to Person 2.) During the study, the researchers were not aware of the identities of the operators and the datasets were randomized. The aim of the study was to find datasets that could be correctly identified by a computer program (neural network) as belonging to the same RNG operator. In a training session the computer was fed a batch of unidentified data from the four operators. When a different batch of the same four datasets was fed into the computer, the program was able to identify Person Two's data more frequently than the other three datasets. Radin and Lubin wrote that Person Two's data was correctly identified more often than the remaining three people. This indicated that Person Two's data had more internal consistency and could be more readily identified from an earlier training dataset. That is, the data had a signature that could be identified by a computer.

1989

JOURNALS

Journal - March 12, 1989 - *Conferences and Travel.*
I have already outlined much of the progress made at the Lab since I began work over a year ago. On a professional level I have contributed both to the Society for Scientific Exploration (SSE) Annual Meeting: helped arrange the program and gave a talk; and became the Editor of the SSE Newsletter, The Explorer.

Last year I traveled to Cornell, NY; to England where I represented the Lab to the British Group at Bristol, to San Francisco; and to a UFO Conference in Connecticut. This year I plan to get out to San Francisco again; to Boulder, CO for the SSE Meeting; and to San Diego for the PA Conference. I have been invited by an old friend, Ginni, to visit her in Kenya, Africa and I am planning a trip for November.

Journal - April 21, 1989 – *The Swami.*
On Tuesday afternoon we had a visit from His Holiness, a Swami, who was visiting various academic institutions. He had been a physicist until four years ago when he became a monk. He arrived at the front door of the School of Engineering, wrapped in a gauzy, orange sari, despite the brisk spring weather. He had chevrons of white clay on his bare legs and arms, an orange cloth over his head and body and sported long hair and a beard. He also had crazy/mad eyes, like "Mad Manfred of Morristown" who I once dated. I prefer to be respectful of other people's religions but there was something about this Swami that was not quite right. I was warned not to shake his hand, in fact not to touch him at all, as he could not touch women. I was very tempted to hug him, but I didn't.

He came down to the Lab and stayed a couple of hours. At the end he suddenly realized who he had been talking with for the past few hours. The Lab Manager handed him some of the PEAR reprints and the Swami remarked "I have heard of these people!" The Manager responded "Yes, that's us!"

When he was talking to the group he was disparaging, chauvinistic and ignorant of simple facts. He would wait for someone else to answer a question and then incorporate their remarks into his own arguments. We were happy when he and his entourage decided to leave.

Journal - April 22, 1989 - *The Bainbridge Ghost.*
Today I went up to Nassau Street in the center of Princeton to the annual Communiversity (Community/University) Fair. I bought several T shirts and necklaces and wandered around for a couple of hours. I passed by historic Bainbridge House, a landmark on Nassau Street and decided to go in for a visit. A lovely old lady showed me around. While we were in the two main rooms, the dining room and the parlor, which were divided by an archway I experienced an unusual event. I was carrying several plastic shopping bags and unexpectedly felt as if someone like a small animal, say a dog, had kicked the bags! I looked around but there was nobody there, of course!

Journal - July 8, 1989 - *The Decline of Parapsychology.*
After many years of endeavor, the various parapsychology groups seem to be progressively "hitting the dust." Over this past year the Psychophysical Research Laboratories (PRL) have struggled to keep the lab going despite collaboration with researchers Peter Rojcevvicz and Maralyn Schlitz and the Julliard School of Music. Now they are closing, as is the Mind Science Foundation. PRL was conducting some innovative work with music and drama students and the Ganzfeld. And they are now closed.

I heard from Rick Berger last week that SURF in Texas is closing and, by an odd coincidence, we had their benefactor visiting us the next day. The Mind-Science Foundation is also struggling to keep its head above water. Early August we will be getting a visit from one of our benefactors Laurance Rockefeller.

The scene isn't any better in Scotland where Bob Morris has the Koestler Chair at the University of Edinburgh. Nothing substantial seems to be coming out of there, I feel. Ed May and Hal Puthoff, formerly of SRI have turned to regular physics although they still maintain an active interest in the Society for Scientific Exploration. PEAR seems to be the only group still moving ahead.

Journal - July 11, 1989 – *Popp's Photon Research.*
Back in the spring, at a conference at Temple University's Center for Frontier Science, the Lab Manager and Director met with a German scientist, Fritz Popp. Popp has been working on biophoton (light

emitted from biological organisms) emissions from cucumber seedlings. There are some interesting excerpts from his recent paper in Experientia, Vol. 44/No. 7, pp543-630, 15th July, 1988: Biophoton Emission: "Most fundamental biological functions, namely cell division, are triggered by a very weak ultra-violet photo current originating from the cells themselves...However, with improved techniques it became more and more evident that actually all living tissue exhibits a very weak photon emission...This corresponds to the light intensity of a candle at a distance of some kilometers...In biological systems excited molecules can transfer their excitation energy to other bio-molecules and thereby trigger amplification mechanisms and/or promote photochemical processes in the dark...From an empirical point of view the most decisive result will be the finding of correlations between biophoton emission and biological functions."

The PEAR Lab has set up a series of tri-polar protocols, with Fritz Popp in Germany, to see if human operators can affect the photon emissions from Popp's photon-emitting cucumber seedlings. This is the next step up from "talking to your plants." Long distance!

Journal - August 7, 1989 – *Bio-PK.*
I did my second remote PK effort to Fritz Popp's seedlings today at 2 p.m. I did the same sequence as last week's effort, high intention, low, and baseline. I first visualized turning on a light over the seedlings so that they would wake up and produce more photons, then visualized the light turning off so that the seedlings could sleep and not produce as many photos, then a non-action baseline. It felt very comfortable interacting with the cucumber seedlings. I have two more to do next week. (We were to later learn that the experiment has some effect, but it was not significant).

Journal - September 30, 1989 – *Soviet Visitor.*
This week we had a visit from Prof. Valery Venda, head of one of one of the major research institutes of learning in Moscow, USSR. He gave us a talk on his learning theories and how they apply to Perestroika, he said, *"There has to be some lessening in efficiency to change over to the new system."* He seemed positive that the changes would be for the good of the Soviets but had to be handled carefully i.e. "timing and acceptance."

The Lab Managers had to take off for another appointment out of town, so the Lab staff was left to show Dr. Venda around, we showed him the experiments and a staff member took him off to purchase a computer. Later we all took Dr. Venda out to dinner in downtown

48

Princeton. We finished the evening with "bear hugs" and he seemed very appreciative of the evening. I had the feeling that we had been instrumental in some way to help heal the rift between two great countries, albeit in a small way.

Journal - October 9, 1989 – *Chaos Resolving.*
Over the past two weeks there has been an escalation of chaos, not only at the University but everywhere. Everyone I have talked to recently has commented on the state of chaos. During this state of chaos, there seems to be a catabolic process going on. A breaking down of the state that was. During this state of chaos, a senior administrative person within the School of Engineering took his own life (for whatever personal reason, he shot himself in the chest).

Now we seem to be in an anabolic state, a rebuilding, a restructuring, a re-patterning. The changes don't seem greatly different, although we will miss our colleague greatly.

The Lab Manager and a few others seem to feel that the chaos is linked to an unusual pattern of sunspot activity. I feel that it is linked to a larger, universal pattern of periodic ebb and flow, catabolism and anabolism that affects both the sun's activity and ours.

I feel that there are peaks and troughs in this activity and, as we explore space, we will find evidence of this cyclic pattern in and around our own solar system – maybe even further afield. It is a cyclic system, so pervasive it affects systems as diverse as the sun's activity right down to the human cellular level. This is all speculation, of course, but even Einstein had to start somewhere!

Journal - October 9, 1989 – *Visit to Africa.*
From November 7th to December 7th, I will be away, traveling in England and to Nairobi, Africa. Since I decided to take up my friend Ginni's offer to visit her in Africa, there have been a series of coincidences. I keep meeting or hearing about people who have just returned from Kenya. Somehow, I feel that visiting Africa, at this time, is important and timely, for some reason. It is said that Mankind (Humankind) has its roots in Africa and maybe I need to get back to the source to find some answers - and even understand the question!

JOURNALS – 1990's Overview

While I was working at the PEAR Laboratory, I gained confidence in my Psi (intuitive) abilities and from 1992 on was being hired as an independent consultant by groups such as Psi Tech and Intuition Services, as well as private individuals and groups. Some of this project information took up to eleven years to confirm and some future perceptions still must be verified. What I have concluded from over three decades of remote viewing work is that this special application of consciousness is valid and useful. It has been employed by police departments, private business, government, private groups, and individuals. Remote viewing data is never used alone but in conjunction with other sources of information. Over the years, through remote viewing, missing people and children have been located, murders and other crimes assisted to find hidden evidence, and, in the business world, remote viewing has given managers an extra "edge."

In 1992, I relocated to Las Vegas to work as a Research Coordinator with Robert Bigelow and from there began my own business teaching remote viewing, researching, consulting, writing, continuing my graduate studies, and helping raise my stepsons. I opened a small office on Flamingo Road in Las Vegas and also taught, wrote and consulted from my home office up near Sunrise Mountain.

Journal - January 1, 1990 – *Happy New Year.*
1989 was a good year with lots of interesting new things: some good and some bad. The TREAT I and II meetings revealed the fragile egos of those in the UFO community. The verbal and written duels between the leaders were disturbing and the field lost many good people. The Lab has seen a constant stream of visitors from all walks of life and from all over the world; fascinating people.

The media has become interested in the Lab, too, and several TV crews from the US and abroad have filmed PEAR. Next week the "48 Hours" crew will be filming the Lab's work. A write-up in the NY Sunday Times magazine was a breakthrough but lacking in its attitude to the Lab and its omissions of the Lab Manager's role in the formation and running of the Lab. Both forms of media coverage have generated much public interest.

My participation at the Lab continues several levels and my level of interaction with the experiments doesn't seem to have declined. Still getting good results.

Journal - January 4, 1990 – *Esoteric Artwork.*

Back in 1979 I did some artwork that consisted of geometric squares and triangles depicting, as I titled it, "Man within God within Man." I didn't know the significance of the symbolism until I read P.D. Ouspensky's '*The Symbolism of the Tarot: Philosophy of Occultism in Pictures and Numbers.*' There I read that "The triangle is God, the Trinity, or the world of ideas, or the nominal world." The point within it all is Man's soul. The square is the visible or phenomenal world. Potentially, the point is equal to the square, which means that all the visible world is contained in Man's (Woman's) consciousness, is created in Man's (Woman's) soul. And the soul itself is a point having no dimension in the world of spirit that is symbolized by the triangle. I have never read this teaching before, about the symbolism of God, Man and the Universe, that we could have these symbols within us, either on an individual basis or a collective consciousness level.

Journal - January 9, 1990 – *Confirmation of Imagery.*

About five years ago I tried doing some mental exercises to look at the idea that, a. we have occult or hidden knowledge available to us and b. that we can tap into it. I did two sessions: one, looking at the speed of light coming from the stars and another regarding light, the pineal gland, aging and grey hair. I perceived that graying or white hair could act as a light detector to aid the pineal gland in its functions.

Feedback: This week I found an article in *Science News* by Ivan Amato entitled 'The Natural Root of Fiber Optics.' Interestingly, the research was done by John Wells of the Berkeley Nuclear Laboratories in Gloucestershire (near Bristol) in England and Richard Hellen (of the Bristol Group) had been telling me about some of their other work when I visited them this autumn!

Basically, the researchers shone light through a gray hair and found that it acted like a fiber-optic cable, transmitting light from end to end! "So, you certainly have a way of getting white light down to the base of the bulb of the hair, in other words to the base of the dermis."

The article ends on a speculative note that maybe retinal photo receptors and head hair may be evolutionarily linked in the waveguide function and may confer some unknown benefit."

Journal - January 16, 1990 – *Sympathetic Magic.*

There have been two occasions when I was able to put "sympathetic magic" to work. The first being that the Lab Manager's son misplaced an important envelope that he needed to return a job application. He spent all day looking at home and at the Lab. I remarked that it always happened that when people usually made up another, replacement envelope and mailed if off, the original envelope would turn up! So, I asked him to give me an old envelope that I "pretended" was a real envelope that I then "pretended' to mail. The Lab Manager and her son play-acted their thanks to me for "mailing" the letter. Lo and behold, about an hour later, the original envelope turned up on the Lab Manager's desk and her son was able to mail off his original application.

Then, later in the week, one of the Lab members misplaced a folder of important graphs that he needed to take to the Graphics department. I told him about the mailing envelope and "sympathetic magic" and that the folder was probably under some other folders. He said that he had already looked. Anyway, we looked again and there were his graphs in the pile of folders. Maybe sympathetic magic works by slowing down the chaos level and allowing order to prevail.

Journal - February 1, 1990 – *ATPseudo.*

The New Year saw a continuation of work at PEAR and residence in Princeton, NJ. The work at PEAR continues several levels: a continuation of assistance with the day-to-day running of the lab; supervising, operators and helping with data processing and checking; and participating as an operator in the lab experiments. My participation in the studies has revealed several significant signatures on the Random Number Generator (RNG), ATPseudo (Pseudo RNG), and Pendulum experiments. Signatures are computer-recognized data patterns that are unique to individual operators. I plan to continue with remotes on the ATPseudo and to do some regular RNG sessions. Since the end of December, I have been doing a weekly remote RNG attempt to Bristol, England. (In accordance with PEAR Protocol, I have not included my Operator ID.)

Late last year the Lab generated some public interest with an article in the *NY Times Sunday Magazine,* that led to some TV coverage of the Lab and Bob and Brenda's new book *Margins of Reality.*

On a personal level I have continued to record instances of synchronicity (coincidences), interesting meetings, spontaneous psi and other anomalies. Unfortunately, my recent interest in the UFO Abduction phenomenon has been put on a back-burner due to the bitter animosity among the key-players. This has meant not attending TREAT2, but colleagues will update me. Various, odd explanations have been put forward for the UFO and Abduction scenarios, the most recent one proposed by Cannon. He claims that the whole scenario is a government mind-game, using the UFO story as a cover. This and other alternative explanations have been stored in my "mental data sorter" to do some signal processing, looking for patterns and similarities.

Ring and Stillings are strongly advocating the 'Imaginal' explanation and the strong associations with childhood abuse and neglect. My basic plans are to maintain course, increase my personal skills and knowledge and add these to further the aims of the PEAR Team.

Journal - April 21, 1990 – *Julian Jaynes.*

Last week I attended a Psychology Colloquium over at the Princeton University Green Hall and had the opportunity to talk briefly with Julian Jaynes (author of *'Bicameral Consciousness in the Breakdown of the Bicameral Mind'*). In his book he proposes that there are three types of consciousness: "the bicameral or God-run man; the contemporary, modern or problem- solving man; and contemporary forms of throwback to bicameralism, manifested as hypnotism, schizophrenia, poetic and religious frenzy, among other phenomena."

I found him quite congenial although I was told he rarely came to these talks. We talked for a while, he assumed I was a student, until I mentioned that I worked at Robert Jahn's Lab! He became derisive, calling the Lab's work "parapsychology" while I was trying to remedy his impression: i.e. that we referred to it as human-machine interaction and human-information processing. He said he would consider coming out to visit the Lab and mentioned that he was working on another book. As I had read his first book *Bicameral Consciousness,* I decided to read it again, bearing in mind my conversation with him.

Journal - April 29, 1990 – *Douglas Dean.*

Yesterday I went up to the Communiversity Day Fair held in Princeton, where the University and Town come together to hold a fair: food stalls, competitions, events, dancing, singing etc. It was a hot day, 95 degrees, and the Fair was bigger than ever this year – great fun!

While walking around I met Douglas Dean (physical scientist/parapsychologist) who also lives in Princeton. Douglas has done some fascinating research work on the healing properties of water from sacred sites such as Lourdes and other holy springs. He has used infra-red technology to assess samples, as well as assessing water held by healers versus non-healers. He has also been interested in Kirlian photography that photographs the energy fields of biological specimens such as leaves and human hands.

Poor Douglas has been quite sick. About a year ago he had a major operation but hasn't quite recovered, as well as suffering from shingles, chest pains, and flu. It seems ironic that someone so dedicated to researching healing, has been so sick himself. He has joined a Reiki healing group where he has been receiving treatment. I gave him two, big, healing hugs which he seemed to soak up!

I was able to talk to him about his experiences at Saybrook University. He completed his Ph.D. as an external student but had problems getting his dissertation work accepted. I told him about my application to Saybrook and he was very encouraging despite his own discouraging experiences.

Journal - April 29, 1990 – *PEAR Lab.*

(According to PEAR Protocol, Operators ID# has not been included with this data)

Over the past two years the Lab has been collecting random event generator (REG) data using a new, shorter protocol (Thou) and looking at each operator's signature with different parameters, hopefully to find conditions where the operator is successful. During those two years, I have discovered personal parameters on various devices (related to intention and focus) where I have achieved a 2.8 significant standard deviation from the average (mean) in the high direction.

Journal - July 12, 1990 – *Cosmic Rays.*

I want to record here an informal experiment that I run each time I go over to Fine Library on the Princeton Campus. In the lobby, near the building, is a cosmic-ray counter. It counts every time a ray passes through detectors and causes a spark to jump. A counter measures each time this occurs. This happens sporadically, on a random basis, and is caused by cosmic rays entering the Earth's atmosphere. I have found that I can stand in front of the equipment and cause it to count at an increased rate. I think the equipment is on display for educational reasons, so I don't think I am interfering with anyone's experiment.

Journal - July 19, 1990.

At the Lab this week we received a copy of an interesting paper entitled '*Parapsychology in the People's Republic of China*' by Leping Zha and Tron McConnell dated June 9, 1990. The Abstract dealt with the development of parapsychological research in China over the last decade. I noted many similarities between the Chinese development of Psi and that of the USA. For example, the initial focus on gifted subjects and disarray in the research field, and, the efforts of a Chinese astro-scientist to put the field onto a more scientific footing. Noted were the problems the field encountered from both skeptics and government.

I noted in the paper, that the Chinese scientist Qian Xuesen, had studied at MIT in the 1930s, did his Ph.D. at CIT (California Institute of Technology), and was the Goddard Professor of Jet Propulsion at CIT's Jet Propulsion Laboratory. Knowing that Prof. Robert Jahn had also held the Goddard Professorship at MIT, he was asked if he had ever met Qian Xuesen? He replied that not only had he known him, but Bob had taken over the Goddard chair from Qian Xuesen!

Neither of them had an interest in parapsychology at that time but had a mutual interest in electric propulsion. Both men, over the next ten years, were to become leaders in aerospace propulsion in their countries and to set up anomalies research programs. Interestingly, another leader in the anomalies field, Andriankin (who will be visiting the Lab from Russia in October) has also held a prominent position in the USSR space propulsion program.

Journal - July 24, 1990.

For several years I have been receiving the *European Journal of Parapsychology* and the parapsychologist Sybo A. Schooten has been on the Lab's mailing list. We learned that, due to financial circumstances, the parapsychological laboratory within the Department of Psychology of the University of Ultrecht had finally closed. The *Journal* will continue to be published with the aid of the Koestler Lab at Edinburgh University, but the *Journal* doesn't show any good, current research from the European sector. It seems that Ultrecht is just another example of Psi laboratories that are going under through lack of support, for example PRL, the Texas group and many others. It seems unfortunate but, perhaps, the closings are part of a general reorganization of the field. 1991

Journal - March 10, 1991 – *Remote Experimentation to Moscow.*

Today I talked by phone with Andrei Berezin a colleague at the Institute for Theoretical Problems (ITP) in Moscow (a branch of the USSR Academy of Sciences.) We set up five remote experiments with the AT Pseudo program from Princeton, NJ to Moscow. The ATPseudo is a computer program that runs a random number generator that takes a "seed" starting point from the computer, unlike the true random number generator (RNG). It has been found that the results for this device are often opposite to intention. For example, when the operator is trying to generator more positive numbers, the result is often in the opposite direction i.e. more negative numbers. The reason for this has not been determined.

I will attempt one series per day, 8-9 a.m. (3-4 Russian time) for five days, Monday through Friday this week. At the end of the week we will fax my intentions to ITP and receive feedback.

Journal - April 23, 1991 – *Preliminary Results from Moscow.*
I talked to Andre today in Moscow and got some preliminary results of my remotes to the USSR. It seems my low intentions were significant below the .05 level, according to Andre. It sorts of boggles the mind to think that human intention can affect a computer program over half a world away! Eighteen months ago, I did a batch of remotes when I was visiting Africa and they were significant in the high direction.

Journal - April 29, 1991 – *AtPseudo RNG Results.*
Received feedback and true to form the Lab ATPseudo went in the direction opposite to intention. My High intention and Baseline were chance, but my Low intention created a score of 100.164 that created a P of 0.0507 – barely shy of significance.

Journal - April 30, 1991 – *Similar ATPseudo signatures.*
When I compare the three sets of ATPseudo remotes from the UK, USSR and the USA they show a very similar signature, all intentions going high and the Low intention going significantly high.

Journal - June 25, 1991- *MacroPK.*
A few weeks ago, when I went to switch on the Murphy computer for the pinball machine, I experienced an interesting phenomenon. A rock about 2" square, and weighing about 8 oz, which was sitting behind the keyboard, jumped slightly and banged down onto the countertop. I think it only jumped about a ¼". At the time I was feeling agitated about something and that could have caused the PK activity.

Journal - July 19, 1991 – *Moscow Trip.*
I have been back about a week from my two week's trip to Moscow and have decided to record some of my impressions. I will also add the report that I completed for the PEAR Lab to the end of this account.

I knew before I went to Russia (and I had discussed it with the Lab) that I would come under some surveillance, but I didn't realize that it would be so blatant. For example, the first day I arrived Andrei and I were touring Red Square and it was disconcerting to look up and find that we were being video filmed from across the road. At the apartment, Andrei was warned several times by telephone, that he shouldn't be there, alone, with me.

Most of the time I had a "babysitter" at the apartment, Erast Andriankin's "niece" who was there ostensibly to cook for me. I noticed a very badly installed "bug" in the bedroom ceiling, nobody had bothered to tidy it up and there were no curtains in the bedroom windows, so there was ample opportunity for visual surveillance.

I seemed to draw a lot of interest from Andrei's colleagues at ITP, especially from ITP's "International Visitor Coordinator" who Andrei told me was KGB. I was given a lot of freedom around the city, but always with an escort. One day Erast Andriankin took me outside of Moscow by train to visit the grave and house of Boris Pasternack (author of Dr. Zhivago). We also visited with a Russian dignitary Victor Semionovich Gorelov and his delightful wife, Ina in Peredelkino. Ina is a superb gardener of roses, vegetables, and fruits. At Pasternack's grave we were accompanied by two American "students" who turned up out of nowhere and were very curious about our activities. They accompanied us to Pasternack's house but left us shortly after.

Later, I asked Andrei about Gorelov. (Erast had already told me that Gorelov was high up in Soviet government but wasn't military.) Andrei told me that Gorelov was someone high in counterintelligence! Erast had told me that Gorelov didn't speak any English but I noticed him react several times to things that Erast and I said. For example, Erast joked in English that "cemeteries are not sanitary!" and Gorelov laughed.

I told both Andrei and Erast that I had a strong premonition that there would be "bloodshed" in Moscow around Christmastime, the third week of December but it would be localized. I don't know if they took me seriously. (Perestroika or 'restructuring' began in 1985 and the collapse of the Soviet Union came about by the end of 1991, December 1991, bringing an end to the Cold War).

Andrei and I visited some wonderful places, swam in the Moscow River with his family, and one day took the train out of Moscow to Zagorsk a medieval monastery town that was founded by Saint Sergei. People now come to Zagorsk for healing and to drink the spring waters. We left Zagorsk feeling very relaxed and refreshed. The visual images of Moscow and Zagorsk that remain with me are of gold and blue onion domes, wildflowers, and multitudes of people on the painted subways.

REPORT: The Institute for Theoretical Problems, Moscow, USSR.

While I was working at the PEAR Laboratory, I had a unique opportunity to visit a country steeped in mystery and intrigue: Russia, then the USSR. In 1991, Russia was in between Perestroika (the policy of restructuring the economic and political system) and Glasnost (the policy or practice of more open government and wider dissemination of information) and it was anybody's guess which way the country would go. Despite the western definitions of these terms, pre-Glasnost Moscow was chronically short of food, had long lines for commodities (when they were available) and secret police and surveillance were the order of the day. There was a certain air of paranoia in the grey, gloomy city but I was made very welcome.

Originally, I was invited to a humanitarian conference which was to be held just outside the capital, but I was also invited to spend some extended time at the Institute for Theoretical Problems (ITP), Located in the Arbat section of Moscow. A Russian consciousness researcher, Andre Berezin, who had previously visited PEAR, offered to be my host and I was housed in an apartment complex in the heart of the city. The apartment was owned by Erast I. Andriankin, head of ITP.

It was a totally different world to the openness of Princeton, NJ. I was escorted everywhere and had a "minder" at the apartment, who slept in the kitchen. Supposedly, she was there to take care of my meals and other needs I had, as I didn't speak Russian, but I was quietly told that she was "assigned" to me during my stay.

When I arrived, I travelled with Andre out to the conference center, but everything was in Russian and the translation service didn't work, so I decided to spend the remainder of my time in Moscow. Andre was happy about this as we would have some time to do psi work in the ITP laboratory and get to travel out to some interesting places around Moscow. The following is an accounting that I wrote up for the Fetzer organization that partially funded my trip.

Institute for Theoretical Problems (ITP)
USSR Academy of Sciences, Moscow.

ITP was in the Arbat section of central Moscow among foreign embassies and behind the Ministry for Foreign Affairs. The four-story edifice was built in the mid-1880s and, at one time, must have been a magnificent building with its wide staircases and large halls. ITP was renting the building but Erast I. Andriankin wanted to purchase the property. I was unable to visit all the building as many of the larger side rooms and upper floors were undergoing long-term restoration work and there was building debris and scaffolding everywhere. The central courtyard of the building was filled with garbage thrown from the upper floors; there was only one working toilet for the entire staff, and the plumbing needed extensive work. Despite these problems, the building was magnificent and had great potential.

ITP Researchers.

ITP employed about thirty people, mostly theoretical physicists/engineers, but also staff for financial and secretarial support. The Institute operated on a contractual basis and maintained some secure areas of the building for military research. I was not allowed access to these areas but was introduced to some of the researchers.

Among the staff at ITP were many who were not only professional but also spiritual: Two had studied at monasteries. Among those I interacted with were Kobarkof, Chudin, and Sutyrin, but few spoke English. The topics being studied on a theoretical basis at ITP included: ionic transfer across biological cell membranes, electro-magnetic effects on DNA, and DNA modeling. According to Andriankin, the Institute was also involved in the modeling of propulsion systems (he had a rocket science background). Apart from the collaborative work with PEAR, carried out by Andrei A. Berezin (and formerly Pavel Kukushkin), there was no other obvious consciousness-related research being conducted at ITP. Andre was also involved in psychotronics: specifically, electromagnetic devices that might enhance human-computer interaction. When I returned to the States, Andre asked me to take two psychotronics devices back to the Lab (I had letters of introduction from ITP to give to customs inspectors). Back at PEAR, the devices affectionately called "Big Bear" and "Little Bear" were run randomly during psi (RNG) studies but no effects were noted, either for success or otherwise.

PEAR-related Research.

During the two weeks that I was visiting ITP, Andre and I collaborated on several series of human-computer interaction studies and, interestingly, while I got some significant runs, they were the opposite of what I was achieving at the Princeton Lab. I noted that at the end of each day, Andre would lock up the computers and other equipment as theft was a big problem and the "black-market" rampant.

There were also opportunities to carry out some remote viewing work between Moscow and Princeton. Back at the PEAR Lab, local sites were chosen, and I remote viewed these and shared my perceptions during phone calls back to the States. They were moderately successful.

It was not all work: Andre invited me out to visit with his family; we swam in the Moscow River and took a visit out to a monastery that had been built on an island. Andriankin took me by train out to the countryside to visit his colleagues and visited cemeteries and local churches. The highlights were visits to Red Square, Lenin's Tomb, to part of the Kremlin that was open to visitors, as well as to more ordinary locations such as shopping malls and restaurants. Food was extremely scarce, and most restaurants only served basic cabbage soups and sandwiches were small pieces of bread with a tiny slice of salami!

What remains with me? The incredible, richly painted interiors of the churches, the colorful domes of Saint Basil's, the great kindness of the ITP staff and people on the street, buying souvenirs on the Arbat, and the deep, subterranean, lavishly decorated subway stations where trains ran frequently but getting caught in rush-hour was scary. Truly, an amazing visit!

Entertaining a Young Moscow Boy in a Local Shopping Mall.

CASE FILES - 1991

The Tunguska Incident, Siberia.
PROJECT: The Tunguska Incident.
METHOD: ERV.
DATE: 1991.

CLIENT: Psi Tech.
TYPE: Application.

During the winter of 1991, I met with a scientific colleague, C. B. Scott Jones, (Scott) who had been working with remote viewing groups to assess future technologies, especially those that could help remedy planetary problems. He asked if I would like to undertake an informal viewing project: this was indirectly for a RV group called Psi Tech. He let me review confidential reports from other projects that he had commissioned from multiple viewers, particularly perceived events surrounding The Tunguska Explosion in Siberia in the 1800s. I was impressed at the degree of concordance between the viewers' perceptions of these events. The client was looking for any new information that might be perceived.

A few weeks later I did a session to look at the Tunguska incident and perceived an explosion that embedded micro-particles in the trees and surrounding soil in the area. I perceived that by examining these particles the nature of the event could be better understood.

Remedying the Ozone Hole.
PROJECT: Remedying the Ozone Hole.
METHOD: ERV.
DATE: November 20th – 21st, 1991.
CLIENT: Psi Tech.
TYPE: Applications.

On November 20 I did the first of two remote viewings of potential future technology for the same colleague who gave me the Tunguska tasking. Again, this was indirectly for Psi Tech. I looked at the future (possibly 30 years ahead) to assess how society would attempt to cope with the depletion in the ozone layer.

I first saw large circular tanks in the California hills. These tanks evolved into a complex of storage tanks and a processing plant for cleaning and storing polluted ozone from auto and industrial emissions. This "waste" had been pumped to the tanks from over and around a large city, possibly Los Angeles. Ozone pollution is produced as a by-product of auto and other pollution when it interacts with sunlight. However, it is "dirty" and needs to be collected, measured, "scrubbed" of particles and measured again, before it can be released into the upper atmosphere. The ozone is "lofted" into the atmosphere by means of upward wind currents off the sea, which produces some natural ozone of its own, and by a solar-assisted thermal venting process. Many large polluted cities could be candidates for this process. The "lofting" mechanism doesn't reach the upper atmosphere but assists the ozone high enough for it to rise of its own volition.

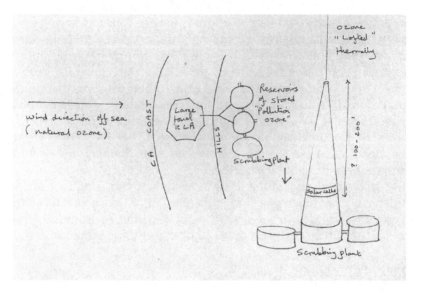

The next day I completed the second remote viewing to locate and identify technical devices to process ozone to supplement the depleted atmospheric levels. However, I felt that both technologies might be implemented too little and too late. Thermally processed ozone sufficiently heated by thermal ocean currents and solar energy could be "lofted" up to supplement the depleted layers. I saw a processing unit which could float on the ocean, possibly constructed from a ceramic material, approx. 30-50' in diameter and covered with solar tiles. It glistened in the sunlight: aesthetic as well as functional.

Descending into the ocean was a rigid pipe to collect filtered seawater. This too was about 30-50' to provide stability. The unit was not tethered but floated in the natural current, rather like a fisherman's float. Rising from the unit was a vent, also 30-50' tall to discharge the processed ozone. Inside the body of the unit was a catalytic process which created ozone from exposure to ocean thermal energy and solar energy. While these technologies might help clean up the atmosphere, will they be in time. Will such technologies come too late?

Feedback: Eight years after doing these sessions, I received feedback from an unlikely source. I was flying back to NV and browsing through the airline's magazine. There was an article by an engineer proposing something like my first scenario, large tanks in the LA hills "scrubbing" the air!

Journal - August 19, 1991 – *The Beginning of Glasnost.*

On the day that Hurricane Bob is sweeping the NJ shoreline, comes the news that Gorbachev has lost power in Russia. Conflicting stories in the media say that he resigned from "ill-health." There have been other rumors that he has been arrested and a military/KGB coup was taking place. When I was in Moscow a few weeks ago I noticed a lot of military activity on the streets and a general dissatisfaction with the conditions that were present: food shortages. We have learned that, now, Perestroika and Glasnost are "on hold." I was fortunate to travel to the USSR when I did and return safely. On TV this morning I watched as tanks face the Kremlin and Russian people throng Red Square opposing military force, supporting the changes and for Boris Yeltsin to take power.

Journal - November 21, 1991 – *PsiTech and WMD.*

Yesterday some information came over email about Psi Tech, the group attempting to use remote viewing on a practical basis. This is the same group that my colleague Scott is working with to establish psi and other talents as human potential possibilities, to foster government and industrial interest and funding.

According to an article taken from an AP report written by Ruth Sinai, entitled '*Psychic Spies: ESP used in an effort to ferret out Iraqi's weapons site,*' it seems that the group, headed by Major Ed. Dames and Major General Stubblebine, are using their groups' talents in accessing intelligence matters, as well as working for corporate customers.

Journal - December 31, 1991 – *End of Year Review.*

1991 has been an interesting year in terms of personal development and discovery. It involved some interesting travel to Russia, England, and California and Virginia in the States, meeting new people and making new friends, and establishing old ones.

1991 also saw a change of address to a new apartment, with a renewed sense of harmony and peace in my personal environment. I needed to establish my own space, apart from the Lab, especially as I am putting substantial time into my schoolwork (I was accepted to Saybrook Graduate School for my Ph.D. in Psychology).

At the Lab, 1991 was an energetic year of data analysis and "spadework" and 1992 should see several papers emerging including a couple potentially written by myself and the Lab Manager, who has asked me to write up the serial position work (First Timer's Effect) and another on the 20/2000 RNG database.

I have also been working on several papers for school. Last summer my Saybrook mentor, Dr. Tom Greening, asked me to write a biography of Russian mathematician/visionary Prof. Vasily Nalimov. I was able to visit with Nalimov in Moscow and have based my paper on that interview. This was an invited paper for the *Journal of Humanistic Psychology*.

Also did some preliminary remote perception/viewing work, on a voluntary basis, with the Foundation for Human Potential in Virginia, a new institute, founded by Senator Pell and funded by Laurence Rockefeller. 1992 has some exciting projects in store, more travel, more collaborative projects and exciting times.

1992

JOURNALS

Journal - January 1, 1992 – *New Year.*
Another year has come and gone and here we are in 1992. What exciting things lie ahead this year? Hopefully, I will complete another six courses towards my Ph.D. and take two leave trips out to California for Saybrook Annual Meetings. I look forward to these trips as I get the opportunity to travel and reunite with my west coast friends and colleagues.

This coming year I plan to have at least two scientific papers published: a biography of Prof. Vasily Nalimov; and a write-up of the laterality research we did in Manchester (with Dr. Jim Smart). The Nalimov biography was an invited paper via Tom Greenings, editor of the *Journal of Humanistic Psychology*, who is also my Saybrook advisor. January celebrates four years at PEAR and, hopefully, more years, at least until I complete my Ph.D. studies.

This summer the Annual Meeting of the Society for Scientific Exploration is going to be held in Princeton and it will be exciting to meet professional colleagues and network. Professionally, 1991 saw the establishment of my career on a more professional level. As a woman scientist it is important to publish and get credentialed. Another exciting potential for 1992 is further involvement with C.B. Scott Jones' group, the Foundation for Human Potential located in Virginia and collaboration with other psi groups.

In November I decided, after four years of sharing my colleague's house, to find my own apartment. It will be good to have a separation from lab and home, so that I can complete my schoolwork and pursue a possible relationship. I found a small apartment in Princeton and this has become my sanctuary. Overall 1991 was an exciting year of work, study and recreation. I traveled to Russia and England and 1992 promises to be just as exciting. I haven't yet planned any more overseas travel but who knows what possibilities are ahead?

Journal - February 4, 1992 – *Gravity Jet.*
Today was both an interesting Zen kind of day and yet a frustrating one. Yesterday I decided to do a couple of series with the new "Down Fountain" or "Gravity Jet" as it is called. This is an experiment with a continuous flow of water that an operator tries to either slow down or speed up, to affect the flow of the water.

We had a staff meeting on Monday and it was decided that if we didn't get some good-quality data with a large yield from the device, then the experiment would be scrapped. I did seven short series today: the first one went a little contrary to my intention but all the other six went in the right direction, high intentions went high, low intentions went low, and four of them had a strong delta between high and low. However, the lab staff didn't seem interested. I think they are determined to scrap the device regardless of what gets achieved.

I feel frustrated because whenever an operator achieves a large effect it causes panic, statistics are reassessed, machines recalibrated etc. The Lab keeps asking for large effects from the machines yet tells media and visitors to the lab that we have no "heavy-hitters," that all we see are "small effects that accumulate statistically over time." The focus of the Lab favors small effects and it seems to be a waste of good psi effort to do otherwise. I'll wait and see what the guys do with this current data before I decide if I'll invest any more time and energy in the Gravity Jet experiment.

Journal - February 18, 1992 – *Drumbeat PK Experiment 1.*
Another new Lab project is the 1:1 Drumbeat Experiment. To date I have completed eighteen series with the drumbeat experiment and have learned something about my personal style. Prior to today, most of my drumbeat efforts were "backwards" (contrary to my intention to put order or entropy into the drumbeat sequences.) I reasoned that I was carrying over some of the mindset from the REG experiments and I was having unintended results on the unattended drumbeat runs. So, I did a mental flip-over of intention to put more order into the attended runs.

Journal - February 26, 1992 – *Drumbeat PK Experiment 2.*

Great! Today, a member of the Lab staff analyzed my Drumbeat 1:1 data and the fourth order series were highly significant in the ordered direction in the attended runs! The graphs look quite dramatic and it looks quite definite where I switched strategy from a REG-mindset to a new psychological set for the Drum-beat experiment for the last three series.

While the Lab member was graphing and analyzing my data, he had a problem adding all the data into a cumulative graph, but he was able to do so. As I was looking at the terrific printouts of the graphs, his keyboard locked up! I think this was some of the random and free-floating PK that we have seen on other occasions.

Last evening, the whole Lab group went to the McCarter Theater in Princeton to see the Kodo Drummers from Japan. They were spectacular! I noticed lots of second and fourth order sequences in their drumming routines. The drumming frequencies were knocking plaster off the ceiling of the McCarter Theater!

Journal - February 26, 1992 – *School Work.*

As we near the end of February, I want to record what a super month this has been! It has been a month for writing: I completed the Soviet Psychology course and completed three long essays for school; completed the second draft of the Nalimov paper for the *Journal of Humanistic Psychology*; completed the second draft of the laterality paper for the *Journal of Development Neuropsychology* (it didn't get accepted); wrote a draft of the Serial Position effects paper for the Lab's *Technical Report*; and wrote a draft for the REG 20 and 2000 Tech Report.

It has also been a complementary month for "right-brain" activities, especially the Lab experiments. We have three new studies running: The Drumbeat Experiment; the Fountain, and the Gravity Jet. In all three experiments I have been able to achieve a greater effect than before, getting Z scores of between 3 and 6, whereas before my maximum score was usually a Z score around 2. I feel that this increased psi ability is attributable to the overall mental stimulus of my school studies and the novelty of the new experiments.

Journal - March 1, 1992 – *Women's Spirituality.*

Last Thursday evening I went over to the Unitarian Church to attend the Women's Spirituality Meeting. This is a new group consisting of the gathering of three existing groups. The Group was opened by "Candus" who sang a Gregorian chant to the Goddesses of the North, South, East, and West as she lit four pink candles. Her voice was strong and pure, and I had the image of her singing in a similar setting many centuries ago. We did a guided meditation regarding spirituality and then each shared what spirituality meant for each of us. I told how, for many years, my spirituality had been defined by others, mainly the masculine dogma of the Christian church. There was a consensus that, as women, we start out in childhood, with an understanding of our own feminine spirituality, a connection with nature, animals, and the seasons, but this was conditioned out of us by society. Now as mature women we were reclaiming our inner feminine mystery and spirituality and becoming stronger in our own right (rite). I think this group will have a lot to teach me.

Journal - March 22, 1992 – *Changes.*

There has been some tension and unease in the Lab as there have been some strained relations between the Lab and one of our funders. In addition, we are on a decreasing scale of funding from our major aerospace funder. We were informed that by June we should have a good idea whether the minor funder will continue to fund us and if we still have jobs! So, by the end of September I may be looking for another position, if the Lab doesn't find alternative funding.

On a more positive note, one of the Lab researchers analyzed my PEAR Pendulum experimental database, separating the pilot from the formal databases. It seems that I have had a significant effect: my high and low efforts are in the right direction (speeding up and slowing down the pendulum) and the delta between the highs and lows is significant with a probability of .036! There seem to be several factors contributing to this success including my strategy of using a "diffuse" attention state while operating the pendulum experiment.

It gives me a great deal of satisfaction to review my database on all of the Lab's experiments and come to the realization that I have had success on most of them, (except for the ATPseudo series that we have found doesn't yield for anyone locally) as follows: On the local REG experiments my high efforts are significant with a Z score of 2.919, p of .002, low efforts significant with a Z of 1.927 and a p of .027, and a Z-delta of 3.427!

The Up Fountain had been significant at around a Z of 3! And now the Pendulum experiment is also showing a good yield. While this knowledge, that I can have a significant effect on devices ranging from micro-electronics to macroscopic, and in many mediums, electronic, water and crystal, is satisfying; I also realize that it carries with it a sense of responsibility and a realization that I need to maintain control over these abilities. (There was also the sad realization, at the time, that if my position at PEAR came to an end, I could not continue to explore these abilities.)

This realization made me more certain that I need to look out for myself, to be prepared with a good resume, my two scientific papers in publication, and prospects ready to be developed. If my position does go under, I need a lifeboat and I need to be constructing one now!

Journal - May 27, 1992 – *Career Changes.*

The Good News: Yesterday, the PEAR Lab Manager commented on how impressed she was by the thoroughness of my laterality paper that I had submitted to the neuropsychology journal *Cortex*. Also, the quality of the serial position paper that I had been preparing for a *PEAR Technical Report* and for the next SSE Meeting in Princeton.

The Not-so-Good News: However, the Lab Manager said she had been feeling that the original position that she hired me for, four and a half years ago was now, way below my capabilities and experience and that they were phasing out my position, as part of their economy measures. It seems I have outgrown the position and need to look around for something more academic and challenging. Although her comments were unsettling, I realize the truth in them, and plan to start a serious job search.

So, like Mary Poppins, who let the East wind carry her away to other adventures when she was no longer needed, I will let the cosmos carry me to a new adventure. There are several avenues I can access, and I plan to talk to and network with other people in the field, over the next couple of weeks.

Journal May 28, 1992. – *First Photon Series.*

I did my first Photon session today and got an almost-significant split between the right and left intentions (1.710). I was hesitant to work with the device at first as it had some instability, but this seem to have been worked out Also I was rather taken aback by Stan Jeffers comment that he was expecting me to "blow the machine away!" I guess one of the Lab members told him about my success on other devices. Between May 28th and July 17th, (I eventually completed 5 sessions with a very significant delta between Left and Right of 4.491.)

Journal - June 27, 1992 – *Job Search.*

All this past week I have been at Belmont, CA attending the Saybrook Annual Meeting to satisfy the residential part of my school commitments. The week was divided up into two major sections; school courses and job interviews. School has been great: courses on chaos theory, alternative healing, Soviet psychology - and meeting everyone again!

On Thursday, I went over to Dr. Ed May's new SAIC Lab in Menlo Park. Ed has been putting together a cognitive science laboratory to study brain correlates of psi function. He was out in Princeton a few weeks previously and we had talked about a possible position in his Lab. Unfortunately, he could not hire me as he has government customers and I am not yet a U.S. citizen. Also, he doesn't have his grant money or equipment in place so isn't in a place to hire anybody yet.

The next morning, I received a call from a job mediator regarding a job possibility in Las Vegas. It seems that Prof. Stanley Krippner had sent him my resume and he was impressed by my background. The mediator came to Saybrook last night and I had an informal interview sitting on the steps outside the party! It seems pretty sure I will be getting a formal interview for the position in Las Vegas.

Journal - July 3, 1992 – *Bigelow Foundation.*
I called Robert Bigelow as arranged yesterday. (He was the job prospect the mediator had mentioned in Las Vegas). We had a fascinating discussion about the possibility of my coming to work for him in Nevada. The job does not entail funding of interviews of abductees (as the mediator had suggested) but was much wider in scope. It appears that Bigelow is setting up a Chair of Anomalous Research at the University of Nevada at Las Vegas and they will be coordinating with PEAR to set up a lab there to replicate the work of the Lab!

Bigelow is interested in all areas of research including psi, UFOs, abductions, and crop circles. He and a team from Nevada will be visiting PEAR at the end of July, early August and I will also see him when I go to Las Vegas for the PA Conference in August. I will then have a better idea of the job and its possibilities by mid-August.

Journal - July 16, 1992 – *Psi Tech.*
Last weekend I was away in Albuquerque, NM for the MUFON Conference, where I talked at length with Ryan Wood. Ryan was acting as a sales representative for a remote viewing group, Psi Tech run by ex-military remote viewer Ed Dames. Psi Tech is now a civilian group trying to actively market remote viewing to businesses and government. I told Ryan about my OBE experiences and about the associative remote viewing (ARV) I did with Targ's group. Also, that I

had taken part in Precognitive Remote Perception (PRP) studies at Princeton. Ryan suggested that I write to Ed Dames, send him my resume, and perhaps meet the group. Ryan also suggested that I attempt a test remote viewing to locate the Ark of the Covenant to send to Psi Tech.

I did the remote viewing and located the Ark in a cave under a house on a hillside in Haifa, Israel. I called Dames to get their mailing address and I got to speak to Ed when he called back. It seems that Bill Higgins (another RVer) had already shown Ed some of my PEAR work and he was impressed. Dames had already spoken to Ryan Wood, too, so he knew about my interest before he called. I typed up my Ark perceptions and send them off to Psi Tech.

Coincidently, my current NJ boyfriend was traveling down to Alexandria, VA to attend some Scottish Games on the 24th and had already invited me to go with him. And Ed suggested we meet for dinner when we were in VA.

Although the group didn't have funds to hire me, Ed said, they would be looking to "contract out" remote viewing projects when they move to Albuquerque later this year. So, things come full circle!

Journal - July 16, 1992 – *Electronic Voice Phenomena (EVP).*
On Tuesday, Robert Bigelow called in response to my letter to him that was sent before I went out to New Mexico. Basically, my letter stated my interest in the Nevada position with his company as a research coordinator. That I was willing to help facilitate the liaison between the University of Nevada and PEAR and asked if there were any projects I could help with in the meantime.

Bigelow responded that he had a project he was currently working on related to Raudive Voices, otherwise called the Electronic Voice Phenomena or EVP. I was able to locate some groups who are currently working with EVP including a German physics professor who is working with technically supported EVP. (EVP is the recording of non-material or anomalous sounds or voices using electronic devices such as voice recorders, radios, and television sets that have been tuned to a non-broadcasting station.) I sent Bigelow a fax of my findings.

Journal - July 16, 1992 – *Ross Perot Prediction.*
Today, America appeared shocked as Ross Perot, the billionaire Texan, who was a contender for the run for the next presidency, decided not to declare himself a contender and to opt out of the race. It seems that this was the last thing anyone was expecting – except me. I have been telling everyone, since Perot appeared on the scene, that he would drop out of the presidential race and that most of the votes

would go to Bush. I told this to my current boyfriend and the guys at the Lab, as well as Ryan Wood at the MUFON Conference. It is possible that we will learn that Perot's decision to run was designed and deliberate, to wake up the electorate and engineer votes for Bush. Keep posted.

Journal - July 17, 1992 – *PRP Results.*

Since the spring, the Lab has been working with a new protocol for the Precognitive Remote Perception (PRP) study. (That is, remote perception sessions are run before the outbound partner even decides where to visit at a specified date and time). Back in the spring, I carried out five trials with a colleague, William Higgins, when he was visiting Korea and Nepal (April 21, 1992 to May 1st, 1992). Since that time, I learned some new information about our results. Unfortunately, the 5 targets that I sent to Bill, bombed – he picked up a lot of subjective material, but it skewed negatively but I picked up most of Bill's data that he sent from Korea. Enough information got through to score significantly at the < .05 level (Z = 1.767). This adds to the string of significant series that I have achieved at the lab, strengthening my nontraditional skills.

Journal – July 18, 1992 – *Update.*

What a bumpy ride the last six months have been; exciting but eventful. The major events have been the necessity to find another research position, due to the Lab funding situation and my own career growth.

Since January, I have continued with my Ph.D. graduate studies in psychology at Saybrook, written up two scientific papers for journal publication, written a technical report for the lab and presented a paper at the SSE Conference. There has been a fair bit of travel, too. I went home to England for Christmas, then out to California twice for Saybrook meetings and to New Mexico to the MUFON Conference in Albuquerque. Next month I am off to Las Vegas to attend the Parapsychology Conference in Nevada and to network. I have had several leads in the job situation.

My best bet, so far, is with a new group in Las Vegas, Nevada, funded and headed by Robert Bigelow. The Bigelow Foundation is set up to study anomalous phenomena including psi and a replication of the PEAR Lab at the University of Nevada, Las Vegas (UNLV). I have been told that I will be the liaison between PEAR and UNLV and part of my job will be to interface between the two groups. However, I need to be patient as Bigelow hasn't yet actually given me the job, nor have Bigelow's group come out to visit.

<u>Journal – July 18, 1992 – *Update Continued.*</u>

During my five years at the PEAR Lab, first as a volunteer, then as a member of staff, part of my involvement has been as an Operator in the psi experiments. To my satisfaction, every device and study has yielded a significant outcome, validating my skills in psychokinesis (PK) and remote perception. However, I don't consider these abilities to be paranormal or unusual but part of my normal cognitive abilities.

I may have the opportunity to put these skills into practical application. Next week I will be meeting with Ed Dame's Psi Tech group when my current boyfriend Brian and I travel to Alexandria, Virginia for the Scottish Games weekend.

Psi Tech is relocating to New Mexico soon and Ed Dames mentioned that they would need new "independent contractors" to carry out remote viewing projects. I'll know more after talking to Dames next week.

<u>Journal – July 27, 1992 – *Psi Tech Meeting.*</u>

Brian and I had dinner with Maj. Ed Dames of Psi Tech in Virginia, and I was impressed with his presentation and his company. Brian was quite skeptical, But Dames was able to assure him of the validity of the work and its applications. As Brian and Dames are both retired Army, this helped.

We discussed the trial remote perception on the Ark of the Covenant that I did for Psi Tech and the sessions that I did for Bill Higgins for PEAR. Dames said that Higgins was very complimentary about my remote viewing skills. Dames told me that he was very proud of his team of remote viewers and that he had the "cream of the crop" working for his company. He asked me to contact them once they were established in New Mexico. Dames asked me to be part of his group, which I feel is a great honor and to be part of their remote viewing team. A while ago I was meditating on the need for recognition – and here it is, someone who recognizes my abilities in this area!

(That evening I received a phone call from Ed Dames and got my first assignment. Dames gave me the coordinates 2259-5152 to work and will send my session tomorrow.)

<u>Journal – August 9, 1992 – *Psi Tech.*</u>

During the past few weeks I have completed some remote viewing work for Psi Tech and Ed Dames. According to Ed, I did well, and my perceptions matched at least three of the other viewers' perceptions.

What I saw, basically, was that a small plane carrying the target person crashed against a cliff as it tried to gain altitude in low cloud cover. The plane crashed near a light house, an estuary, a river and small town. The person got ashore but the plane, in three pieces got swept into deeper water and carried by the tide down the shoreline. Ed said he would send some copies of the transcripts so that I could see how my remote viewing matched the others. He said I would be "amazed."

<u>Journal – August 14, 1992 – *Viva Las Vegas*.</u>

Here I am, all checked out of the Hacienda Hotel waiting for my ride to the airport to catch my flights back to Princeton. (The old Hacienda casino on the Las Vegas strip was eventually demolished to make way for the Luxor). What a whirlwind of a week. My meeting with Robert Bigelow went very well and we seemed to hit it off. We spent a fair amount of time talking, attending the PA Conference, visiting with the UNLV folk and networking with colleagues.

Mr. Bigelow took me to look at some apartments and found one within reach of shops, buses, etc. with roaming room for my cat, at a subsidized rent. The Bigelow office building is a lovely old house, built by Bigelow Holdings in the style of a mansion and I'll have my own office downstairs where we are going to put together a library and computerized database of papers and reprints. We will also be liaising with the University to set up several research groups within the Schools of Health Sciences, Physics, and Psychology.

Bigelow Corporate Offices on S. Eastern Avenue, Las Vegas.

Journal – October 3, 1992 – *Para-Physics, Inc.*

My first days in Las Vegas and my first visit to socialize with likeminded people. On Thursday, the day I arrived, Robert Bigelow and I had planned to attend a meeting of a psi group that met on an informal basis. The leader, Alan, works as an engineering specialist for EG&G Energy Measurements. Alan runs a private group called Para-Physics, Inc, which runs every few weeks for the purpose of private research and exploration.

Unfortunately, Bigelow couldn't attend so I got a ride over and it was an interesting evening. Alan has one whole wall of his living room, taken up by a large-screen TV that he uses as a computer monitor and film screen. The group consisted of me, Alan, a UNLV psychology professor, psychic friends and several work associates of Alan's.

The evening was taken up mostly by Alan's psychic friends and the UNLV professor doing psi readings that Alan recorded. One colleague of Alan's, Dave, was particularly good and Dave turned out to be more than just a friend over the next few years! Alan had planned to give an electroencephalograph (EEG) demonstration that evening but his equipment wasn't ready.

Journal – October 24, 1992 – *Quakeline.*

Ryan Wood, who had formerly worked with Ed Dame's Psi Tech group, called me to chat. He had sent me a picture of a painting that had been stolen (along with others) from the Isabella Stewart Gardner Museum in Boston. Ryan is hoping to get a contract to remotely view the location of the lost paintings. I told him that I felt they were currently in Canada and that the painting, in question, was hidden under another old painting. If he gets the contract it would be interesting to do an extended viewing.

Ryan also told me about his company, Quakeline, that collects predictions of potential earthquakes. He asked me, as a viewer, to look at the next big earthquake and would pay me a small fee. Eventually he sent a list of questions related to the viewing.

I went ahead and did the viewing for Ryan and visualized a location for the next large earthquake. I saw fire and Asian people running. The city was modern with tall buildings and some neon lighting. Several foreign locations came to mind but could not pinpoint a location.

I realized that Ryan, who lives in California, needed more information than I had given him regarding this large earthquake. He needed the location of the next "catastrophic earthquake." The project title outlined specifically that the impact and timing of future earth changes was important. I told Ryan about flashes I had of NY and ruined buildings. The remote viewing that I had of the devastation in NY was appalling. The City was split in two, fires raged, and it was centered close to China Town and Little Italy.

(Now that I look back on this remote viewing, I am left wondering if what I viewed was the destruction of the Twin Towers, while not a natural earthquake, it certainly had the power and destruction of one. And the location was correct).

CASE FILES - 1992

PROJECT: Double-Slit Photon Experiment.
METHOD: Applied PK.
DATE: May 28, 1992 & June 17, 1992.
CLIENT: PEAR Lab.
TYPE: Research.

Earlier this month researchers Stanley Jeffers and John Sloan were at the Lab and brought with them an experiment that uses a split-screen photon-detection device. This experiment is based on findings in physics related to the behavior and detection of photons. The study took about an hour and we needed to complete five sessions each.

PROJECT: Drumbeat Experiment.
METHOD: Applied PK.
DATE: April 18, 1992.
CLIENT: PEAR Lab.
TYPE: Research.

One of Robert Jahn's theories is that human consciousness has its own "signature" or beat – and he initiated a drumbeat experiment to test out this theory. During 1992 I carried out a total of twenty drumbeat sessions with a mechanical drum that was programmed to function in several different modes: such as the amplitude mode and four different applications: soft versus hard beats; + versus - , on versus off, and randomly distributed.

The operator puts their consciousness into the task of ordering the random drumbeat output compared to unattended baselines. On this experiment, I obtained a good result, at the significance level, on the fourth order of the experiment. I have also completed a further five sessions in the frequency mode of the experiment. In this protocol, drumbeats are interspersed with pauses and the output is randomly distributed. Yesterday, the Lab analyzed my results and discovered that these new five series were also significant at the .05 level. This gives me a good feeling that the Lab is onto some significant information regarding the form and function of human consciousness.

PROJECT: Psychic Reward.
METHOD: ESP/PK.
DATE: 1992.
CLIENT: Houck, Wood and Vaughan.
TYPE: Research.

In the early 1990s, colleagues Jack Houck and Ryan Wood introduced me to researcher Alan Vaughan and their new intuitive software Psychic Reward. What an interesting program! This was in the days of floppy disks, small computer disks were just coming in, and PCs were still slow and cumbersome. In Psychic Reward, users viewed a wheel on the computer screen with letters of the alphabet arranged around a circle. Using either the psychokinesis (PK) option (influence the computer to choose the letter you pick) or clairvoyance (ESP) option (pick which letter the computer has already chosen) users clicked on letters and received musical tones as feedback.

This was a fun program and I had some statistically significant success, in both the PK and ESP options! I decided that I wanted to try the PEAR format (Baseline, High, and Low scores) with Psychic Reward. My attempt at a Baseline revealed a middling score, my attempt to get a High score was significantly high, and the low score was low but not statistically significantly. The percent increase between the high and low scores was significant with a Z score of 2.47! Jack Houck and Alan Vaughn wrote up their results in 1993 and again in 2000 for the *Journal of the Society for Psychical Research*.

PROJECT: Area 51.
METHOD: ERV.
DATE: 1992.
CLIENT: Bigelow Foundation.
TYPE: Applications.

How would you access information about an area of land that was not even supposed to exist? Through remote viewing maybe? Many people have asked me if I have remotely viewed that controversial area of the Nevada Test Site named Area 51, also called Dreamland. I can respond honestly that, yes, I have viewed Area 51, but there wasn't really anything too exciting there. The following is a report of a viewing that I did in the fall of 1992, commissioned by the Bigelow Foundation.

As I had some idea of the kind of terrain the area was situated in, I decided to look for unusual activity in and around the location. There was some busy activity up in the far north-westerly corner where I saw dynamiting and explosions occurring in the mountain side. There was activity to excavate into the hillside in order to build part of the facility underground or under the hill. Most of what is on the surface of the area, i.e. hangars and outbuildings are only partially functional, and most of the activity is underground.

I did see some fascinating engineering projects. There were the standard V-shaped aircraft but with an upwardly curved back, like a lateral arch on the back surface. There were also half-circle craft with this same arched, curve in the back. They looked like a horseshoe crab – without the tail. There were a few craft which had two arched curves cut into the back surface and looked bat shaped.

PROJECT: Ark of the Covenant.
METHOD: Natural RV.
DATE: July 15, 1992.
CLIENT: PsiTech.
TYPE: Applications.
COORDINATE: Ark of the Covenant.

In July, 1992, I met with a colleague, Ryan Wood, who had been working with Major Ed Dames' group, Psi Tech. Ryan suggested that, as an introduction to Psi Tech, I might submit a remote viewing project, notably "the current location of the historic Ark of the Covenant," that would be of interest to Psi Tech. This was completed as a voluntary applications project.

In mid-July, I completed the project, looking at the Ark's current location but not at its use or composition; just its "real-time" location. I perceived it to be in Haifa, Israel - in a cave located under the cellar of a house on a hillside. I perceived that the lower part of the cave could be accessed through the cellar, but the main entrance had collapsed and was filled with debris.

I perceived the Ark to be empty, that the contents had been distributed to thirteen elders when the Ark was stored in the cave. The lower cave originally had two entrances – one in a higher hill cave and the other one lower down. Knowledge of the caves was passed from son to son, until a house was built over the lower cave entrance.

The higher cave entrance was perceived as being surrounded by fruit orchards (olives and oranges) and the cave was used as a storage area for the fruit and its products. A tunnel led to the lower cave; it was full of debris but could be passed through. The lower cave was dry, but a stream ran underground across one corner. Knowledge of the cave under the house had almost been lost. Older, local people knew the story of the caves and the tunnel but don't realize the significance of what is there. Psi Tech liked my work and signed me up to do further projects.

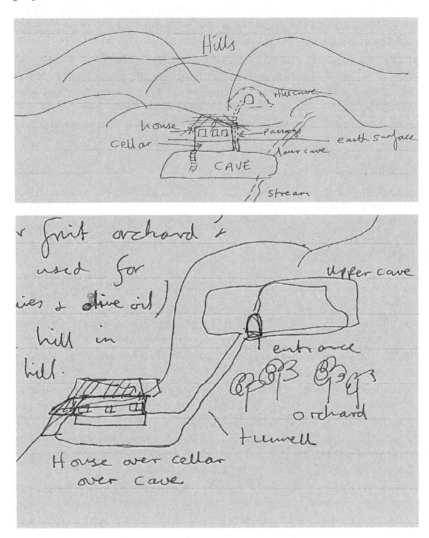

<u>The Little Prince.</u>
PROJECT: Plane Location and Recovery.
METHOD: Coordinate Remote Viewing.

DATE: July 28, 1992.
CLIENT: Psi Tech.
TYPE: Applications.
COORDINATE: 2259 2152

In the summer of 1992, I was able to meet Ed Dames in person in Virginia and was impressed by his energy and enthusiasm. He called me, in Princeton, shortly after, and arranged for me to carry out my first technical remote viewing as a consultant for Psi Tech. Ed explained that, while I had not taken his training, I had enough natural talent and discipline to be included in his team. I was thrilled to be participating. This was an unpaid, exploratory project.

That week, using just the random numbers (called a coordinate), 2259 2152, that Ed gave me, I attempted to remote view the target. I felt excited and challenged. My energy level was so high during the work that a psychokinetic event occurred. As I finished the viewing, something seemed to implode on the desk next to my bed, causing a hanging plant to swing and a pen to roll off the table. My cat stared at the spot, eyes wide with fear, for several minutes and would not be distracted. I have learned that stray outbursts of psi energy can often be associated with high energy levels, so the event did not alarm me.

A few weeks later, I carried out another viewing of the same target to focus on specific factors that Ed needed for his final report to his client. Eventually, I received a copy of the report, with my viewing included, and I was absolutely amazed at the concordance between information that other viewers had accessed and my own. This further confirmed my belief that this stuff works!

Little Prince RV Session.

I lay on my bed in my small apartment in Princeton, NJ, trying to relax my body and let my mind focus inward. Ed had given me a coordinate, a random series of letters and numbers, and nothing else, connected to a specific target and my job was to locate the target information. I had learned that relaxation is the best way to carry out my latest tasking – to find the location of a downed aircraft.

Lost at the end of WWII and piloted by author Antoine de Saint Exupery, the military mail plane was traveling south of the French coast and the weather was fine. Saint-Exupery was a well-known aviator and writer, the author of the children's book 'The Little Prince.' He was a seasoned pilot but had crashed several times before in Africa and France. Now in his forties, overweight, and in poor health, he had convinced the French military to rehire him to fly dispatches along the Mediterranean coast. During the flight the plane was lost, presumed crashed. Despite searches and inquiries, the loss of the plane and pilot remained an enigma for nearly fifty years.

I knew none of this as I lay relaxing, just the case number for the project, a coordinate consisting of random letters and numbers, attached to a hidden tasking: to locate the downed plane, to describe the location and any landmarks. This is called "blind tasking" to avoid leading the remote viewer.

The Princeton room was quiet, curtains drawn, my cat Sophia settled into my side, as I used the coordinate to mentally travel to the correct location. I immediately visualized high white cliffs. I next saw a beach, a lighthouse, rough water, and perceived strong currents and tides. There was an estuary and a small town nearby with houses lined up along a main street. Evergreen trees dotted the landscape around the small town and atop the white cliffs. I perceived that this was the correct location and wandered around observing and mentally recording my perceptions.

Next, I perceived a figure staggered ashore, dressed in a heavy, brown wool uniform. The figure wore steel-rimmed, old-fashioned glasses and had trouble walking. He came ashore, not at the estuary or the lighthouse but near a wooded valley that came down to the water between the white cliffs. I perceived that he felt very sad and that he would not see his family again. He was crying and fell on his knees. I realized that he was dying and stayed with him. Perhaps, at the time of his death he released some sort of energy because at that moment, in my Princeton bedroom, there was a very loud noise, my cat flew off the bed, items rolled off the bedside table, and a hanging plant started swinging wildly.

I am not a great artist, but I made sketches of what I had perceived; the huge white cliffs, the ocean, the estuary, the lighthouse, the vegetation, the small town and houses and wrote up an account of my perceptions that I mailed off to Major Dames. A few months later, I received a copy of a Final Report that included feedback about the project and the collected perceptions of eight remote viewers, including myself. As I read through the Report, I experienced an epiphany: This stuff works! Remote viewing works!

There was a high degree of matching between the viewers' perceptions. All the viewers had pretty much viewed the same location, one had even sketched the plane, and most of us described the lighthouse, the white cliffs and the estuary. It was one of the most important moments in my remote viewing career.

Feedback and Follow-up.

Further feedback was given to the viewers in the form of a newspaper clipping of a story involving the plane crash and disappearance of a Lightning P-38 during World War II on July 31, 1944. The pilot of the plane was the French author Antoine de Saint-Exupery.

No further feedback was available until November 1998 (six years after the fact) when an article in *Paris Match,* a French magazine, indicated that a trawler fisherman had found the location of the downed plane off the Cote d'Azure, in the south of France. An inscribed bracelet discovered at the site confirmed the plane as the one crashed by Saint Exupery. A request to the French authorities provided a great deal of feedback regarding the locale and landmarks in the area of the crash.

Additional feedback was provided in the form of an article published in the Smithsonian magazine *Air & Space,* dated May 2001. The article entitled *'Fishing for Saint-Ex,'* and authored by Joseph Harriss, examined the evidence recovered from the submerged plane in 1998. The data that pointed to this being Saint-Exupery's downed plane were that an oval air intake, particular to the F-5B turbo supercharger, found on the submerged plane, was like the one on Saint-Exupery's plane. The submerged landing gear was also like that on the plane that was piloted by Saint-Exupery. However, the French authorities and the family of Saint-Exupery have discouraged further investigations, declaring him a national hero, erecting statues to him, celebrating the 100-year anniversary of his birth in Lyon, and issuing a postage stamp with his likeness.

Psi Tech and Intuition Services.

Over the next year or so, I completed several more projects as a consultant viewer for Psi Tech and then things seemed to take a difficult path for the company. Ed moved Psi Tech from Virginia to New Mexico and focused most of the group's efforts on remotely viewing extraterrestrial activities. At this point, Ryan Wood and several other significant board members left the group. Ryan was in the process of setting up his own company, Intuitive Services, Inc. (ISI) in California and asked if I would like to join his team. ISI accepted projects as varied as looking for stolen art treasures, accessing information about future technologies, attempting to generate lottery numbers, evaluating the impact of major earth-changes brought about by earthquakes, and locating targets identified only by geographic coordinates.

1993

JOURNALS

Journal – January 27, 1993 – *New Year's Update.*
It has been several months since updating this journal and a lot has happened in the interim. One of the major concerns right now is; did I made the right decision to move to Las Vegas? Although one great thing to come out of the move was meeting David Smith!

The position with the Bigelow Foundation has not evolved as was originally planned. Before the move, I was assured that the position would involve research and would not just be administrative. However, most of my time is taken up with administrative duties. Also, my job description was originally presented as being a liaison between PEAR at Princeton and UNLV in Las Vegas and a replica PEAR Lab being built at the local university. This has not happened and there is no sign of it even being discussed. I am not a complainer, but my position could be taken over by a competent administrative assistant. I feel very frustrated: I miss working as part of a team and feel isolated down in my back office. Perhaps it is time to see what else is available in Las Vegas although I am not hopeful. Perhaps it is better to stay where I am for the time being.

Journal - January 27, 1993 – *Project Z and Relationships.*
Over the past few months I have completed some remote viewing projects for Ryan Wood and his new company Intuition Services. In November, Ryan asked me to remote view the Rings of Saturn for a representative from Lockheed. While doing that project, I was able to perceive the potential presence of a new alloy, consisting of two known Earth elements that we have named Z. Ryan and the engineer were very excited about this and asked me to do another viewing to see how this alloy was manufactured.

Ryan said they would try and manufacture some of this alloy and perhaps patent it (and that my name would also be on the patent).

However, he almost managed to blow up his garage when he tried first time to create Z!

It is a small world! It turns out that David's brother is remote viewer Paul Smith, who is also a Psi Tech viewer. I had been telling David what I did at PEAR and he mentioned that his brother Paul, who was in the U.S. Army, did "something similar." I also remembered Paul Smith's name from our computer database at the Lab, as he had requested reprints of PEAR's research.

When I mentioned this connection to Ed Dames, he said *"No way!"* But he checked, and indeed Paul Smith is David Smith's brother. David related to me that Ed Dames had told Paul that I was one of his "best viewers."

It is a small, strange world with all these characters interacting. Paul and David also know Hal Puthoff and Hal has been out in the Nevada desert sky-watching for UFOs using detection equipment created for specific frequencies.

Journal – January 29, 1993 – *Advice.*

I have been thinking about my decision to change jobs and have made the decision to hang-on for a few more months. However, if anything else comes along in the meantime I plan to reconsider. The following is some advice I wrote down for myself before taking the Las Vegas position and it applies equally well now:

"Be a strong decision-maker. To reach your goal you must gather all your resources together and organize them. Carefully consider the long-range consequences of temptation. They might not be so bad. Being more perceptive and courageous will put you in a position of power."

Journal – January 29, 1993 – *Wouldn't it be funny if...*

Yesterday I was playing a mind-game/exercise with myself "Wouldn't it be funny if____, and one of them was, "Wouldn't it be funny if the distance to the planets was shorter than we thought." We measure the distance to the planets in light years assuming that nothing travels faster than light. But what if that theory was wrong and "things" could travel faster than light, the distance would be much, much less. I have a problem with the notion of travel being measured as "light years." For example, a bicycle, car, and rocket can all cover the same distance, but the bicycle could do it in one hour, the car in ten minutes, and the rocket in one second. They will all have covered the same distance, but we don't refer to the distance as "bike miles" or "car miles" or "rocket miles," just miles per hour. Something infinitesimal might travel faster than light and traverse time and space as we know them and significantly shorten the travel time between "here and there."

Journal – February 3, 1993 – *Update on Z.*

I talked to Ryan Wood yesterday and they are very enthusiastic about the potential for Project Z. They envision heat-resistant ball bearings as well as other devices that could be manufactured from Z. The advantage of Z and Project Z are tremendous. These are some of the ideas that Ryan's group has been "kicking over:"

It would be announced that Z was discovered as a result of technical remote viewing, thus giving credibility and kudos to the skill. It could lead to new technological advances in superconductivity and devices that currently overheat at high temperatures could be made from the new alloy, such as car engines that could run on less fuel and oil; it might aid our "race for space" with coatings that could withstand high temperatures;

The project could prove financially healthy if, when it is patented, a benefactor might be willing to finance the application, or the patent could be sold to the highest bidder. I made a positive affirmation that these speculations would come to pass.

Journal – February 11, 1993 – *Test Site Visit.*

Yesterday Robert Bigelow and I traveled with a group from UNLV to the Department of Energy Test Site north of Las Vegas for an educational visit. As the test site was closing some of its departments, they were donating equipment to the university and the visit was for the departments to see some of the equipment. However, the visit was much more than that and we got to see a great deal more than the usual visitors to the Test Site.

We were picked up early outside of UNLV and drove up to Mercury where we received our badges. During the morning we attended talks and presentations on the monitoring at the radiation labs and visited some of the facilities. The highlight was one of the shielded rooms that contained a total body radiation counter.

We lunched at the Mercury staff restaurant and then traveled north by van to one of the control sites (where the original bomb tests were coordinated and monitored.) We watched videos of the underground tests and it was impressive to see the ground rippling and eventually caving-in of the blast holes. In the afternoon we traveled much further north to the P Tunnel, where devices had been irradiated under blast pressures to test their effectiveness, to Sedan Crater which was blasted to look at the nuclear potential for engineering projects; to Frenchman's Flat, where the first above-ground tests were conducted,

84

and to the areas where underground tests had caused enormous craters.

It was all intriguing and fascinating! I remember seeing films on TV of the first above-ground tests and seeing the site yesterday was amazing. There is a current moratorium on nuclear testing at the Test Site, but we were told that things were set up to move again, if the need arose. There are plans to put the site to peaceful purposes in the future, such as the development of solar energy.

Journal – February 18, 1993 – *Alternative Medicine Seminars.*
Yesterday evening was the first talk of the UNLV series entitled Alternative Approaches to Health Care and Janet Quinn was our inaugural speaker. She told us how research has proven that Therapeutic Touch enhances the relaxation response in cardiac patients, lowers diastolic blood pressure, significantly decreases pain, decreases anxiety in patients, increases human hemoglobin levels, and hastens wound healing.

Therapeutic Touch is healing through the human energy fields, takes about fifteen to twenty minutes and is used in major hospitals without the need of physician's orders. The talk and videoing of the presentation went very well, and the audience was very enthusiastic.

Next month we have Barbara Dossey talking on Holistic Nursing and health alternatives and, in April, her husband Dr. Larry Dossey will be presenting on medical alternatives and new paradigms. I was worried that the whole effort would come collapsing down around our ears but this first one went off so well that I have great hopes for the continuation of the series.

Journal – March 19, 1993 – *More Z Project.*
I finally got to talk to our Lockheed contact when Ryan called me on Tuesday. Ryan says they are still looking for the correct mineral powders to conduct an experiment to produce Z. It has been decided that Col. John Alexander of Las Alamos will test any product that is produced.

Our contact was quite profuse in his thanks, over the phone, for the information that I was able to retrieve through remote viewing. Ryan says that their patent search is complete, and it doesn't look as if any other groups or persons have tried to make this product. The plan is to go ahead and patent the idea in our three names.

Journal – May 5, 1993 – *Psychic Reward.*

For about a month now, I have been playing a psi computer game sent to me by Ryan Wood called Psychic Reward. It was developed by Alan Vaughan and Jack Houck through their company Mind Technology Systems. After playing with the software for a while I discovered that there were various tactics, I could use to produce high and low number scores.

Recently I have been experimenting, to try and do a tri-polar series (like the PEAR protocols): first trying to generate a low number effect, then a baseline in the middle, than a high effort to get high numbers, as a third attempt. This seems to have worked well. The low attempt generated a Z score of -1.32, the baseline -0.31, and the high intention generated a Z score of 0.93. While these individual scores were not significant the delta or split between them was.

What was more interesting was that if all the scores were added together to get an average, the overall score would be basically "chance," and what one would expect in a "conservation" model.

Journal – May 21, 1993 – *Dinner with Ingo Swann.*

Robert Bigelow had arranged for me to go to Manhattan for a few weeks to assist Budd Hopkins who had been sick and got behind with his correspondence and writing. We made a big dent in his backlog and I had some personal time to explore Manhattan.

On May 20, I had dinner with Ingo Swann (later to be called the Father of Remote Viewing) and found him to be a charming, soft-spoken, gentle man in his fifties. His art is colorful, dynamic, and outrageous and must be a representation of the "inner" Ingo. At dinner he asked if I would be willing to do some remote viewing projects for him on an occasional basis and if I could work from coordinates. I told him, "Yes, on both counts." Wow! To be asked to participate in remote viewing by one of the most illustrious viewers in the world is a great honor. Ingo also agreed to write the foreword to my book that eventually became *Remote Perceptions.*

Journal - June 4, 1993 – *Update.*

Amazing that I am starting the 15th volume of my psi journal. It started back in 1978 as a means of recording my OBE investigations (after attending the "Outer Limits of the Mind" class at Manchester University), then recommenced in 1984 when I was living in Orange, NJ (after watching a British TV series called The Omega Factor about parapsychology).

Such a lot has happened in those intervening 15 years. This new chapter in my life, here in Las Vegas, has introduced me to the beauty and wonders of the desert, mountains and hot springs of the desert southwest. Also, a host of new friends and an interesting job as a research coordinator in the fields of Parapsychology, Ufology and alternative health. I now have the time and space to do my writing and schoolwork with a possible opportunity for publication, various opportunities to do technical remote viewing with groups such as Psi Tech and Intuition Services. There is also bi-weekly participation in psi groups (Psi Club) such as Para-Physics, Inc. and communications and interactions with many interesting and wonderful people in the fields of science and medicine.

This summer I will have two important scientific papers published and may get, at least, one of my potential books accepted by a publisher. This week I have been getting my home office ready for the onslaught of writing for school and my books, which should start in August or September.

Journal - June 14, 1993 – *Project Z.*

Over the past two weeks I have had several calls from the folks at Intuition Services updating me on the progress of their attempt to create Element Z from my remote viewing efforts. (Back when I remote viewed the Rings of Saturn, I detected a new element that might be useful to humanity. I did a second remote viewing to perceive how it might be processed from two basic Earth elements. That process will not be reviewed here.)

The Intuition Services folks had been trying to produce the element in a garage but had already blown up their equipment trying to get the right pressure! I was getting concerned about the progress on this issue, particularly as they had asked another group to look at the process and this group was also trying to produce Element Z. A retired colonel from Los Alamos was also asking for information about the process. So, Z has been generating a lot of interest.

I called Intuition Services yesterday, to try and persuade them to find a qualified lab that they could trust, to undertake the preliminary processing and production of Z. It seems that they were going that afternoon to meet with Prof. Bill Tiller. Later, IS reported that Tiller was interested and would like to take on the project. I was pleased about this as I was concerned about the IS folks either blowing themselves up or never getting down to developing the element.

The IS folks were getting a bit out of their field and losing interest but, now they seem more excited about the project. They say they have a benefactor willing to put up production money, once there is a sample. (Unfortunately, in the decades since its discovery, Element Z has either not been produced or has gone deep into some "black" project.)

Journal - June 4, 1993 – *Art Recovery Project.*

Over the past few weeks I did some remote viewing for Intuition Services/Psi Tech regarding the stolen art from the Isabella Stewart Art Museum in Boston and they had passed on this information to the investigation team looking for the art, to the FBI, and to the Canadian Mounted Police. These groups reacted strangely to this information, being very skeptical, almost abusive, challenging Psi Tech to bring the art to their door! However, with the information from IS they were a bit more interested and put one of their "minor minions" onto the case!

In the meantime, IS gave another west coast viewer, Charles Nunn, the same project and he corroborated many of the things that I viewed about the art, its theft, and its current location. It was uncanny how many correspondences there were. There is a cash reward for the recovery of the art, and it is possible that our team could collect some of the money if the stolen art was recovered.

When I talked to Budd Hopkins (an accomplished artist himself) he knew about the art theft and was surprised that I was involved in remote viewing its location and trying to assist in its recovery. (To this date in 2016, the art has not been recovered although more is known about the actual theft.)

Journal - June 18, 1993 – *Project Z Continued.*

Intuition Services called today to update me on some of the projects we have ongoing. As well, as having Los Alamos and Bill Tiller interested in the Z Project, it seems we now have Lockheed interested and they will be having a meeting soon with IS officiating. One of the group members has learned to electroplate and is still in the process of accessing the right elements. He feels that it is OK to share information with these groups if they sign a non-disclosure statement provided by IS. (To date, 2019, nothing more has been heard about Project Z.)

Journal - June 18, 1993 – *Area 2000 Radio Show.*

Yesterday, at the Foundation, we had a meeting regarding Mr. Bigelow's idea about having a weekly radio program dedicated to the anomalies field, the UFO field. It seems that he has finally located a talk show host: Mr. Art Bell, from KDWN-720. Art is planning on airing Mr. B's program on Sunday evenings from 8-10 p.m. starting July 4!

George Knapp was able to locate Art Bell for the show and the meeting worked out some of the legal issues and how I would participate in locating weekly guests who had contributed professionally to their fields: Ufology, parapsychology, and alternative medicine. We still need to come up with a directory of potential speakers, which I am working on, a title for the show, and some theme music. I have generated a list of some potential titles (the one that we eventually went with was Area 2000).

Journal - June 30, 1993 – *Nalimov Paper.*

A week ago, I received copies of the *Journal of Humanistic Psychology* containing my published article on Russian mathematician/visionary Professor Vasily Nalimov, which was great! I had visited with the Nalimov's in Moscow, a few years ago and interviewed them for the article. Now I am waiting for my laterality paper to be published in the neuroscience journal *Cortex*, probably in August.

Yesterday I received a fax from Alfred Dorof of ISI Press. They publish *Current Contents*, a publication that goes out to millions of professionals all over the world and features a reference for all the Contents pages of all the scientific journals around the world that relate to the social sciences and psychology. They are going to publish an abridged version of my Nalimov paper with a foreword about the Nalimovs by Professor Eugene Taylor.

Journal - July 21, 1993 – *Ingo Swann.*

When I was visiting Manhattan a few months ago I had the delight of meeting and having dinner with Ingo Swann and had a wonderful evening. I was saddened to hear how disillusioned he was with psi research and the progress of remote viewing. He promised to send me an autographed piece he was writing, which arrived last week (he signed himself "Ingo Bingo"!) Then today his new book *Your Nostradamus Factor* arrived and inscribed "To Angela, a visionary, love Ingo." I had tears in my eyes as I read it.

Journal - July 21-22, 1993 – *Leukocyte Experiment.*

When my friend Dave and I were in Santa Fe, NM, we were intrigued by Col. John Alexander's talk about his research with Cleve Backster's Lab. Basically, Backster took cells (oral leukocytes), isolated them from the donor and monitored their activity. The Lab found that the leukocyte activity spiked in response to the emotional state of the donor.

When we got back from Santa Fe, Dave and I called Cleve Backster who was delighted that we were interested in replicating his work and sent us a reprint of his initial research. Last Thursday, at Psi Club, Dave and I carried out a pilot project. I donated some spit and we joked about "spitting for science!" This was centrifuged down to locate the white cells that were then placed in a shielded container. Their activity was monitored by computer and we watched the cells' movements on the Psi Club leader's giant wall screen.

After the solution had settled down to a steady state, we tried to affect my cells. They didn't react until Dave threatened to stick me with a pin and we got a lovely response spike! We got a few more spikes when I thought about emotional topics and when Dave tickled me but nothing more.

Then I decided to actively interact with my cells saying, "Come on, little cells, wake up" and they started producing some activity spikes again. Then we threatened to put them down the garbage disposal or douse them with mouthwash and they went crazy!

The activity from the cells produced continuous large spikes for about five minutes, and then the spike activity decreased with cycles of stabilization creating a "pulse" effect. It looked like a heart-beat trace. Finally, the trace settled down to a steady, almost flat state. The group leader monitored the cells for half an hour after we left but, he said, there was no further activity.

Yesterday, I called Cleve Backster and he was interested to hear about our pilot test. However, he said that just spitting into the tubes wasn't enough but oral washing with saline was needed to harvest the leukocytes. He is sending us some further supplements with instructions for the oral washings.

Journal - August 21, 1993 – *Update.*
This has been an interesting couple of weeks with lots of activity, both at work and at home. At the Bigelow Foundation we have continued the Sunday radio show, Area 2000, and to date Art Bell has interviewed John Alexander, Linda Moulton Howe, Brian O'Leary, Ian Stevenson, Budd Hopkins, Walter Uphoff, Bruce Maccabee and Raymond Moody. There hasn't been a lot of public reaction but the feedback we have received has been positive.

Each week it has been a challenge to hunt around and find UFO news for George Knapp to announce at the beginning of the show, but it is surprising how it all comes together. I have become quite adept at "surfing the nets," scanning the UFO and Paranormal computer bulletin board systems for newsworthy items. Today I found some literature on the Mars mission and its failure to communicate with Earth and news of Russian UFOs. I was able to share the Mars mission info with Brian O'Leary when he called as he had written about the "Face on Mars" theory and I mailed him what I had printed off the BBS. I hadn't heard about the communication failure and wondered if it had suffered the same fate as the Russian Phobos Mars probe which also lost communication. Brian is planning to come to Las Vegas sometime in September to meet with Mr. Bigelow. He may also attend one of the Psi Club Meetings and show us how to bend spoons with psi, which would be great.

My citizenship interview went well on the ninth and I am now waiting for information about the "swearing in court" ceremony.

Journal - October 1, 1993 – *Anniversaries.*

Today is an anniversary. One year ago, today I moved to Las Vegas to begin working for the Bigelow Foundation and one year ago that Dave and I met at the Para-Physics Psi Club meeting. A lot has happened during this past year as well as many things continuing to happen.

This fall I resumed my courses at Saybrook towards my Ph.D. in Psychology and have a total of nine courses to complete before working on my pre-dissertation essays and then onto my dissertation. This semester I am taking the statistics course again, critical thinking, and neuropsychology and learning disorders. These will complete my required courses so I will be able to choose six other courses that I can do quickly. I plan to get my course work completed by the end of next summer, essays completed in the fall semester, next year, and the dissertation completed the following spring semester. (It took longer than expected and I graduated 2001).

It is hard to believe that I have been at the Foundation for a whole year. Since July 4 the focus of the Foundation has been the radio show, Area 2000, sponsored by Robert Bigelow and featuring professional speakers from the UFO, the abduction field, the near-death and reincarnation fields. We have a continuous roster of speakers from July 4 through December 26 of this year.

Journal - October 13, 1993 – *Guest on Area 2000.*

After almost four months of booking guests on the radio show, Robert Bigelow asked me to appear as a guest, which is quite an honor. So, last Saturday, between 8 and 10 p.m., I was Art Bell's guest on Area 2000. We talked about the Bigelow Foundation, the PEAR Lab, Out-of-Body-Experiences, remote viewing, ghosts and psychokinesis and the two hours went by very quickly. Dave stood by with support, orange juice, love, and funny faces!

During the call-in portion of the show, the listeners asked some very pertinent questions and I was able to give them some information on each topic. Monday, we had about a dozen callers, many asking for additional information. George wasn't around to give his news segment on the show, but Linda gave an interesting interview with Debbie Tomey and some of Linda's recent sightings. People who called the office on Monday were very complimentary and said they enjoyed the show.

Journal - October 13, 1993 – *Disinformation?*

About a month ago, I received a phone call from a local Ph.D. psychologist who expressed an interest in working with abductees and doing regression therapy with them. He came to the office and we did some UFO video and audiotape swaps. At about the third visit he let slip, in conversation, that he had a "brother" in the "service" back east who had some information that there were several MJ12 members about to retire and he sort of tickled my interest with the information. He also mentioned that he had some friends in the CIA. At the next visit he leaned forward and asked, *"If someone wanted to give some information to the public without panicking them (about UFOs and aliens) how best could it be done?"* My reply was that information should be given to several top researchers and professionals in the UFO field and let the information "trickle down" gradually until it was accepted into the general knowledge of the population. He leaned forward again and said *"...Like your radio show?"* The last time he came to visit he was reluctant to talk about his ideas but said he was off to Virginia to see his brother...stay tuned. (Nothing came of this, but the therapist and his wife continue to send Christmas cards, as of 2016.)

Journal - November 30, 1993 – *ESP Games.*

I continue to work with several Psi software programs such as Dome (Jon Gaborioult), ESPTEST and Psychic Reward (Houck and Wood) on my computer. I have been getting some good results, particularly in the clairvoyant and ESP mode. I sent off some significant results to Jon. I have also called Princeton to participate in some remote PK programs, but they always say they are too busy to set them up.

Ryan Wood and his colleagues are still researching the art thefts and the Z Project (which Lockheed and Los Alamos are both interested in). Ryan was going to send me a video of the possible location of the stolen artwork, but I haven't seen it yet. On the positive side I find that my remote viewing and positive affirmation skills have been useful lately in locating restaurants and house hunting!

Journal - November 30, 1993 – *Moving Households.*

Dave and I have been talking about merging households for some time, but we put it off until after his divorce and until we found somewhere nice. I had several remote viewings of a house that had a coat closet in the entryway and a step down into the living room, with lots of rooms. We had looked through the newspapers and found possibilities but nothing that really appealed. The first one that we went to see was too near the smells of the Las Vegas city garbage dump. Then, a few weekends ago, Dave and I were driving around up by Hollywood Boulevard in Las Vegas and saw a house that was being repainted and for rent. We went inside and the painters let us look around. It had a hall closet in the entryway and a step down to the living room, lots of rooms and we both liked it right away. It had an enclosed back yard with two lovely trees, patio space, roses in the front yard, four bedrooms and a big living room. It was difficult coming up with the security deposit and first month's rent but using positive affirmations we got everything together (and we were even able to pay the rent early which the landlady appreciated). My new affirmation is that my old condo will rent out soon so I can move all my belongings to the new house. Dave will continue renting his old apartment until the New Year, and then we will merge households.

Journal - November 30, 1993 – *Dean Radin.*

Last month Dean Radin visited to meet with Mr. Bigelow and discuss his ongoing "psychic switch" research. Dean has now joined the Bigelow team and has set up his office over at the Harry Reid Center at UNLV. Dean has worked for various engineering companies as well as doing psi research at Stanford Research Institute and at Princeton University. Dean was also President of the American Parapsychology Association. He has been working on the development of his "psychic switch," using computer neural networks, for several years and this will give him an opportunity to go into further development. When it is in the applications stage I may go over and take part in some of his pilot studies. Mr. Bigelow's plan is to establish a center at UNLV and bring other scientists "on board" as it expands.

Journal - November 30, 1993 – *Area 2000 Closes.*

Since July 4, Mr. Bigelow and the Foundation have been funding a radio program on Sunday evenings from 8-10 p.m. called Area 2000. It has been a great success and has focused on two main areas of interest: the UFO field and near-death or after-death phenomena. We have had a great variety of speakers from both areas and we get many calls from listeners who hear the show. However, I think Mr. Bigelow is losing interest even though the host Art Bell and the listeners are very enthusiastic about the program. There may be some changes ahead.

George Knapp has opted out of the news spot at the beginning of the show and Linda Moulton Howe may incorporate his spot with hers. Also, Art Bell will soon be moving his studio from Main Street, downtown Las Vegas, out to his home in Pahrump, Nevada. This might affect the show although everything is done by telephone. It will mean reaching a bigger audience as Art will be linked by fiber optic cable to a stronger relay in Washington State. We may also go for a more varied program where speakers have the option to have listeners call in and we could have more than one guest on at a time.

Journal – November 30, 1983 – *ESP Testing.*

For the past month I have been conducting ESP testing in the office at Robert Bigelow's request. He received a set of Zenner (ESP symbols) Cards and scoring sheets from the Parapsychology Institute in Durham, N. Carolina. He decided to test the staff of Bigelow Holdings, on a voluntary basis, to see if we could get some results.

So far 114 people have participated in the clairvoyant section (that is just guessing what card comes up next in a stack) and 9 have completed the telepathy section (with me looking at the card and the staff member taking a guess at the card).

Overall, in the clairvoyant section of the test, the staff members scored marginally above chance, but a few members of staff did much better. One staff member, who has studied Transcendental Meditation (TM, a form of meditation), did well. One of the positive things to come out of this experiment is that Mr. Bigelow provided funds to purchase a comfortable recliner for the office which makes a nice addition.

Journal – November 30, 1993 – *UNLV Student Survey.*

When we knew that Dr. Dean Radin was coming to Las Vegas, Robert Bigelow was curious to see whether there was any interest among the students and whether courses on psi, healing and UFO research would be acceptable at UNLV.

Six thousand survey forms were sent out to all the Schools within the University and the response was good. We got over 1,200 responses and there was a six to one response in favor of the courses. What was interesting was the choice of topics that most student chose: Psi and

Dreams was the most favored with Alternative Approaches to Medicine, Remote Viewing, and UFO Research also popular choices.

About 20% of the students added their names to the responses and address for follow-up if courses were offered. Understandably there were some unfavorable comments such as: "Why waste money on such courses?" We need parking lots not more courses," and one respondent wrote "Shame on you!" across the form.

This response was encouraging for me, too, as I am giving similar courses at the Southern Nevada Community College in the New Year and it is reassuring to know of this interest.

CASE FILES– *1993*

Cortex Laterality Paper.

Prior to immigrating into the United States in 1981, I had worked for three years at the Department of Child Health located within the Faculty of Medicine at the University of Manchester, England. There I had worked as a Research Nurse while carrying out research towards my Master's degree. I finally wrote up my findings and gained my degree. My Professor, James L. Smart suggested that he and I write up the research for a scientific journal. I suggested Cortex, one of the most prestigious neuroscience journals, but Dr. Smart was doubtful that they would accept a Master's graduate paper. I went ahead anyway, applied and they accepted our paper! In 1993, Cortex published '*A Prospective Study of the Development of Laterality: Neonatal Laterality in Relation to Perinatal Factors and Maternal Behavior*' - Cortex, (1993) 29, 649.

The Mars Observer is Lost!
PROJECT: Mars Observer.
METHOD: ERV.
DATE: August 1993.
CLIENT: Bigelow Foundation/Independent.
TYPE: Applications.

In August of 1993, NASA's Mars Observer was on its way to view the Martian surface when it suddenly and inexplicably went dead. No communication was heard from the Observer after its system was shut down in order to pressurize the fuel tanks. As an avid computer bulletin board system (BBS) "lurker" I followed reports of NASA's efforts as they tried to communicate with the errant craft and get it back into communication.

The UFO community, particularly Richard Hoagland's group, had suggested that NASA may have deliberately sabotaged the Observer to prevent further pictures of the famous "Face on Mars" from being filmed. There were wild speculations that NASA had secretly turned the Observer back on and that pictures of Mars were being relayed to a secret location where clandestine surveys of the Martian surface were being carried out. In a radio broadcast at the end of November, Hoagland made a prediction that the Observer would suddenly regain communication by January 8 or 9, 1994. However, January came and went, and nothing happened. I did a quick remote viewing session that I relayed to the NASA BBS. After the fact, NASA issued a report and what they think may have happened to the Observer. My observations of dust and dirt particles becoming trapped in flaps that looked like cat-doors could have been correct. NASA commented in their report as dust and dirt may have entered the Observer's system sometime before launch, causing it to shut down.

Location of the Roswell Wreckage.
PROJECT: Location of Roswell Wreckage.
METHOD: ERV.
DATE: April 1993.
CLIENT: Intuition Services.
TYPE: Applications.

In April of 1993, I was asked to do a viewing by Intuition Services to locate the whereabouts of the Roswell wreckage. It has been widely speculated that a UFO crashed in Roswell, NM in 1947 and that the event was covered up by the government. The group wanted to know the current whereabouts of the wreckage and to locate a paper trail that could lead investigators to information regarding the Roswell cover-up.

As usual the group supplied me with a list of non-leading questions, looking for new information, to which I gave the following answers:

1. Where is the majority of the Roswell crash wreckage now? Where is it being studied now?
Large pieces of triangular and strut-like pieces of debris, wrapped in green cloth (surgical drapes) and over-wrapped in tarpaulin are sitting on dusty shelves in a warehouse at Wright Paterson Air Force Base. They are very high up, to the very end of row S. This row is the farthest right as you enter the front entrance to the warehouse. The

warehouse door is open to the light and, currently, not closely guarded. People come and go through the open door. There is an office space to the left of the front door (as you enter) and all the itinerary of the warehouse is coded in a locked file cabinet. In the cabinet are references to documents located in a locked file in a two-story stone building on the base.

Documents there are dated 1958 and are yellowed with age around the edges. They relate to physical examination of the debris. The documents have a decal on the top left, of a circle with a horizontal stripe through, and writing is superimposed on the design. The debris is not currently being studied but there is renewed interested from Los Alamos.

I did not see any round (flying-saucer shape) debris. When Brazel reported the debris to the military and they issued the initial press release, the debris that Brazel found was reported as a "flying saucer." This was purely a case of misinformation and confusion brought on by people not communicating clearly. Immediately, it was assumed that a round-type UFO had been discovered and sparked all the conjecture and stories that followed about the finding of a UFO.

There were one or more non-human bodies found near the Brazel ranch and these were removed immediately they were found. The finding of these bodies caused a great deal of panic and anxiety, miscommunication, misunderstanding and general chaos. At one time, the bodies were "lost"; it was reported that they had been rerouted by accident to another military location but were eventually recovered and studied. There was paperwork prepared for the removal of the bodies (at least two) but they indicated that the remains of two dead airmen were being moved. The names given were something anonymous like John Doe and James Doe. There was a rumor around that the bodies were of German paratroopers that had lain undiscovered after their plane crashed during the war.

2. Describe any living civilians that were aware of the crash before the military arrived. Male/Female? Age? Occupation?

Besides Brazel and his family, and people who have been described in the literature and in the media, there were two other people who had knowledge of the debris; a young boy who was at the ranch shortly after the crash, maybe a young nephew. There was also a young woman, a friend of the wife (housewife, wife of a neighbor) who was shown the debris. She didn't say anything because the wife showed it to her without Brazel's permission.

3. Is there a private source who has proof of the early July "74 crashes? Describe that person and his home.

There were various surgeons, pathologists and medical personnel, with military connections, who were sent samples of biological tissue and debris to analyze after the crash. One such person is a heavyset man with a florid complexion who lives in the New York area and works in New York City. He has several homes, including one in Westchester County.

4. Is there important documentation to be found about the crash in non-secret vaults, such as government archives or presidential libraries? If so, which ones?

All the important documentation related to the crash is still in secret vaults and not available to the public, yet.

5. Are there other crashed UFOs on the planet that have not been recovered that could be? If so, where are they?

Yes. Peruvian Andes, Colorado Rockies, Russian Urals. Round shapes have been recorded on spy satellite images of the Rockies but have been dismissed as anomalies or geological formation. Maybe the mountainous areas cause crashes due to misjudgment of height, weather conditions, and geomagnetic anomalies. Despite their advanced technology, the craft pilots do make mistakes!

6. What caused the Roswell crash(s)?

An electrical storm combined with fluctuations in the electromagnetic field of the Earth i.e. an electromagnetic anomaly in the geography around the Brazel ranch?

7. Describe the aftermath and activities of the personnel around the crash site at the Plains of St. Augustine, NM and at the wreckage area near the Marc Brazel, Foster sheep ranch?

There was a great deal of anxiety and confusion, miscommunication, misunderstanding of orders, dereliction of duty, reporting sick and general disturbance among the military personnel. Nobody knew what anybody else was doing, orders were given and rescinded, personnel were ordered to one location, then told to return as soon as they got there, a general feeling of incompetence and confusion.

8. Were there live or dead non-humans at each site? Where are the corpses now? Are they or were they actively studied by humans? If

98

so, what are/were the surroundings? What are/were they studying? DNA structure?

At least two non-human bodies were found. Cell structure was studied as well as morphology. DNA wasn't discovered until 1953 and by then the bodies of the aliens had been cremated. (The bodies got so disgustingly putrid after thawing for tissue samples that they had to be burned). The testing of the tissue samples did not take place in one location but were sent out to multiple labs. The individuals doing the testing were not told the specific source of the samples, just to analyze them as a biological sample and make a report.

9. *Is there a key witness or document that will "break-open" the Roswell case in the future? Please describe the document or the person. What is the color of the markings at the top/bottom of the document?*

Wings. Blue. The Manager of the Wright Paterson warehouse has been there a long time and knows what is on the shelves. Maybe when he retires, he will be willing to give information.

1994

JOURNALS

Journal – January 3, 1994 – *New Year Update.*

What an interesting year 1993 turned out to be! This time last year I was ready to quit my job and had no idea what I was supposed to be doing here in Las Vegas and, particularly, with the Bigelow Foundation. However, over the past year the job has become more interesting, especially with the support of the Area 2000 radio show back in July. However, there is still not a lot for me to do and, consequently, I am under-utilized at the office.

On the plus side I get a lot of free time when I can complete schoolwork towards my Ph.D. in Psychology at Saybrook. This semester I completed two courses; Critical Thinking, and Neuropsychology and Learning Disabilities.

Over Christmas I talked with Dean Radin and expressed an interest in doing some research with him when he is hired over at UNLV at the Center for Advanced Cognitive Science.

Journal – January 3, 1994 – *Update Continued.*

There hasn't been much happening in the psychic line except a recent project from Ryan Wood. Part A involves remote viewing

99

random picture targets located at his California home and getting feedback. The first was, that I completed on Friday, was of an arrow and Ryan felt that I was 80% on target.

Part B of the project is a latitude and longitude remote viewing of a location in Nevada to find "treasure." This is frontloaded but my goal each time is to look for new and unknown information.

Finally met our Lockheed contact, a husband and wife, RB and SB, last week. RB was on the Psi Tech board but resigned and re-aligned with Ryan Wood's new company. We talked about the art theft project with ISI and the Z project. I voiced my concerns about Ryan potentially blowing himself up trying to manufacture some Z product and the idea that the concept might get stolen. I hope that Ryan, RB, Lockheed, or some other Lab produces some Z this year so they can get it patented.

Journal – January 10, 1994 – *Coordinate RV.*

I received a remote viewing project from Ryan Wood and the only information (frontloading) provided were the coordinates and the word "treasure." At first my imagination gave me the site of "Treasure Island," a new casino in Las Vegas but I reasoned that it could not be that easy.

When I did the actual viewing, I saw a location north of Las Vegas, a military installation located between several narrow valleys and surrounded by mountains. I later learned that two UK researchers had initiated the project. Ryan said he would try and get me some feedback on the project.

Journal – January 10, 1994 – *Area 2000, Final Broadcast.*

It was announced last week that February 6, will be the last Area 2000 interview. I wasn't surprised as Robert Bigelow seemed to be losing interest in the program over the past few months. He decided that it would be too difficult to get another six months of quality speakers (although I had a schedule for the next six months of professional speakers.) Also, George Knapp had dropped out of the show a few months ago.

I talked to Art Bell before the last show and he told me that his plans are to carry on the show from his Pahrump home studio, as there is a great audience and he wants to syndicate the show across the country. I think Art will do fine and all that is needed is a change of name and disclaimer that the Foundation is no longer connected with the show. I have arranged and listened to every show since July 1993.

Despite its short six-month run, the show was great for networking and getting to know new people.

Journal – January 10, 1994 – *Mars Observer Update.*
Back in October, I did a remote viewing of the Mars Observer that had ceased communication. I viewed a piece of grit that got caught in a "cat door" type of pressure valve and that when the craft was pressurized to mix fuel the doors failed to shut, and the systems failed to come back online. I had documented this session with Michael O'Neal at NASA and had told Art's radio audience about it, too.

Yesterday, in the local paper, there was a report that it was speculated that the Observer developed a leak and fuel was wasted, which sort of ties in with my viewing. When they locate the craft NASA will report on its condition.

Journal – January 18, 1994 – *More on the Mars Observer.*
Today, I logged onto the NASA Bulletin Board System (BBS) to find a press release dated January 5, 1994 regarding the Mars Observer and its speculated demise. Although the team could not "point to a particular event that caused the loss of the Observer" they did write that the "most probable cause" was a rupture of the fuel pressurization side of the space craft's propulsion system resulting in a leak of helium gases. This interrupted the stored command sequence and did not turn the transmitter back on. They also stressed a lack of post-assembly procedures for verifying the cleanliness and proper functioning of the propellant pressurization systems.

Journal – January 19, 1994 – *Nevada Coordinates Feedback.*
On January 6th I carried out an RV of a site identified only by coordinated of a location in Nevada. There was a frontloading of "treasure." I have since learned that the group who commissioned the viewing were George Wingfield, the English editor of *The Cereologist*, Michael Brein of Infopreneurs-Informed Sources, and another unknown researcher by the name of John Haddington. George Wingfield provided Ryan Wood with feedback that indicated:
"I was both impressed and disappointed with the RV report on our Nevada target...The description of the classified military base is remarkable and sounds very accurate...There is one extraordinary hit in the report...the feeling that he (she) triggered some sort of alarm. This is spot-on! The immediate vicinity of our treasure is dotted with electronic alarm systems which emitted radio signals."

Michael Brein's feedback letter included the following: "First I would like to say that the initial results of our test are very, very promising.... you just don't know how good your initial results are!"

This feedback was very helpful to me. I had also indicated in a later session that there was a black triangular object and that there was a connection to a pyramid. The group provided a picture of the "treasure" that was buried at the site.

(Later I learned that the group had buried a plastic bag from the Luxor Casino along the dirt road leading to the entrance to Area 51. The bag depicted the Luxor Casino building that is in the shape of a pyramid. While on the dirt road they had triggered one of the electronic sensors and prompted the appearance of the security vehicle in the area. My colleague Dr. Barbie Taylor also took part in the viewing, got the site right, and perceived "a silver dollar in a jar." The target contained 4 quarters in a cup! So, she was right on target!)

Feedback Photo from the Nevada Treasure Project.

Journal – July 1st, 1994 – *Mid-year Update.*

Major changes have taken place since I last updated this journal. In mid-April I decided that my role at the Bigelow Foundation was over and I gave my notice on April 11. I had decided to work through to the 22 or until the end of the month, if that was what it took for to find my replacement. However, Robert Bigelow decided that I should leave on the 12th and I packed up my books and set up my home office to continue my writing, studies and consulting work.

My Saybrook graduate courses are continuing with the completion of the Statistics course, and registering for a Social-Health course, Eastern Psychologies, and Prof. Stanley Krippner has asked me to work with him on updating his Introduction to Parapsychology workbook. All of this will complete my course credits towards my Ph.D.

(Unfortunately, Dr. Krippner and I could not locate the original of the workbook, so we could not work on it).

Now that I am at the end of my coursework, I am preparing for the essay and dissertation stages of my doctorate. I have decided to write my essays on Human-Computer Interaction, Expectancy Effects, and (a Saybrook requirement) a critique of another student's dissertation proposal.

Journal – July 1, 1994 – *Dissertation News and SSE.*

I am working on my Saybrook dissertation proposal and SIRB approval and plan to start running subjects for my study at the beginning of January. When I returned from the Society for Scientific Exploration (SSE) Conference in Austin, TX, I got a heartwarming response from the PEAR Lab that they unconditionally approved my borrowing one of their portable Random Event Generators (PORTREG) and using the Lab's software and methodology for my dissertation study. I will be going out in September for a refresher course. It will be good to see Princeton and the Lab again.

Journal - October 5, 1994 – *Back to Work.*

The summer of 1994 was wonderful! I took five months off to work intensively on my book *Where Angels Tread* and finished up the coursework for my Saybrook Ph.D. in Psychology. (Originally, I had worked with Bluewater Press to publish the book, but it was eventually published with Hampton Roads as *Remote Perceptions*.)

My schoolwork raced ahead, and I finished all the required course work towards my Ph.D., as well as one of the pre-doctoral essays. The first one was a review of Expectancy Effects in the Psychological Literature. The second one, I have planned, is a review of Human-Computer Interaction related to Psi Research, and the third will be a critical review of a Saybrook student's dissertation proposal. Finances have been tough with no job, but school loans have helped.

There was a possibility of working with Dean Radin at the Cognitive Sciences Lab at UNLV, but the financing didn't come through for him to hire me. Since Dean set up his consciousness lab at UNLV, I have been down several times to participate. He has several studies set up, mostly psychokinesis (PK) including a novel application in which a small robot is linked to a random number generator (RNG). The participant in the experiment uses PK to influence the robot which picks up a candy and places it in a cup. Usually it takes a lot of concentration and can take between seven and an infinite number of moves to complete its task. I was able to do it in nine moves!

At the end of October, Dave and I will be flying out to the east coast to spend some time at the PEAR Lab at Princeton University, For my Dissertation research, I will be using one of the Lab's RNGs (PORTREG) and doing a research project on PK and Expectancy Effects, here in Las Vegas.

Journal - October 16, 1994 – *Spoon Bending.*

Last weekend we had Alan Vaughan and his student Chris Lindsley staying here for the Whole Life Expo. I attended as Alan's guest and went to several talks including one given by Dr. Timothy Leary! Dr. Leary is now an old man and I was quite disappointed with his talk, as he waffled on about nothing. (I was expecting to be wowed!)

In the late afternoon, I attended Jack Houck's Spoon Bending Party, to learn how to use PK to bend silverware. I had never bent cutlery before, but I bent three spoons and a fork. I was able to put two sideways turns in two of the spoons. I didn't think I was going to be able to bend them, at first, but as others began bending, the metal on my first spoon got soft and warm and I was able to bend it easily. After that it was easy to bend several more. I'm glad I wasn't one of the attendees not able to get a bent spoon. Afterwards Dave and I went with Jack and Jean Houck to have dinner at the Holy Cow restaurant in Las Vegas.

Dave's theory is that the spoon-bender gets into an altered state of consciousness and can tap into subconscious layers that allow the participant extra energy to bend the cutlery. However, there are studies that show the metal goes through a "warm-forming" and the crystalline changes are different than when the spoon or fork is bent through forcible or cold-form bending.

Journal - October 16, 1994 – *Intuition Training Software.*

Recently James Spottiswoode posted a paper by Alan Vaughan and Jack Houck outlining the development and testing of their Psychic Reward software, designed to develop psychic abilities. Ryan Wood had given me several complimentary copies of the Psychic Reward software and I sent Jack Houck one set of three series where I felt I had done well. Jack and Alan decided to include the data in their paper, along with several others, to illustrate how the software was able to generate significant results. Eight test subjects showed a significant improvement from their first to their third series and three subjects (including myself) achieved significant increases. ($z = 2.51$, $p = .006$).

Journal - October 24, 1994 - *PORTREG.*

Last Friday I received a package from John Bradish at PEAR containing the portable REG (RNG) device: PORTREG, connectors, software and documentation that I will use for my Ph.D. study. Unfortunately, the calibration software wasn't immediately operable, but I completed a few series with the device connected to the computer that I will use for my first pilot project. As soon as I can document the calibration software, I will start running calibration series. I was very excited to receive the box and feel well on the way towards my dissertation.

CASE FILES - 1994

The Unabomber.
PROJECT: The Unabomber.
METHOD: ERV.
DATE: 1994.
CLIENT: ISI.
TYPE: Criminal Case.

In 1994, Intuition Services contacted me with another project. They were requesting information about the Unabomber, who was only known, at that time, by his initials left on a package bomb. We now know that Theodore Kaczinski was responsible for sixteen bombings since 1978 but was still unknown to the public in 1994.

Intuition Services sent a series of questions, which requested unknown information about the Unabomber. Some of these questions were related to a physical description of the Unabomber: Describe his age, height, weight, color of eyes and complexion.

I perceived that the Unabomber was late 30s to early 40s (he was early 50s). I also reported that he was over 6' tall, skinny and gangly. He was under-weight for his height. He had dark blond to light brown hair and an "expressionless" eye, like there is no light there. This was a realistic description.

I perceived that he "worked at home, in a rural area, in a shack-like residence among trees. I got the feeling that he worked alone and was in sympathy with environmental groups but was not active with them. He subscribed to the "political philosophy behind environmental actions and ideas." He was eventually found to have written a Manifesto of his political and social ideas.

My data, along with other perceptions from other viewers was given by Intuition Services to the FBI but whether it was acted upon is unknown. (He was found through other means.)

Gold Coast Properties Assessment.
PROJECT: Gold Coast Properties, Australia.
METHOD: ERV.
DATE: 1994.
CLIENT: ISI.
TYPE: Real Estate Evaluation.

To get to Couran Cove, QLD, Australia, you must take a small speedboat taxi from the Gold Coast resort across the bay to a small rain-forested island. Here, developers had been working with ecologists to build a resort in harmony with nature. In 1994, two colleagues, connected to Intuition Services, decided to invest money in the venture and asked me to do a remote viewing project for them. The investors wanted to know which of the three types of residences would be their best buy, would any of the structures have problems, and what would be the return on their investment in the years ahead?

I did a viewing of the site, found some problems with the supports on one of the types of structures and advised them to purchase one of the other units. It was perceived that they would have a very good return on their investment. One of the purchasers, when he went out to Australia, notified the builders of the problem with the supports and this was corrected. Both investors bought property, one later sold at a good profit, and the other investor still has his property.

In 1997, I had the opportunity to visit the location and the new structures when I toured the Gold Coast and took the water taxi across to the island. Couran Cove was beautiful with a natural rain forest in the center, white sandy beaches at both ends and wild kangaroos playing tag with the golf carts. It was good to get some tangible feedback.

The Big One in the Big Apple.
PROJECT: Earth Changes.
METHOD: ERV.
DATE: 1994.
CLIENT: Intuition Services.
TYPE: Applications.

By 1994, I had been working for about a year with a remote viewing group in California, Intuition Services, which also solicited earthquake information, and ran a 900-service called Quakeline. The group was interested to see if I could predict the impact and timing of future Earth changes using remote viewing. The following remote viewing was specifically focused on future earthquakes that would cause major Earth changes. There has been speculation that "The Big One" - the next gigantic California quake would separate most of the California coast, sending it into the Pacific Ocean. What I viewed, however, was an Earth-changing event that may occur on the East coast of America. Ryan Wood sent me a list of questions related to the viewing that needed to be accomplished and these were my responses, which pointed out that the next "Big One" could very well be in the "Big Apple."

The problem description from Intuition Services said the following: Data from several independent sources have predicted cataclysmic volcanic and earthquake activity to occur throughout the world. A specific sequence of events has been hypothesized leading up to the final sinking and re-arrangement of the west coast of America. Gather the remote viewing scenario for Earth changes and compare/contrast with existing data. The following questions were supplied by Intuition Services to which I responded with the following answers:

1.   *Specifically, when and where will the next major quake occur with significant damage/drastic implications for the U.S. or the world?*
The next major quake which will occur with significant damage/drastic implications for the U.S. and the world will be in the New York and New Jersey area, specifically affecting New York City/Manhattan, although other major cities and towns will suffer severe damage.

2.   *Describe in detail the geography of destruction (faults, hills, cities), how will water, power, pipelines, communications, and transportation be affected, both short and long term?*
Manhattan lies in the path of a major fault that created the foothills of New Jersey. There is a fault that underlies central Manhattan that has been active in the past. Manhattan was once two islands, but surface activity filled in the rift thousands of years before the arrival of the Europeans, who found it one island.
The destruction will be catastrophic and was difficult to view because of the viewer's feelings of horror at the extent of the damage, both to property and life. Loss of life in the subway system is

107

particularly appalling. The quake occurs in the dark and it is cold, which hampers rescue efforts. The island is basically split in two across the middle, first affecting China Town and Little Italy. The quake pushes the two halves of the island apart laterally causing property damage up and down-town. Water, power, pipelines, and transportation are all destroyed but some communication, which does not rely on power lines, will be maintained.

3.   *Describe the aftermath, fires, logistics problems, flooding or any other significant problems. What are the things or skills that are needed most to speed recovery and repair?*

Prior to the quake, many, puzzling, small ground fires arise in the New Jersey and New York areas, which are later found to be due to natural gas leaking to the surface and spontaneously combusting. Looking out over Manhattan from the New Jersey foothills, before the quake, a much heavier than usual haze lies over the city, making the lights shimmer.

The aftermath of the quake is terrible: many major fires, roads are torn up and twisted and communication and power lines are torn apart as the island separates. The major change that occurs is that water from the rivers on either side of Manhattan flood into the central rift causing it to flood. This central waterway will eventually be named the Manhattan Strait (some will affectionately call it 'The Canal').

The skills most needed to speed recovery and repair will be a. airborn lighting (the waterways around the island will be too disturbed for waterway assistance), b. air-born water-delivery systems for the many fires (some will advocate letting the city burn), c. medical and humanitarian aid to deal with the injuries and loss of habitation of millions of people, d. political and PR systems to defuse the public attitude that the city somehow deserved the catastrophe, this attitude could hinder financial and other aid to the city's recovery, e. psychological assistance to enable the remaining residents to rebuild the city, taking advantage of the rift, the strait, and encouraging the rebuilding of communication and building of bridges between the islands.

4.   *How will the average quake victims deal with the trauma? What are their fears, anxieties and hopes?*

The average quake victim will be either dead or severely injured. The primary goal of the survivors will be to get medical aid, food and shelter. Dealing with the trauma, their fears, anxieties and hopes must wait until after their immediate survival needs are met. The devastation will be so great that, for a time, there will be a communal sense of total helplessness and apathy. Dealing with this aftermath will require a concerted and skilled effort from the rest of the nation.

5.   *Determine the timing of major/significant damaging quakes/Earth-changes for the following cities: Tokyo, Southern California, San Francisco/bay Area, Seattle, Missouri, New Year and London England.*

Other major/significant damaging quakes/Earth-changes will occur in Beijing, China; Denver, Colorado; the western coast of south and central America, specifically Santiago, Chile; and Mexico City, Mexico. Lesser quakes, in view of damage to persons and property, will occur in Alaska, the Ural Mountains, and in Samoa. All these will occur within the next twenty years. I did not see any devastating damage occurring in other areas, i.e. Tokyo, southern CA, San Francisco/Bay Area, Seattle, Missouri, or London, England, although minor quake activity will continue.

6.   *Describe the sequence of geological events, what starts first, how do the changes progress significantly and what are the final series of quakes before a long multi-year quiet.*

Quakes will be preceded by anomalous events such as small ground fires, caused by the leakage and combustion of natural gas. Haze, before major quakes, will be characterized by its increasing density and its propensity to hug the ground causing fogs. Water levels will fall, then rise dramatically. The quakes will increase in strength and proximity to each other in a westerly to easterly direction across the globe and will drift upward from the southern hemisphere to the north. The quakes will then lessen in intensity, followed by a long quake-free period.

7.   *Will any new large land masses be formed? If so where and how big?*

The only land masses that I saw formed were the two separate islands caused by the splitting of Manhattan.

8.   *Describe the implications/changes that result from volcanic eruptions? Which eruptions have the most impact on communities/countries both logically and globally?*

I   did not remotely-view any volcanic eruptions. I was focused on quake activity.

9. Are there any magnetic pole shifts in our short term 50-year future? If so describe, direction, new poles and impact on current and future society and commerce.

I did not detect any magnetic pole shift although the fact that the quake activity shifted from the south to the north hemisphere could be a prelude to a later shift. I have no comments currently on the impact of such a shift on current and future society and commerce.

Feedback.

While this viewing does not rule out a major quake on the west coast it does point to a major impact on the east coast including devastating earth changes. Following this viewing, I heard that several other remote viewers had also predicted the "Big One" in the "Big Apple." In addition, old maps were found from around 1933 that clearly showed three major fault-lines running centrally across Manhattan through the Bronx Park, Central Park and lower Manhattan.

An interesting article appeared in the New York Magazine of December 1995, written by Fred Graver and Charlie Rubin, and entitled *'Earthquake: Not only can it happen here - but it will.'*

More than eighty people from different disciplines were interviewed for the article. The authors stated that, although these individuals had "wildly competitive agendas" they all agreed on one thing, maybe not today, maybe not tomorrow but a big quake is coming, and New York is not ready for it! The authors also said that although the interviewees disagreed on how big, how devastating and how soon it would come, nobody denied that New York was going to see a major earthquake.

(As we know, on September 11, 2001, the NY Twin Towers fell in a disastrous terrorist event. Some people have asked me if this was what I was predicting with the Big One in the Big Apple, as the falling towers created an earthquake-like impact on the island. I have to say, I am not sure, and that maybe the Big One is still yet to come.)

Sephoris Excavation.
PROJECT: Sephoris Excavation.
METHOD: Coordinate Remote Viewing.
DATE: April 1994.
CLIENT: Intuition Services.
TYPE: Applications.

Remote viewers have been tasked on many projects to locate historical sites and hidden treasure. For example, in 1994, Intuition Services hired several remote viewers, at the request of the Albright Institute for Archaeological Research, located in Jerusalem, Israel. Under the auspices of the USF, the Institute had partially completed the excavation of a site at Sephoris, Israel, thought by many to be the birthplace of Mary, the Mother of Jesus. This information and other relevant facts were withheld from the viewers. They were only provided with a grid-map of the site and asked to determine (a) if it was worthwhile for the archaeologists to continue the excavations and (b) what would be found at the site?

Using the grid numbers on the map provided as coordinates I perceived a bath area, artifacts, structures and possibly human remains at the site. These perceptions were confirmed upon further excavation.

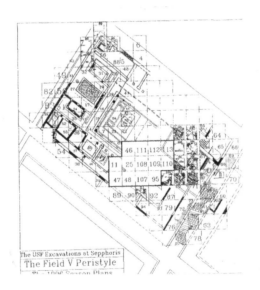

The USF Excavations at Sepphoris
The Field V Peristyle

The Four Corners Enigma.
PROJECT: Four Corners Enigma/NORAD.
METHOD: ERV.
DATE: 1994.
CLIENT: Intuition Services.
TYPE: Applications.

On January 12, 1994 an incident occurred that was noted and followed by NORAD for a week. The event caused a great deal of concern in the Four Corners Area of New Mexico. Basically, a large thermal signature was noted by tracking satellites. A large fire was suspected but when the area was checked there was nothing to be found. In August 1994, Intuition Services commissioned me to do a remote viewing of the site and provided a list of non-leading questions that required responses per their protocol.

Frontloading: *This remote viewing investigates the "NORAD" incident which started on January 12, 1994 at 2:55 pm and continued for about a week. The location of the incident is 37 degrees 30 minutes North Latitude and 106 degrees 18 minutes West Longitude.*

Following are my responses based on a remote viewing of the event.

Preliminary perceptions:
   A planned, staged event. A covert operation.

1.   *What caused the large thermal signature that NORAD detected? Did it pass into the Earth, or crash killing the occupants? How did the event end?*
   What NORAD detected was not a thermal signature, but it was interpreted by their technology as "thermal" because of its unusual nature. There was no crash, no occupants killed, and the signature originated above the surface at about several hundred feet. The signal was an interaction between a new energy technology and known electromagnetic signals already being generated in and around the area. The signal was generated and registered by a set of three towers set in a triangular, or trigone, pattern set about a hundred miles apart. The energy produced a plasma, amorphous in shape, and spread over patchy areas of about fifty to a hundred miles. The concept was like Tesla's original idea of long-distance energy transfer. The event ended by the signal being turned off so that the results could be analyzed. The event may have been detected at night by the appearance of apparent lightning, when no storms were evident. The lightning appeared greenish or bluish. It is possible that people in the area biologically detected the energy and suffered from minor conditions such as headaches, ringing-in-the-ears, stomach-aches, and peripheral neuritis i.e. pins-and-needles in the hands, feet and limbs.

2.   *Is there an underground military or ET base in the sighting area? If so, what is its purpose and function? Describe the size of the base and the access procedure to the base from someone walking.*

There are underground bases but not in the Dulce/ET sense. The bases are strictly military and designed to access satellite information and to detect and analyze military activity. Access to these sites would be difficult as most are accessible either by air or by heavy four-wheel drive vehicle. Some are on reservation land or military land (covert use) but one or two could be walked into. They are not readily recognizable by eye but look for new plant growth over heavy vehicle tracks. Most of the bases are small, usually only one or two story deep, and their primary functions are tracking and accessing satellite or radar information.

3.   *Did the helicopters searching the area a few days later find anything interesting? Were they really US military helicopters or just images that appeared that way?*

A variety of craft were sent into the area, both small airplanes and helicopters, military, government, and civilian. None found anything unusual although a few reported instrument disturbances of aircraft controls.

4.   *Is the incident of November 30, December 1, 1993, in the La Garita area associated? Is so, how? Was there a crash? Any recoverable hardware evidence?*

Sorry, to disappoint you but no, no and no. The incident in the La Garita Area was the result of natural phenomena, local talk and exaggeration. The incident did not cover such a large area as the 1994 incident and did not generate as much attention.

5.   *How many active and inactive ET bases are there in Colorado and New Mexico? What is the purpose of the inactive bases? What is the mission of the active bases?*

There are no actual ET bases (as described by the UFO community, such as the one at Dulce). ETs appear to come and go regularly but do not appear to have established a permanent site as a base. There are favored touch-down places such as lakes and mesas.

6.   *Are there joint US Military and ET bases? What is the purpose of such cooperation? Describe the nature/scope and specifics of any technology transfer that occurs at these underground bases?*

There are at least two bases, not underground, on apparently inactive military sites, which house at least one occupied UFO each. One is housed in a large building, which has steps up the side, which lead to a side door, onto a walkway inside which looks down onto two large rectangular pools of water. In one is a saucer shaped UFO. ETs of the slender gray variety can enter and exit the craft more easily and the water pressure (providing buoyancy) prevents internal damage to the ship and the occupants when they are inside. There are rooms to the side of the larger building where ETs and humans can interact for short periods. There has been an exchange of information and both humans/ETs are learning about each other. Some of the ETs wear human clothing when interacting with the humans. This was decided by the ETs and humans to facilitate psychological acceptance by the scientists and civilians that meet the ETs.

7.   *Has there been any active misinformation given about the NORAD incident? If so, what is the falsehood and why as it seems, with most government agencies, NORAD does not have access to other agencies and their current activities?*

So, it is quite possible that NORAD had no idea what was happening in the area. During the actual operation and after it would not have been possible to ascertain what has happening in the area without specialized signal detection equipment. NORAD happened to pick up the signals and their instruments misinterpreted them as "thermal."

8.   *Is there some distinct electronic method of detecting an ET underground base? How does this method work?*

If ETs work in an ultraviolet light source (as reported from contact stories) it might be possible to look for radio emissions that signal the generation of such light sources in areas where ET bases are suspected.

PROJECT: Hidden Cache.
METHOD: ERV.
DATE: July 1994.
CLIENT: George Wingfield.
TYPE: Applications.

People are always curious about what remote viewing can and cannot do, particularly when some groups within the field claim 100% success rates. This leaves the rest of us open to suspicion and criticism. Such was the case when I was approached by two researchers in July 1994 with a proposed test. As one of the researchers was known to me, I decided to participate, on the understanding that it shed some light on functioning of remote viewing. The project involved a small group of researchers who had visited a hidden location north of Las Vegas and had hidden a cache of small objects. The remote viewing task was to identify the objects and their location. The viewer, (myself), had no up-front information about the nature of the target except the word "treasure."

During the viewing, I perceived a triangular-shaped object that was hidden in a side canyon up near the infamous Area 51. I also perceived that, as the group drove up to the location, they disturbed sensors along the road that alerted authorities to their presence.

Feedback from the group revealed that they had buried a small plastic sack from the Luxor casino in the dirt along the side of the Black Mailbox road, leading up to one of the entrances to Area 51. They had, indeed, perceived sensors along the road and had stopped to inspect them. While there was no triangular-shaped object in the sack, the bag clearly depicts the black triangular structure of the Luxor. We considered the project a partial success.

A Long-Lost Love.
PROJECT: Missing Person.
METHOD: ERV.
DATE: May 1994.
CLIENT: Medical Professional.
TYPE: Applications.

Using remote viewing to locate missing persons is one of the more important uses of remote viewing. However, how do you find a person who has been "missing" for 20 years? In the spring of 1994, I was contacted by a Californian medical professional who had come to the US around 1974 as a student. During his early years in the US, on a Greyhound bus, he happened to catch the eye of a young woman. Being shy and new to the States, he did not talk to her but felt that this was his "soul-mate" and that they had been destined to meet! In 1994 he revealed to me that he deeply regretted never having talked to her and he had thought about her every day for 20 years!

Now, he was looking for information on where she might be and if there was any way he could contact her. We had no name, no location, no contact information, just his story. So, twice during May, I did an "open search" casting my mind around the States for her. I perceived a woman that "felt right" living in Manhattan and saw that she was happily married with children and a career. I did not go the extra step to locate information that would identify her name or address because I felt this was an invasion of her privacy. I had already gone beyond the boundaries of conventional remote viewing in accessing her.

JOURNALS

Journal - March 9, 1995 – *Update.*

It's spring! In more ways than one. The trees have new spring green leaves on them, my rose bushes have buds, I have seen new birds in the yard, and the weather is getting warmer. I love this time of year. Also, financially, things are getting better! Last summer I left the Bigelow Foundation to work on my school courses and essays and my book. I am now completing my final pre-doctoral essay and getting ready to start my dissertation research.

After taking off the summer, I had hoped to get back into full-time employment, but I found that I was overqualified for anything Las Vegas had to offer. Finally, I found a temporary, part-time job as a receptionist in a local office that managed homeowners' associations but that ended when they hired a full-time receptionist. I've signed up to give some classes for the Community College of Southern Nevada, first at Sierra Health Services on business-related topics.

Since the New Year I have been giving occasional classes to private individuals and a weekend-long workshop to four individuals, three of whom came from LA for the weekend. They said they had learned a lot and the weekend gave me some practice in conducting workshops, as well as giving me some good ideas for future ones. It would be great to give a week-long workshop and use art as well as audiovisual to supplement the learning process.

Journal - May 25, 1995 – *Cryptographic Study.*

I received an interesting project from an ex-military intelligence member that linked perceived images with symbols and eventually letters of the alphabet. Not quite sure how this will work but it got my interest! The results of the project were inconclusive.

Journal - May 31, 1995 – *Lyn Buchanan attends my Workshop.*

Recently, I held a remote viewing weekend at the house and several students attended, including Lyn Buchanan from Virginia, one of the ex-Star-Gate remote viewers. It was an interesting weekend and I taught the group various methods for achieving an Out-of-Body-Experience (OBE) and Extended Remote Viewing (ERV). Lyn gave us an impromptu talk on remote viewing by coordinates. Unfortunately, Lyn had to leave the workshop early as he had a family emergency.

During the weekend, Dave gave a spoon bending workshop and we had about eight people attend. I had attended three previous workshops and was able to get the handles of spoons soft enough to twist but I had never collapsed the bowl of a spoon. This weekend I was able to collapse two spoon bowls across the midpoint and I was very pleased I could do this. What happened was that the bowl got soft enough to gently push over and bend down the bowl.

Journal - June 4, 1995 – *RV Study.*

I have been doing another round of projects from the ex-intelligence colleague that he had designed with another colleague which involves precognitive viewing a pair of physical objects on six successive days. The objects are in the colleague's house in Springfield, VA.

I did the first one today. I lay down (with the three cats on the bed) and tried to view what the colleague had put in the target space (a box lid on a shelf at his home). At first, I didn't see anything in the box and then realized, silly me, that I was looking at the box - today! So, I projected to next Sunday and saw the following. As I looked at the box, I couldn't see anything protruding over the box so figured there were flat objects in the box. I saw red and something soft and flat and felt something like a towel in my hands. Then I felt like I was holding a bolt in my hands.

Later, I was sent a set of two sets of picture targets, Set A and Set B, to match against my perceptions. I noticed that one of the sets had a soft squidgy Pooh Bear with a red jacket so chose that and the bolt as the perception targets. Not sure if I am correct or not. The targets were a spoon, brush, bowl, cap, bear, basket, box, glove, glue, roll of TP, a glass, bolt, hanger and a towel. But not sure if I identified the correct ones today and viewers do not always get feedback.

Journal - June 5, 1995 – *Second Session.*

Did the second RV session today and right away perceived a green disk box and shoe brush – two hard objects. I felt the shapes in the box with my hands. However, this project did not work for us. And we discontinued the effort.

Journal - June 9, 1995 – *Emotional Contact.*

Agreed with the colleague to remote view four sets of pictures with an emotional content. He attached numbers to these pictures as a type of Associative Remote Viewing (ARV) project. The colleague had sent a copy of "The Family of Man" – a book of black and white photographs collected over the last century and asked me to pick out twelve pictures that I considered to have emotional content and to assign numbers to them before mailing the book and the numbers back to him. However, by June 19, the colleague couldn't get the project to work as he wanted it to, and we did not complete the project.

Journal - July 18, 1995 – *PSI Targets.*

Every month or so Lyn Buchanan puts out a remote viewing newsletter full of very interesting articles and news. He kindly put in a piece about my remote viewing workshop. Lyn also puts a simple RV project in the newsletter, designated only by a number or a short description such as "950042 is a picture of a natural location. Describe the location." I tried one but will have to wait until next month for the feedback. "I got dark, drab scene, grays, blues and black. Waves and rays, spray. Water, rain, sea. Fabric and wood. Sadness, calamity, disaster. Distance, depth." (The picture target was a ship in a storm).

Journal - August 19, 1995 – *A True Story.*

Yesterday, on the bus, I noticed a young boy of about nine years old and obviously mentally challenged, who was touching everybody who was getting on the bus, and then waving goodbye at everyone. I was sat behind him. Several people were annoyed at his touching them. I had heard that autistic and mentally challenged children often appear psychic, so I decided to see if he was telepathic.

I mentally thought to him *"Hi there, how are you doing?"* He sat back in his seat, looked around, and looked thoughtful.

I then said *"You know, it's OK to touch your Mom and Dad, your brothers and sisters and other relatives but it's not OK to touch people on the bus or in public unless they say it is OK."*

He looked thoughtful.

I continued: *"I bet you can't sit still and not touch people. Don't touch people who get on the bus, OK?"* The bus stopped and two people got on. The boy who had touched everybody getting on the bus, up to this point, just sat back and looked at the people getting on the bus. I sent him the message: *"Good boy! You did it!"* And he grinned from ear to ear. However, he then touched the next people who got on the bus and I sent him the message *"You forgot didn't you"* and he grinned to himself again. I then sent him the message, *"Why don't you give your Mom a hug"* and he looked at his Mom in the seat next to him and hugged her! Unfortunately, she pushed him away and he went back to touching the people who got on the bus. Sad but true.

JOURNALS

Journal - January 4, 1996 – *Saybrook.*

There have been some new developments and projects looming:

School: Even with a new Dissertation Chairperson, progress has been slow. I had to change Chairpersons because the male psychiatrist I had chosen, did not know about the psi subject, or even approve of my dissertation plans and was very derogatory about women scientists. So, as it was early in the dissertation process, Saybrook let me switch to a new chairperson. Maybe it is traditional for chairpersons to "nitpick" or maybe she is apprehensive as I am her first Saybrook Ph.D. Candidate. Hopefully, within the next few weeks she will sign off on my proposal and I can get a copy filed with Saybrook and my application to the SIRB. In anticipation, I have been collecting pre-study RNG calibrations and making a list of potential subjects to call.

RV Projects: 1995 was quiet regarding RV projects but now, in the New Year, things are picking up. Intuition Services have talked about some projects they want to send me. I have also had inquiries about doing some RV projects for Dr. Jeffrey Mishlove of the Noetics Institute and James Spottiswoode of SAIC who wants me to do some ARV sessions.

Galileo Probe: Ten years ago, I had remote viewed Jupiter and, finally, the Galileo Probe has reached Jupiter and plunged into the planet, sending back data. Preliminary information coming back indicates the presence of water, which I predicted in my perceptions of Jupiter! It is good to get some feedback!

Journal - January 5, 1996 - *ARV Bandwidths.*

This past week I had a phone call and an email from Jeffrey Mishlove and James Spottiswood, both doing Associative Remote Viewing (ARV) research, to test a new theory. It seems that the wider the field of potential targets, the more "noise" there is in the system. Similarly, with small target groups, like Zenner Cards, the signal is too small. So, both Mishlove and Spottiswood are carrying out ARV projects to try and find an optimal bandwidth in terms of targets pools to get optimal results.

Journal - January 8, 1996 – *ARV Feedback.*

I was able to finally get online to get my ARV feedback yesterday and found that I did well. What I perceived were concentric red circles on a black background that I interpreted and drew as a hotplate. The feedback was a round, black box with a circular red design on top. Interestingly, the design was a Phoenix ascending from the fire! So, although I interpreted the item incorrectly, I got the color and shape and fire correct.

James Spottiswood related that only viewers with a good track record (including the ex-military viewers) had been invited to participate in these trials. The very first lottery session that the group carried out was highly significant but, as it was a pilot study, no money had been bet! I came in a few series after the project had been started.

Journal - January 8, 1996 - *Intuitive Diagnosis.*

About two months ago I heard about a project being run By Dr. Larry Burke, who is a professor of Radiology at Duke University. He was looking for dowsers who would look at records and radiographs of women patients and decide, based on dowsing, between four patient diagnoses: cancer, osteoporosis, etc. He was mainly looking at the ability of dowsers to detect medical problems from X-rays, but he also felt that other intuitive methods might work.

So, I emailed him back, even though I am not a dowser, to let him know that I would be interested in taking part. He is sending me five trial cases.

When I was a nurse, I used to pray over some of the very sick babies and felt that part of their recovery might be partly due to prayer. For example, one six-month old baby was dying of a severe infection and the parents had called for a priest to anoint the baby and baptize her before she died. They were worried that she would die before the priest came.

I attended the baby and sent the parents out of the room while I changed her diaper. I also made the sign of the cross on her forehead and prayed for her. Whether it was because of my prayers or not, she was recovering by the time the priest arrived. I didn't tell anyone about my intervention.

Although Burke's project is not about faith healing, it is along the same lines and it will be interesting if remote viewing can be applied to intuitive diagnosis.

Journal - January 8, 1996 – *Lamp Posts!*

Last Friday on my way home I stopped off at Nellis and Bonanza (Las Vegas) to deposit a check, planning to take the Nellis bus and transfer to the Lake Mead Blvd. bus home from there. However, the Nellis bus was very late and the Lake Mead bus was already gone by the time I got there. As the buses only run every hour, (the service has improved since then) I called Dave, but he wasn't home yet. So, I decided to walk home, and I was feeling annoyed!

As I was walking, I noticed that the streetlights, first one, then two, were popping out as I walked under them. I had heard about the phenomenon and wondered if I could make a third one go out, which it did as I approached it. The light didn't go out like a house light, immediately off, but gradually dimmed to nothing. I got another one across the street to go out, too, before Dave came by to pick me up, he had finally got my phone message.

I have heard that psychokinesis or PK causes streetlights to go out, either by disrupting the electrical system or popping the bulb filaments. It was only when I went under the first streetlight that they began popping. When the first one popped, I was fuming about the bus leaving, when the second one popped, I was nervous because a man was walking behind me, (but he crossed the road), and the third and fourth lamps I deliberately tried to affect.

Journal - January 16, 1996 – *ARV Feedback.*

This weekend I completed the second set of ARV pilots for Mishlove and Spottiswood of the Laboratories for Fundamental Research (LFR) with some moderate success. I perceived a coffeepot-like shape with a green circle behind for James's target. However, when the feedback target came up on my computer screen it showed a half-cut "orange." My video card in my computer interpreted the colors as orange, even though it was described as a circle of green lemon. Interesting that I should pick up the green circle from the actual target and not the "orange" feedback that I saw on my computer. This persuaded me that RV is picking up the source information rather than the feedback.

Journal - April 18, 1996 – *RV Update.*

For the past fourteen or so weeks I have been participating in ARV studies with James Spottiswoode in Palo Alto, CA. Each Sunday morning, I try and view the ARV feedback that will come up on my screen later. I fax my perceptions and drawings to James. Lately, the impressions that have seemed to be the best matches appear as if overlaid on a grid matrix. Color and shape appear to be accessed easier than other data.

Once or twice I would have had a direct hit if I had written down all my perceptions, but I edited them because I thought they were overlay. I was a little despondent because I thought I wasn't doing well but James said that my results had the "highest effect size" than all the other participants and of the group overall! This was reassuring.

We took a break over Easter week and will start up a new pool of geographic coordinates next Sunday. After each viewing session on Sunday, I log on Monday morning and view my visual feedback. Before Dave upgraded my computer memory and video card, this was a long process (dial up!) and I didn't get true colors. But now it loads quickly, and I get true feedback. I have learned that when I am stressed and tired my results drop off but when I relax the results improve.

Journal - April 18, 1996 – *Unabomber.*

The media seems to think that the FBI has caught the Unabomber, but I am not so sure they have. I did a couple of viewings for Intuition Services and picked up the wooded area, the shack, the fact that he was a wood carver, that he had no car, and the tall, thin person, as well as much more data. All these facts seemed to match some of the profile of Ted Kaczynski, the man they picked up for the Unabomber crimes.

However, there are several discrepancies that have crept in, such as the fact that Ted has not yet been charged with any of the Unabomber crimes and materials listed as taken from his cabin state that none bears any Unabomber description i.e. no Manifesto. (It was later reported that he had indeed written a Manifesto). It is possible that Ted is the Unabomber and our perceptions were way off, or they may have picked up the wrong man? I have the feeling that Ted will be charged and tried as the Unabomber and possibly convicted. (Which he was).

Journal - April 18, 1996 - *Pyramid Mountain.*

I recently spoke with a colleague, Dr. Barbie Taylor, who has a friend, Celeste, who has an interesting project. Celeste has friends out at Kingman, AZ, the other side of the Dam, who own some land with a pyramid-shaped mountain on it. Supposedly, at the top of the mountain is a hole that goes down a long way and people have heard voices and other sounds from the hole. There are rumors of gold or a subterranean chamber, possibly. I'm keeping an open mind!

Next Tuesday, Celeste and I will be spending the day out at Kingman and we will see what we will see. I will take a panoramic camera, to see what I can capture on film. I tried remote viewing the site beforehand and this is what I perceived: that the area was once revered by an ancient people and was a site of worship. People who sleep at the site are haunted by dreams of a "black shape" that drives them away. The hill needs to be climbed in a spiral (like at Glastonbury Tor) to merge with the vortex of energy that surrounds the hill.

Journal - April 18, 1996 - *Teaching the Associates.*

In March I began teaching with the Adult Outreach division of the Nevada State College System. This has recently taken me to the Ethel M Chocolate factory, part of the Mars Group. They have been pulling fourteen to sixteen workers (Associates) off the line for a month of schooling. The plan is to get all the line employees through the program by the end of August. They are receiving industrial Math and English, leadership and public speaking etc. I am teaching them stress management, conflict resolution, defusing, and creative thinking.

The first group was very quiet to begin with and then gradually blossomed. This second group is bawdy and noisy and a totally different energy. This doesn't matter so much for my classes that are very interactive, but some of the instructors of the more structured classes have had a problem. However, this group is growing and blossoming, too! They will graduate next Friday with certificates and a graduation party!

The reason for the classes is participation in a Governor's Award program, where companies are putting resources into their employees' welfare. However, some of the associates didn't even graduate from high school so it is hard for them. The first week they typically look "shell-shocked" but loosen up as the weeks proceed. One of their favorite parts of the stress management course is when I take them on "field trips" around the Ethel M cactus gardens and through the chocolate factory tour, on the visitor side of the glass partition!

Journal - July 31, 1996 – *Paul Smith Visit.*

We had an interesting visit with Paul and Daryl Smith who have been here for the Smith Family Reunion. Paul shared with me some of the RV project transcripts that he worked on while he was still in the military (nothing classified). He is on the verge of retiring and wants to write a book about his experiences. The method he uses is a form of Technical Remote Viewing (TRV) that I also saw from Ed Dames' work. Paul has done a lot of RV, in much greater depth than I have, but I feel I have a greater breadth of knowledge of different forms of remote viewing. There was some discussion at the Family Reunion about the possibility of combining our talents to teach RV sometime in the future.

Paul has been writing about his RV experiences under the pseudonym of "Mr. X" and trying to correct some of the erroneous information that is out there. Once he has retired from the military, he will be able to write under his own name although I'm sure there is still classified RV material that he is not able to share.

While they were here in Las Vegas, Paul and I visited Dean Radin and Janine Rebman at UNLV and Paul filled us in on some of the very interesting history of the RV government program.

[Note: Unfortunately, I did not record my journals for the remainder of 1996 as I was busy with school, writing and raising my stepsons. But following are case notes of the major projects conducted during 1996.]

CASE FILES – 1996

Laboratories for Fundamental Research (LFR).
PROJECT: Lottery ARV.
METHOD: ARV.
DATE: January 1996
CLIENT: LFR.
TYPE: Research.

The Laboratories for Fundamental Research (LFR) are in Palo Alto, CA. In 1996, researchers Dr. James Spottiswoode and Dr. Edwin May conducted a research project to assess a remote viewing protocol called Associative Remote Viewing (ARV). For example, in predicting the stock market ARV can indicate whether a stock will rise, drop or stay the same. It is not a foolproof protocol and needs to be carried out very carefully to be effective.

LFR had already conducted several trials when I was invited to participate in January 1996. I learned that only viewers with a "track record" were being invited to participate. They had initially conducted a pilot session with a group of validated viewers and hit all the numbers of a lotto game, the problem was that they hadn't bought tickets for the game, because it was just a pilot session!

From January 7, through to May 12, 1996, I participated in sixteen ARV trials. Basically, I would retrieve a coordinate (a case number) sent by email and carry out a remote viewing session. I would then fax my session to LFR, and the researchers would judge which of the picture targets (associated with several different outcomes) best matched my viewing. When the outcome of the prediction was known, I could then retrieve the "winning" picture on my computer and see how well (or poorly!) I had done. Trials two through four were 4-target studies: that is there were four picture targets associated with four potential outcomes. Trials five through sixteen were 5-target ARV studies. My job as a viewer was to view the picture correctly associated

124

with the actual outcome. My sixteen sessions showed a 94% success rate (Overall Stouffer's Z = 1.57, p = 058).

A further five sessions investigated a finding in remote viewing called Local Sidereal Time (LST) that had discovered a possible connection between the timing of a viewing and its success. In this last phase of the research viewers were randomly allocated to do their viewing either at specific LST times or non-LST times. A later paper by Spottiswoode and May reported that, over all the participants, the study was not successful and there was no indication of any LST effect, contrary to their findings with an earlier database of thousands of remote viewers. My thoughts on this are that viewers with a good natural ability, who are well-trained and practiced, can overcome many social and environmental effects that might adversely affect their work.

[Note: Similarly, to the end of 1996, I do not have a record of Journal entries until the summer of 1998 when they were recommenced. Being busy with school, writing and family, some things had to take a back seat. The following Case Files fill in some of the missing dates.]

CASE FILES - 1997

The Las Vegas Riots.
PROJECT: The Las Vegas Riots.
METHOD: ERV.
DATE: July 1997.
CLIENT: Independent.
TYPE: Prediction Feedback.

During a class exercise in July 1997, a target was given to the class to identify what was happening on New Year's Day, 2013 in Las Vegas, NV. I did several Extended Remote Viewing (ERV) searches and perceived a disturbing picture that I described as the Las Vegas Riots.

What I perceived was a dismaying picture of fenced-in areas: the airport, the university campus and an area stretching from the Luxor up and past the Stratosphere. All around the fenced-in areas was derelict and burned out. There were gates where service personnel could come and go, and a monorail extended from the airport to the Las Vegas Strip. There were gates at the four corners of the university, UNLV but both the university and the Strip were still struggling to survive.

In addition, I perceived that satellite cities outside Las Vegas: Primm (now Stateline) and Jean were serving as embarkation and arrival points for planes and passengers. It was also perceived that the City Council only sat on alternate years at UNLV and the Strip. I hope I am wrong about this but civil unrest across the World has shown how easily, crowds can get out of hand and create mayhem. Since 1997 we have seen Las Vegas go through some very difficult times with foreclosed houses, jobs lost and unemployment rising. Let us hope that cool heads within the LV community can keep this from happening.

Feedback: Since 1997, Primm (Stateline) was slated to be the site of a new, International airport but the plans were shelved due of the recession. Much of Las Vegas, off the strip, is fenced in due to old casinos being demolished. A monorail has been built since 1997 and it now connects many of the Las Vegas Casinos. There are plans to extend it out to the airport. Las Vegas is struggling to survive the recession and I still perceive the riots as a potential threat to Las Vegas.

What is interesting about these types of predictions is that they often are right about short-term events but can get off-target when an event is for an event farther in the future.

Treasure Caches.
PROJECT: Treasure Caches.
METHOD: ERV.
DATE: July 1997.
CLIENT: Independent.
TYPE: Treasure Hunting.

There are problems with treasure hunting using remote viewing. Very few treasure hunters have the up-front funds to pay for exploratory RV sessions and there is no guarantee that the viewer will be paid when any treasure is found. If treasure hunting projects are taken on, it should be for the thrill of the hunt and of being included on the trip to find the treasure.

A new case came into my office from a colleague that targeted an area that might harbor treasure. Front-loading provided with this project was that, as far as known, all the targets were on land that was available for treasure seeking. The target consisted of confirming that caches of treasure were located at the three locations, confirmation of the size, and directions to each treasure, landmarks or visible objects. Due to the varied locations, the project was performed in three stages. The main question asked was to confirm whether treasure caches existed at Big Bend, Tillamook, and Bond in Oregon.

Remote viewing perceived that there had been a treasure cache at Big Bend but that it had been retrieved about fifty years ago. I described how I had perceived and followed a dirt path and observed seven men who retrieved wooden boxes and bags from a cleft high in the hillside. The cache was held at a cabin before being collected by a mule team. The cache consisted of coins, silver ore and a little paper money and it came from the theft of a bank shipment from one county to another.

At Tillamook it was perceived that there was a large cache located in an old worked-out mine. The hill in which the mine was located was overshadowed by a large hill that looked like two angel wings spread out, especially at dusk. There was a large, old, leaning tree near the entrance to the mine. The front of the mine was built up from tailings that have a green color, indicating that copper was once mined there.

I described the interior of the mine and a passageway and felt that this might have been a Spanish mine. There was a cave-in of debris within the mine that might once have been a trap. Two bodies were perceived under the cave-in of shale and debris. The "treasure" consisted of smelly cloth bags containing Spanish coins, probably silver and there were dangers of further cave-ins.

There was no cache perceived at Bond. What was seen was an area that looked like Goldfield, NV. Lots of rough, rocky, scrubby ground with stake claims all over. There may have been the occasional nugget of gold and copper ore found here but no big hidden cache was perceived. The area appeared quite desolate and there was nothing really exciting here. Nothing more was heard from the treasure hunters once they received this information.

Nevada Treasure.
PROJECT: Nevada treasure.
METHOD: ERV.
DATE: July 1997.
CLIENT: John L.
TYPE: Geological Investigation.

In 1997, two remote viewing projects were carried out for a Nevada mine owner to investigate a sinkhole on his property to determine if it contained historic artifacts and/or precious minerals. The mine was found to contain silver, quartz, and garnets, but no treasure.

Stock Market Trends.
PROJECT: Future Stock market Trends.
METHOD: ERV.
DATE: July 1997.
CLIENT: Australian Couple.

TYPE: Financial.

New clients, a young, Australian, professional couple, needed information regarding stock acquisitions. They were undecided whether they should proceed with their plans as they had heard conflicting information from several different stockbrokers. Basically, they needed to know whether they should go ahead and invest their money or wait. Based on remote viewed information, I advised them to wait, and not invest in the largest potential investment and cited several reasons. The following email was received from the couple a few months later:

"Concerning the project, we designated ***** (the one about the special bank trading programs), we've decided in light of your information to not progress this idea any further. Ethics are important to us and, after what you told us, this project no longer sits comfortably with us."

A year or so later they sent the following information:

"Well, firstly, the "Trading Programs." We took your advice and did not get involved. Since then, the Australian authorities have cautioned people about these types of so-called investments. I'm told that many of these programs are promoted through networks of Church people. Consistent with your advice to avoid them, the Australian authorities are telling people who will listen that they're really a major scam."

The All-Seeing Eye.
PROJECT: The All-Seeing Eye.
METHOD: Book Review: Remote Perceptions.
DATE: 1997.
CLIENT: Henry Reed, Edgar Cayce Institute/
Atlantic University

My book *'Remote Perceptions: Out-of-Body Experiences, Remote Viewing and Other Normal Abilities,'* was not published by Hampton Roads until 1998, but the manuscript had been floating around the remote viewing community for about a year. In 1997, Henry Reed, Ph.D. of The Edgar Cayce Institute for Intuitive Studies and Atlantic University decided to have his students review all the available books in the remote viewing field. He wrote:

"The All-Seeing Eye, this remote viewing omni-reader gives you an opportunity to read quick summaries of most every book written on remote viewing, as well as its precursors and some experimental offshoots. Atlantic University students read the books, summarized them in their own words and we've collected them here, along with some other articles related to remote viewing."

"You'll read quick versions of the books written by the main players in remote viewing, from the laboratory, the battlefield, the archaeological, and the crime scene. The reader provides you with omni-vision, being able to see from multi-perspectives simultaneously."

I am always reluctant to read reviews of my work and rarely watch or listen to my radio interviews. However, I steeled myself to read the reviews of my book by the students: Sue Beardslee, Patricia Parks, and Denise Dahl.

Basically, they gave a good overview of the many aspects of the book but focused more on the predictions and remote viewing exercises. They concluded that:

"The predominant theme of this book is Smith's search for a legitimate, scientific study of remote viewing with an emphasis on obtaining optimal results, that when applied ethically and responsibly, will benefit humanity. She has combined seventeen years of private research, seven years of scientific research, five years as a consultant on remote viewing, two years of teaching and more...Her journey to discover our human potential in the field of remote viewing continues."

Henry Reed, Ph.D. (1987), *The All-Seeing Eye: A Remote Viewing Omni-Reader: Original Summaries of the Books on Remote Viewing.* Published privately by The Edgar Cayce Institute for Intuitive Studies and Atlantic University.

Papoose Lake, NV.
PROJECT: Papoose Lake, NV.
METHOD: ERV.
DATE: July 8, 1997.
CLIENT: Class Project.
TYPE: Exploration.

From 1994 through the early part of 2002, I was teaching remote viewing at my home near Sunrise Mountain in Las Vegas. At the same time, I was helping to raise my three stepsons, working on my Ph.D. studies, writing books, consulting, and doing remote viewing research.

During class, I would ask the students to write down locations that they would like to explore with remote viewing. In one July class we had explored off-planet and Earth-based locations. While the class was on a roll, looking at sites, it was decided to look at an area north of Las Vegas, the Nevada Test Site, more specifically a location known as S4 or Papoose Lane. I also took part in these sessions and recorded my perceptions of these unknown locations.

A remote viewing of the area showed hangars and office areas to the north. There was no runway in front of the hangars, but it was perceived that the whole white flat (dry lake) was a runway. To either side were perceived mountains with black silt leached down onto the dry lake from the mountains. Off to one side, nearer the hangars was perceived blasting into the mountain "Boom, boom, boom!"

A second viewing on the same date showed the hangars with offices and utilities in between and a long, cylindrical rocket-shape half-in and half-out of the central hangar. A closer look at the central hangar showed it to have a rounded room with overhangs that came down over the vertical sides. There were windows up under the overhangs.

Whether this was correct, or even if we should have been viewing the area at all, is uncertain.

Back Side of the Moon 1.
PROJECT: Back Side of the Moon 1.
METHOD: ERV.
DATE: July 8th, 1997.
CLIENT: Class Project.
TYPE: Exploration.

There is a great deal of mystery and ambiguity about the Earth's moon, especially the back side of the Moon. Often talked about as the "Dark Side": the part of the Moon hidden from us has kept people wondering for decades. The lunar probe Clementine photographed the Moon, back, front and sides, many times over but finding detailed photographs of the back of the Moon is difficult. Also, the back of the moon is not the "dark side" it gets as much dark and light as the front of the Moon.

Ingo Swann, in his book, 'Penetration,' wrote how he was tasked with the Moon and perceived strange things on the surface. In 1997, as remote viewing class project I "took a look" at the back of the Moon and perceived some interesting and unusual features. For example, large patches of dark vegetation, like "black broccoli" were perceived. Also "walkways of light" between two large, upright, cross shapes. Lastly, three mountains were seen to ring an irregular shaped plateau. On this plateau were perceived mounds of large stone balls, some circular and some football shaped.

Back Side of the Moon 2.
PROJECT: Back Side of the Moon 2.
METHOD: ERV.
DATE: August 4, 1997.
CLIENT: Class Project.
TYPE: Exploration.

Another look at the same area, the back of the Moon by ATS, in August 1997 perceived some unusual structures that seemed unaffected by gravity: if they had been constructed on Earth, they would have fallen. These were structures that were top-heavy. They were tubular and squared but with rounded corners. For example, there was an arch that seemed to twist itself halfway and come down in a different orientation. It would be interesting to see what other viewers perceived of this area.

Europa.
PROJECT: Europa.
METHOD: ERV.
DATE: July 8th, 1997.
CLIENT: Class Project.
TYPE: Exploration.

In the same class as the Moon perceptions, I looked at Europa. The night sky looked light, but the ground area was very dark. There appeared to be lots of dark "lollipop" trees. I felt as if I got "stuck," as if I was stuck in a Venus Flytrap and had to retreat from the site.

My second look took me to an ice-flow in an ocean and I looked under the surface. Here I perceived a biological like oceanic plankton or krill but huge! The creature was three-armed with a large central eye and flagella or feelers that furled out from the three arms for movement.

The Stone Goddess.
PROJECT: Geological Formations, Helena, Montana.
METHOD: ERV.
DATE: November 23, 1997.
CLIENT: RV Class.
TYPE: Exploration.

During 1997 and 1998, I had the opportunity to travel to different parts of the US and aboard (Australia, Canada, and New Zealand) to teach remote viewing. One course took place in Helena, MT and I loved the little town and the people there. In addition to teaching, I was asked to provide some remote viewing data to the organizers.

Just outside Helena the land opens to its aptly named, Big Sky Country. Here are the Black Hills, cattle ranges, ranches and stables, and ancient rock formations. One of these, the Stone Goddess, is an enigmatic Neolithic site. A small group of us braved a freezing-cold day to visit the site and perceive information about the location. My perception was that the site was originally dedicated to a cat-worshiping group with a leading cat-headed goddess. Unfortunately, very little is known about the site, so we were not able to get feedback.

The same day we spent some time searching for agate geodes in large, white bentonite-clay cliffs before one of the group members split and polished their internal beauty for us. Bentonite is formed from the weathering of ancient volcanic ash and it was mind-blowing to visualize this huge cliff as the fall-out from a nearby volcano.

I was also able to perceive information on original land boundaries for another leader of the group, a local rancher. While we were walking the land boundaries, the rancher showed us an exquisite, black obsidian, Clovis point, a hand-ax, that had been found washed out of a gully. As I held this ancient artifact in my hands, I felt surges of energy going through my body! What a day! Montana was full of treasures.

Visiting the Stone Goddess Stone Circle in Montana.

Mount Olympus.
PROJECT: Mount Olympus.
METHOD: Coordinate Remote Viewing.
DATE: December 3rd, 1997.

CLIENT: Civil Engineer.
TYPE: Historical Applications.
COORDINATE: 13808S

An engineer client gave me a historical project, working "blind" with only a coordinate: Coordinate 13808S. During this viewing I perceived an ancient time with small people using "silver" spears. The project feedback was the historical past of Mount Olympus in Greece.

The client was touring in the area, visited a museum at the location and was able to verify much of the perceived information including that the people of that time used "silver spears." They even had some of the artifacts on display in the museum!

1998

JOURNALS

After a hiatus of a few years when I didn't maintain my journal, I recommenced it at the end of June 1998. I was preoccupied with school studies, writing my books, traveling, raising my stepsons, getting married to David Smith, researching, consulting, and teaching remote viewing.

Journal - June 30, 1998 – *Back from New Zealand.*
Since returning from New Zealand, life has been gradually slowing down, so I can take a "breather" and reassess where I have been and where I am going. New Zealand was a fantastic adventure teaching and traveling but now life is a lot quieter. It took me about two weeks to get over jet lag and I had a persistent cough when I returned, which has now gone completely, thank goodness.

The week I got back, it took all week to unwind from the trip, sort through all the mail, answer all the emails, clean the house, give Dave and the boys some TLC, and prepare for some students the week of June 21. Only one of them was a paying student and I have been thinking how to remedy this situation. The class went well but I really feel that the teaching needs to be given to a larger group to be productive. I have also been thinking along the lines of getting some office space to give classes.

Journal - July 1, 1998 – *Mailing Lists.*
For a long time, I have thought about sending out email notifications to many of the people on my email list but didn't have the knowledge on how to do this. Recently, I came across a free list server

that distributes email messages to whatever email addresses you request. Today I came across another group that lists go out to for free. I can send information on courses, classes, travel, the newsletter, info about the book etc. Hopefully, I will be able to stay in touch with a larger number of people who are interested in remote viewing activities, gain new students, perhaps find some research or start-up funding. The name I have chosen for the list server is (no longer in service) and I am now an official list owner. I sent out invitations today to a group of email addresses and hope there will be a good response to the invites. I know there will be some people who won't want to be on the list, but I am also sure there are a lot of people who would love to be included. It will get remote viewing information out to a much wider group of people.

Journal - June 1, 1998 - *New Opportunities.*

About ten years ago I did some contract work for Psi Tech, which was then set up as a business. Unfortunately, I was told, PsiTech as a business has folded and the group is now operating as a teaching organization. Ron Blackburn and Ryan Wood (once part of the Psi Tech Board) set up another organization, Intuition Services in California. Now Ron Blackburn, Jack Houck, Skip Atwater, possibly funded by businessman Stanford Burberick, will be setting up a new entity like Psi Tech. Ron and Stanford say they would like me to be involved at some level. What I am hoping is that I will be paid a salary. Dave keeps on about me getting a "real job" so perhaps this will satisfy his need to have another full-time income coming into the home. I am also looking into renting an office full-time, nearer town. I am finding that having an office at home is great in terms of convenience, but it is detrimental to getting any real work done. My colleague Dr. Wendy Altamura says that there are small offices becoming available down on Flamingo, where she works as a psychotherapist, and it would be convenient to work there. I love working from home, but it is time to get back into the workplace.

Journal - July 16, 1998 – *Using the RNG for Predictions.*

Before I went off to New Zealand, I did a couple of remote viewing projects for two colleagues. One of these was to perceive the ups-and-downs of the US stock market. I decided to experiment using the random number generator (RNG): a device that electronically produces a series of plus and minus pulses that show up as a random line feedback on the computer screen. The line goes up for more plusses and down for more minuses.

According to one of the colleagues, the predictions that I generated for him using the RNG were quite successful and followed the actual stock market trends. They even had an independent analyst check the plots and the trends. I generated predictions for three stock quarters. The first quarter RNG quarter tracked the actual stock market. The second quarter the prediction started slipping and by the third quarter it was off track. The lesson here is to do predictions in small batches, close to the actual outcome of the event you are tracking.

Since then, the two colleagues have suggested another project, that of detecting human consciousness, using the RNG. Like measuring the "Footprint of Consciousness." For example, an individual would travel mentally to the location of an RNG. If the RNG ran significantly high or low, that might be an indication of the presence of human consciousness. No visit or an interrupted visit might show no effect. The PEAR Lab had done experiments to this effect with great success, for example their remote RNG studies.

So far, four subjects have attempted to RV target envelopes in my office while the RNG was running. Two had successful visits and affected the RNG, one with a statistical z score of 2.5! The other two did not complete their RV session and only got a chance result on the RNG. The calibration data was also within chance expectation. This could form the basis for a new study!

Journal - September 23, 1998 – *New Office on Flamingo.*
For the past six months I have had the idea to set up a professional office for Inner Vision, but it wasn't possible during the summer as Dave was away working and I was looking after my stepson Daniel. When Daniel started school again and Dave returned, I went down to Flamingo/Pecos and inquired about available offices. We settled on Suite #310 which is one large room with two large windows and a nice view of the Sheep Mountains. At the end of August, I put down the deposit and moved my office down to Flamingo. I love the new space and have been very productive.

Journal - October 9, 1998 – *The Stargate Yahoo List.*
For about six weeks I have been moderating an online Yahoo list for folks interested in remote viewing and psi. The original RV list was run by PJ Gaenir and her husband Lu in Seattle, but PJ decided to close the list when they moved to Texas. A UK colleague, Steve Creitzman, took up the challenge and resurrected the list calling it the Stargate list after the RV Army Unit's last project name. He ran it for about six months until one of the Intel guys started to give him a lot of trouble, "flaming" other subscribers' posts etc. Steve unsubscribed him from the list, but

the Intel guy threatened to sue Steve, so Steve was going to close the list.

Steve asked me if I wanted to take over the list, which I did. I felt it deserved to be maintained. The last six weeks have been an experience! Steve had re-subscribed the Intel guy back onto the list and he continued to cause grief to everyone, so I unsubscribed him - again. Consequently, the list got spammed and flamed and I was ready to give it up. The Intel guy tried subscribing through false names and online addresses and through his cronies, but I caught these as they came through. We survived all the spanning and flaming and other shenanigans and eventually the list became healthy again with an intelligent traffic. Steve and I have now decided to share moderatorship of the list. He is the main moderator and I will take over when Steve needs a break or if he must be out of town. It's a good project to be involved with and I've enjoyed the challenge.

Before I went up to Seattle to hold the weekend course, I was approached by an individual who been subscribed to the Stargate List, who went by the name of Greg, also Kopfjammer (Head Hunter in German). He sent me an email saying he was collecting together a group of talented RVers and OBEers to conduct projects that could bring in up to $25,000 for the viewers. This was exciting as paying RV projects are scarce.

Greg gave me a practice task to locate his fiancée (who had given her permission to be remote viewed). I did three RV sessions and was correct on two of them but haven't received feedback on the third yet (2019, I was correct on that one, too). I think he was impressed, and I asked him to put me onto a "real project."

However, I think he has hit a dilemma. He mentioned that he had recruited the world's best on-demand viewer (name withheld) in Berkeley, CA. But, in the meantime, she had been causing problems on the Stargate List. I had unsubscribed her and she was also bounced off Art Bell's List. This had caused a problem for Gregg who wanted to work with her and me. I will tell Greg that I am still willing to work with him regardless of who else he hires. We'll see how this little drama works out.

Journal - October 9, 1998 – *EEG and Remote Viewing.*
When I was up in Seattle visiting with Lew and Hanna Hollander, I was able to work with some of his biofeedback equipment and recorded several sessions using two EEG leads while doing OBE/RV.

In the first session I just did some calibration data, deciding what I was going to do for the next sessions. The data from the calibration sessions showed equal brain frequencies over the whole range including high beta up to 39+ Hz. (gamma).

Next, I did a couple of short OBE sessions of a few minutes each and noticed that the EEG brainwave data was bilateral in the lower ranges (theta, and delta) with not much happening up in the higher ranges (alpha).

Then I did a short CRV session and another pattern emerged consisting of a periodic contraction and expansion over all the range. It was quite interesting to watch. When I was acquiring data, the bilateral data was in the theta-delta range, and when I was recording the data, the data showed a beta/alpha pattern. This was only pilot data and I would like to get some EEG equipment of my own to carry out some further studies.

Journal - October 9, 1998 – *New Writing.*

My new book *'Remote Perceptions'* is already doing well in presales. When I called Hampton Roads at the end of September, they had presold 1,200 copies. This covers my advance, so I don't owe Hampton Roads anything. When I talked to Pat Adler, she said that the book had been delayed because the printers got the book color wrong and it will be the end of October before I see copies. I would rather wait and have the book right rather than rush it out. Hampton Roads says that reviewers had received advanced copies of the manuscript already.

In the meantime, I have been having thoughts about a second book which I will call the *'CE4 Enigma: A Scientist looks at the Alien Abduction Phenomenon.'* I wrote up a short one-page proposal and cover letter and will mail it off today. (It eventually got published by Hampton Roads as *'Diary of an Abduction.'* Both *'Remote Perceptions'* and *'Diary of an Abduction'* are currently out-of-print but I am working on getting them republished.)

I mentioned the book to Frank DeMarco, when I was visiting them in May, and he said he might be interested and to let him know when I was ready to work on it. The book is based on a series of journals, like this one, that I have been writing for about twenty years. They cover many areas: parapsychology, ufology, etc. I think this second book would be a great seller and generate a lot of interest for experiencers and researchers.

Journal - October 9, 1998 – *A New RV Society.*

A few weeks ago, I called a colleague, Dr. Wayne Carr in Reno, NV to give him my new office address and he mentioned that he had taken over the American Association of Remote Viewers (AARV). However, he felt that he didn't have much time to work on it at any length and offered the Presidency of the organization to me! I was flattered but decided to decline the offer. The AARV was started by Army RVer David Morehouse, and several others specifically for their students and it never really got off the ground.

I talked to Paul Smith about Dr. Carr's offer. Paul said that I should call another friend of his who was interested in funding a new society run by some of the individuals involved in the early development and training of CRV. We came up with a short-list and decided to invite these folks for a one-day workshop to discuss setting up an association. The invitees would then stay on to offer a talk to a group of CRV students.

Paul's friends advised me to call Lyn Buchanan in Alamogordo and we discussed the location (NM) and the timing (next spring) and Lyn seemed happy with the potential short-list which included Ingo Swann, Lyn Buchanan, Paul Smith, Hal Puthoff, Jessica Utts, Skip Atwater, Joe McMoneagle, and Dean Radin. Others to be included were myself and Paul's anonymous friend who would provide financial aid for the initial meeting.

I called Ingo on Wednesday and he seemed pleased to hear from me. I asked him if he would like to be on the start-up of the new society and he didn't give me an outright no, just said he didn't know what he would be doing next spring and to contact him nearer the time.

Lyn and Paul both said they would be involved, as did Skip Atwater. The other folk haven't yet returned my calls. Jessica Utts is on Sabbatical. So, half of the list have given a positive response. When I talked to Lyn, he had great hopes for the Society and felt it would add credibility to the field, would set some standards for training and applications, and would recognize the leaders in the RV field.

Journal - October 9, 1998 - *Searching for Opal.*
Over the summer I have been working with Jim Francis to locate areas in South Australia (Coober Pedy area) to locate opal. Jim originally sent me a map of the region, but I asked him for a grid of the area. The map had too much information. I used Associative Remote Viewing (ARV) to locate several areas where he and his colleagues could locate opal. Using the gridded paper and a green pencil associated with opal, I marked off several areas where Jim could search. I faxed off this information to Jim in Australia.

Jim responded by email and a videotape showing how they had dug down and found basic opal (potch) where I had RV'd it. They are now looking for a better quality of opal. The video was very helpful for feedback as it showed the area, the exact location where they dug, even underground where I had RV'd a seam of opal. In fact, Jim had called me from the site, when they were excavating and I have viewed the excavation face and told Jim indicators, (a diagonal seam of darker material) of where to dig.

Jim eventually sent me two small pieces of opal. He also wanted me to sell some raw, uncut opal for him in Las Vegas, but I declined as I didn't want to get into the selling market. Jim is a great entrepreneur and I am always willing to help him when I can.

Journal - October 9, 1998 – *Remote Viewing Feedback.*

In the remote viewing field, there has been some discussion about the concept of "feedback." Some CRV projects and training methods require feedback as a mandatory part of the protocol. There has been some discussion on whether the student is picking up precognitive information about the target from the picture feedback that they will be shown, or whether they remote view the target.

A colleague is planning to set up a web page for an experiment to examine this question. There will be a total of nine to ten targets, half of them will have actual feedback available to the viewer. The other half will give false feedback to the viewer. The real target picture will be hidden in a sub-file. The viewers would email their perceptions to me after viewing the coordinate. When have a certain amount of feedback data, it will be analyzed, and we'll have some information on the feedback problem. (This never got set up but it's still a good research idea).

Journal - October 9, 1998 – *More on the Footprint of Consciousness.*

About two months ago, I ran a pilot project for a colleague to detect "non-local consciousness." Remote viewers attempted to view a target envelope located at the Inner Vision office. We had eight subjects: four who did the viewing on time and four who either forgot or who were not able to do the study.

The four individuals who viewed the envelopes did well on the experiment. While the viewing was in progress, a random number generator (RNG) was running and recorded any deviations away from chance expectation when the subjects were actually "visiting" the target. This gave us some preliminary information that "something" might actually be detected by the RNG. Two of the viewers had an impact on the RNG. We decided to look for some funding grants to do a larger study. (The study is still pending, 2016, but others have begun running RNGs during training and practice remote viewing sessions).

J

<u>ournal - October 11, 1998 – *The RV Family Tree.*</u>

For the past two years I have been working on a large graph, The RV Family Tree, with outlines of all the key individuals and organizations involved in the development of the remote viewing/remote perception field. Ingo Swann and Janet Mitchell claimed to have coined the term, remote viewing, at the American Society for Psychical Research (ASPR) in NY but the first published account of the term was by Puthoff and Targ at SRI.

The RV Family Tree got enlarged and is now called the Remote Perception/Remote Viewing Family Tree to cover all the preceding and ancillary individuals and organizations. I got a quote in 1995 to print the Family tree but didn't have the money. Then Stanford Burberick, a retired businessman wanted to add the Family Tree to his book as a pullout section. In return he said he would have 1,000 posters run off for me. This plan fell through as his publisher wasn't keen to add the pull-out to the book as it would add to the cost of the book. I had another possible benefactor but the cost of printing the posters far exceeded the donation.

(The Family Tree is no longer available in computer-sharable format.)

<u>Journal - October 11, 1998 – *Remote Viewers Support Group.*</u>

For two weeks I have been running a Remote Viewers Support Group at the Flamingo office to give some support to students of RV and to provide some additional training and practice. The first week we did a free-form RV practice target of the Pyramids, and the group did quite well.

I showed them Jim's tape of the Coober Pedy search for opal using remote viewing and we played the Psychic CD software package *Psi Explorer* that was developed by Mario Varvoglis in France.

Last Tuesday we played with Jack Houck's intuition software training, *Psychic Reward*, and did a remote tracking exercise. One of the students got himself into a bit of trouble filming one of the other tenants in the building but we apologized, and it was OK.

Next week we will do a PEAR Out-Bounder Technique and on the Tuesday close to Halloween, we'll do a spoon bending evening and some Halloween activities. We'll light some candles, play some eerie music and perhaps play the Australian spoon bending video tape.

<u>Sephoris, Israel.</u>
PROJECT: Burial place of Mary.
METHOD: Extended Remote Viewing (ERV).
DATE: September 1998.
CLIENT: PH, New Zealand.
TYPE: Humanitarian.

This project explored the concept that Mary, the Mother of Jesus, was buried in Turkey, where Mary, supposedly, spent her final years. The client needed landmarks to help her identify the site. This project followed a Controlled Remote Viewing course in Wellington, NZ: The Tasker was the wife of a NZ diplomat and University Professor. No feedback has been received apart from the client noting that the perceived data was consistent with information seen at the supposed burial site in Turkey.

<u>Spanish Treasure.</u>
PROJECT: Spanish Treasure.
METHOD: ERV.
DATE: July 1998.
CLIENT: Independent Client.
TYPE: Treasure Hunting.

In 1998, another project came along for a different client who was looking for gold, silver, and historic Spanish artifacts in Arizona. Although the clients confirmed that the remotely, viewed perceptions correctly identified surface landmarks in the area, no feedback has yet been provided as to the location or finding of treasure.

Treasure hunting, using remote viewing, can be quite exciting and some good quality information can be perceived. The colleague, in this case, felt that there was enough information to plan a trip. Unfortunately, like many treasure-hunting ventures, it was never completed.

<u>Sophia PK.</u>
PROJECT: Sophia PK.
METHOD: Natural RV.
DATE: December 1998.
TYPE: Animal Psi.

I have included this account in this section because it really doesn't fit anywhere else. It gives an example of animal psi (animals showing paranormal abilities), telepathy, and psychokinesis (PK). My cat Sophia who had traveled with me from Princeton to Las Vegas, NV was a very smart cat and we often seemed in tune with our moods. Nevada winters can be quite chilly, so when Sophia was lost one cold December, I became worried when she was missing at bedtime. She always came into the house at night, particularly in the winter.

After calling and calling, I eventually went to bed but slept fitfully, worrying where she was. I fell into a light sleep only to be awakened in the early hours of the morning by my old dot-matrix printer pouring out pages of nonsense characters and spooling out rolls of paper onto my office floor. The computer and the printer had been turned off before I went to bed. It had never malfunctioned like this before.

After turning everything off and scrapping all the wasted paper, I decided to call Sophia one more time at the front door. This time she rolled out of the rose bushes onto the lawn, very cold and with her front paw trapped in her cat collar. I don't know how long she had been there, but the bushes were right under the office window where the printer had run amok.

I picked her up, took off her collar and freed her paw, wrapped her in a warm towel and cuddled her until she warmed up enough to drink some warm milk. I really feel that her energy turned on the printer, to get my attention!

A few years later, I asked Dr. Dean Radin about this event and he agreed that this might have been Sophia (animal-PK) turning on the printer in her distress to get my attention or I may have picked up her distress and triggered the printer myself (telepathy and PK).

Instrument Enhancement.
PROJECT: Instrument Enhancement.
METHOD: ERV.
DATE: October 19th, 1998.
TYPE: Technology.
CLIENT: Business.

In 1998, I received several treasure hunting projects. These are not my favorite type of projects as there is so much "mental noise" involved. To begin, there are client expectations hinging on your results: will we find the treasure, and will it be financially profitable? Then, there are the expectations of any other viewers involved: will we get a share of the proceeds? After being burned several times by clients taking off with the RV results and never ever being seen again, I pick and choose which projects I will take on.

The following project was a little different, the client was interested in finding ways to simplify finding treasure, rather than just with remote viewing. The client was a dowser and wanted to find ways to create a synthesis between body and mind to find lost treasure.

He asked the following questions:

1.   *Look into the future and see, what is the best way to modify or improve the instrument (dowsing equipment) for locating and sensing gold and silver at a long distance.*

What was perceived was a modification of the current equipment to include an element of randomness. As has been shown by experiments at the PEAR Laboratory at Princeton University, human consciousness can interact at the quantum level with certain electronic random systems. A random output system, such as a random number generator, needs to be linked to the current system to either run concurrently and in synch with the current system.

A random event or number generator puts out series of plus and minus pulses in a random fashion. Using specialized programs these can be converted into one and zeros that can be calculated. Run over a certain period as a calibration, the device puts out pluses and minuses that equal a chance distribution, that is, it does not exceed the average. However, when human consciousness is included in the equation, the random number generator tends to put out more pluses or zeros in response to a given situation.

There needs to be a three-input system consisting of the current device (the client's current dowsing system). (1) Which is run by an individual. (2) Alongside will run a random number generator. (3) Which may or may not be physically linked to the current system. When a question is asked such as "Is there gold here at a certain location?" the current system should be employed as usual. The random number generator, which is being run concurrently, (if there is gold present at the site) should respond with a deviation from its normal functioning with excess streams of pluses or minus pulses. It should be possible to install some sort of audio signal to indicate whether the signal output from the random event generator is deviating from chance expectation. A good electronics specialist should be able to build this for the client and I mentioned that he might want to contact the PEAR Laboratory at Princeton University for some of their published papers.

2.   Look for methods by which we can use an electronic sensing method i.e. we use dowsing rods now to sense signals, need an electronic device that will sense signals instead.

What was perceived was an interacting system that used the L-rods in combination with Galvanic Skin Response or GSR (as used in biofeedback work). The Galvanic Skin Response measures the electrical conductivity of the skin. When a person becomes aroused, the GSR level rises and can be measured electrically. Usually, metal L-Rods are encased in some sort of holders, which allow the rods to swing freely. These holders should be composed of some electrically conductive metal that is linked to a GSR-measuring instrument, which also employs a tone to indicate changes in the GSR. When the L-Rods or dowsing rods are asked to locate gold. The GSR device should indicate the presence of gold by causing the tone to go up or down as the individual's skin conductivity changes.

3.   Look at current methods used by others for sensing objects at a distance.

There are a variety of methods that others use for sensing objects at a distance. The most common of these employs a method called psychometry. In psychometry, an object is held in the hand and information is accessed from the object. However, for remote sensing, I perceive a modification of this method. A small piece of real gold would be held in one hand as an "identifier," the other hand would be linked to the GSR device. The hand holding the small piece of gold would be moved over a location map and the question would be asked "Where is the gold?" As the psyche or human consciousness perceives the location of gold, the GSR should rise in tone and indicate the location of gold on the map. This might take some practice with prior known locations to calibrate the individual and the GSR device.

Color Coding/ Associative Remote Viewing or ARV.

The psychometry method could be modified to use colors instead of gold. Sometimes our emotions, expectations, and needs act as barriers to the accessing of accurate information. In this adaptation, the individuals involved would decide which color would be designated to represent gold (or any other metal/mineral). For example, a green crayon may represent actual gold. The green crayon is given to an individual (who may or may not know what green represents, it doesn't matter) who is also linked to the GSR. The green crayon is held in one hand, the GSR is linked to the other hand. The hand holding the crayon is moved over the location map while asking "Where is green?" When the GSR indicates a physiological arousal, the map is marked with the green crayon.

All these preceding methods are based on the hypothesis that the human central nervous system (CNS) can act as an antenna for accessing information. When knowledge is accessed the natural response is for the body to react in some way (often resulting in the micro-movements of dowsing L-Rods). The galvanic skin response (GSR) gives a readily accessible audible signal that indicates the aroused state of the CNS.

Vietnam MIAs.
PROJECT: MIAs in Vietnam.
METHOD: Coordinate RV.
DATE: October 1998.
CLIENT: Mike Van Atta.
TYPE: Applications.

In October of 1998, a colleague, Mike Van Atta, sent me a request to remote view the possible locations of several soldiers missing in action in Vietnam - MIAs.   In both cases, I perceived that there were Vietnamese people who knew where the bodies were, and I remote viewed potential locations for my colleague. I hoped that he would find the information helpful in supplementing or confirming known data. He later confirmed that the data matched what was known about the selected MIAs and that the additional unknown information could be helpful. Sadly, to date, there has been no further feedback on these cases but, it is hoped, the information could supplement what is known and may one day provide closure.

The Boat in the Castle.
PROJECT: Mirabel, Spain.
METHOD: Coordinate Remote Viewing.
DATE: 1998.
CLIENT: T. Emerson May.
TYPE: Historical Exploration.

During the latter half of the 1990's a researcher and writer, T. (Ted) Emerson May, was following up on readings given by the famous "Sleeping Prophet", Edgar Cayce. The readings involved the fabled land of Atlantis and that "evidence for the existence of Atlantis would be found in three places in this century: in the Caribbean, in the Pyrenees

Mountains and in the Yucatan Peninsula." Many of Cayce's readings were very accurate, so Ted decided to follow up the Atlantis readings with his own research.

Using a combination of remote viewing and spiritual clairvoyance, May established a dialog with an entity called Magnus through colleagues, Charlotte and Mary. The readings focused on Mirabel, Spain and pointed Ted to locations in the Pyrenees, a mountain and a ship that appeared to be abandoned on the mountain. Inside the ship's hold was perceived to be slabs of stone about ten feet square and that the slabs had some sort of markings on them.

Ted now reached out to other remote viewers over the Internet looking for someone to mentally "travel" to Mirabel, Spain, to confirm the perceptions. He first found an American, Richard Rader, who was married to a Spanish woman, and lived in Malaga, Spain.

I was another remote viewer included in Ted's outreach. He tasked me with the project (I was not privy to the location or his other findings) and I perceived a castle on a hill south of Malaga, Spain. Ted felt that the ship, perceived by another viewer, was inside the castle but none of the other viewers had seen the castle in their viewings. Interestingly, the group later found ruins of a castle at the physical site that had not been previously reported. Ted and another viewer, Patty, asked for more information about the castle but, by this time, I was too front-fronted (had too much up-front information to be objective) and declined. I had seen too many castles in the UK and felt my viewing would be too analytical.

Water on Mars.
PROJECT: Journey to Mars.
METHOD: ERV.
DATE: 1998.
CLIENT: T. Emerson May.
TYPE: Exploration.

T. (Ted) Emerson May also tasked me with another "blind" (no upfront information, just a case number). What I perceived was a high vantage point that reminded me of the Valley of Fire, north of Las Vegas, a place of dry, hot, red sandstone. During my remote viewing session, I perceived water from a hot spring flowing down the hillside to rapidly sink into the dry, dusty earth forming a mud pool. I sent this data to Ted and received feedback that this was a viewing of Mars, around 50,000 years ago! Ted informed me that he had sent the data to Dr. Hal Puthoff.

<u>Finding Opal at Coober Pedy.</u>
PROJECT: Opal Location.
METHOD: Coordinate RV.
DATE: July 17th, 1998.
CLIENT: Jim Francis.
TYPE: Geological Search.

In 1998 my friend Jim was off to search for opals in Australia, at a location called Coober Pedy. Jim asked if I could do a remote viewing to locate the best spot to dig. He sent me maps of the area in South Australia, which I knew wouldn't work, as they had too much topographical information, too much "frontloading" to do an objective viewing. Instead I constructed a graph of small squares on a plain sheet of paper that I superimposed over the map. I asked myself what color I associated with opal and came up with "green," and then chose a green pencil to mark where I perceived the best opal to be.

Using a hand-dowsing technique, holding my hand over the squares and "feeling" for the right location, I outlined one major area in green (that covered several squares) and a smaller area. The grid was faxed to Jim and off he went to Coober Pedy. At the site, Jim used a dowsing instrument to narrow down the location, and then got to work on the excavation.

Working with a mate, he began using a backhoe to begin the construction of a large hole. When you look at Coober Pedy, explained Jim, these excavation holes are all over the place (as well as a whole city constructed from underground tunnels and caves!) Jim told me that miners can dig up to twenty of these holes before they hit "potch," the precursor mineral to opal. Jim hit "potch" on the first try and his email to me proclaimed "Eureka!"

However, Jim was having trouble getting to the opal and called me in Las Vegas. He told me that he had hit a wall of dirt and wanted to know how to proceed. On the phone, I remote viewed that the wall of dirt had a darker, diagonal line slanting down from the top right to the bottom left. I told Jim, that if he dug in an S shape at the bottom of the diagonal line, he would hit the opal, he did- and he did! Jim sent a video tape of the unpolished stones that they pulled out of the excavation and he sent me one of the smaller polished stones.

Over the years since, Jim has been a steady friend and colleague and we have promoted each other's work. Jim asked me to write a forward to his Mind Power book and I have called on him many times to promote my new projects. Jim has also consulted with me on many

147

different projects including real-estate ventures, business evaluations and solving criminal cases.

University Project.
PROJECT: Research Target for a Skeptic.
METHOD: ERV.
DATE: March 1998.
CLIENT: University of Texas.
TYPE: Research.

In the March of 1998, I took part in a series of remote viewing sessions for an academic at the University of Austin, TX. He was one of my trainer Paul Smith's colleagues and a skeptic. I don't mind skeptics if they play fair. This one didn't!

After doing a couple of sessions with moderate target contact, I did a session that turned out to be right "on target." Despite a cold and sore throat, I did a solo session and drew an unusual ideogram of a flat line with a sharp peak, a divot, in the middle. I got gestalts of a "landscape"

As the session progressed, I perceived that the landscape was "grey and monotonous, bleak, windswept, expansive and sparse." I drew the ideogram again, larger, a flat line with a sharp peak in the middle. The sketches morphed through several shapes but each coming back to a sharp, triangular structure. I wrote "definite structure."

I decided to make the sketch three-dimensional and drew parallel lines up one side, declaring an AOL (analytic overlay) of a pyramid. I then sketched a definite pyramid and declared it to be "Cheops" and ended my session.

My session summary read: "Rising up out of a bleak, sparse landscape is a solitary, solid structure. Colors of black, white and grey. Initially tower like, the sketches morphed into a triangular structure like the Cheops Pyramid. The structure is in a bleak, windswept, expansive area which was grey and monotonous. Bands or lines run horizontally around the structure. At the top the lines radiate out around the peak of the structure. Solid structure."

I faxed off my session, as I had done with all my other sessions, to the researcher and, when instructed, I logged on for my feedback picture – which turned out to be the Cheops Pyramid! I was pleased and called David to see my session and feedback picture.

Unfortunately, the skeptic said that he had never received my session, even though he had sent feedback, which is only done in response to a received session. He may say he never received it, but I know I hit the target!

Years later, when visiting with Ingo, he showed me Cheops Pyramid sessions done by the military team at Fort Meade (all unclassified). There was the same ideogram, time after time: the flat line with the sharp spike in the middle, which I thought was uniquely mine!

Calibrations Sessions.
PROJECT: Where is Zoe?
METHOD: ERV.
DATE: September 10, 1998.
CLIENT: Private Investigator: Gumshoe.
TYPE: Missing Person.

Another case that I received during the time I rented the office on Flamingo, was from a retired private investigator, who described himself as a "gumshoe!" I had never heard that term before and it struck me as sort of quaint. The case involved a missing child: a little girl who had been abducted by her biological mother who was described as a felon. However, before I searched for her, Gumshoe wanted to test if I really could locate individuals using remote viewing. OK! I was getting used to people wanting to see if this skill really worked, even when working for free on a humanitarian case!

Gumshoe had the permission of his girlfriend, Zoe, and she became the focus of three attempts to describe her locations. Interestingly, she didn't go to too much trouble to hide her activities and I found her in her office, and at other domestic locations, describing the building and the interiors. Gumshoe said he was impressed and decided to give me the missing child case.

1999

JOURNALS

Journal - January 8, 1999 – *Finishing up my Ph.D. Dissertation.*
1999 started off with a flurry of effort to get my Ph.D. Dissertation finished. I worked on the extra stats and writing during December. I finished New Year's Eve in time for Dave to take me away for the weekend to the Caliente Hot Springs Motel, NV. It was lovely to relax in the hot spring waters and get all the muscle kinks out. Dave sprung for a suite so we had a kitchen and large bathroom with our own large tub that we could fill with spring water. We also had the use of a larger private bath which could have fitted a small group of people! We drove

back home along Rainbow Canyon, which didn't save us much time, but we did see some lovely scenery.

The Dissertation was a monster job and eventually became a two-inch manuscript with thirteen appendices. I mailed it off to my Dissertation Chairperson, yesterday morning, so she should get it on Saturday or Monday. When she has approved it, I will be able to send it to the other Committee Members, Prof. Stanley Krippner and Dr. Robert Jahn, for approval. Then, it goes to an Outside Reader for their approval. The final hurdle is an oral exam which we might be able to do by telephone conference call. It feels good to have the bulk of the work finished! There might be some minor changes and corrections but, basically it is finished. I plan to graduate this summer.

Journal - January 8, 1999- *Book Signing.*

My book *Remote Perceptions* was finally released by Hampton Roads at the end of November. At the time they had presales of 1,400 copies and I felt happy that it was selling. Since then I have been on a few radio shows and this has given some additional promotion to the book. I have a book talk and signing set for next week at Borders Books in Green Valley. This is the first one I have ever done. Kathy Cooper of Hampton Roads says that there might be a lot of people interested, or just a few, but not to be discouraged, or take it personally. I am just treating it was a fun thing to do! Hopefully, as it gets more publicity there will be an opportunity to do some more.

There was the possibility of doing a TV show in Canada (The Dina Petty Show, Toronto) but they wanted me to do a live demonstration, which I was reluctant to do. So, I am not sure if the show will happen or not.

I recently sent sample chapters of my second book *The CE4 Enigma* (later to become Diary of an Abduction) to Hampton Roads, as they were interested in seeing the work, but I haven't heard anything back from them yet. I have decided to go ahead and work on the rest of the book chapters. If Hampton Roads doesn't want it, perhaps I can market it to another publisher.

Journal - January 8, 1999 – *Formation of IRVA.*

In the fall I was approached by Dr. Wayne Carr who wanted me to take over the running of the American Association of Remote Viewers. I declined and discussed starting a new one with one of Paul Smith's colleagues who offered some financing. The plan is to hold a one-day meeting in March in Alamogordo to discuss the formation of a private Association that will accredit RV and psi practitioners. The folk who have agreed to attend are Lyn Buchanan, Paul Smith, myself, our benefactor, Skip Atwater, Dean Radin, Jessica Utts, and Hal Puthoff. We will also be inviting Brenda Dunne and Charles Tart as Ingo Swann and Joe McMoneagle have declined to attend.

The one-day meeting will be followed by a two-day conference organized by Lyn Buchanan and PSI, at which some of the one-day attendees will give talks and presentations. This should be an auspicious few days. Our sponsor is arranging the financing for the venture and I need to look out fares, accommodations, etc. for the attendees and speakers. It will be a great opportunity to help get the new association off the ground and help in bringing some respectability and credentials for psi practitioners and teachers.

Journal - April 8, 1999 – *Road Blocks.*

I notice that the last time I wrote in my journal was back in January and a lot has happened since then! A small group of us have formed a new association: The International Remote Viewing Association. I took part in the first remote viewing conference in New Mexico and attended Lyn Buchanan's Intermediate Controlled Remote Viewing course in Alamogordo, NM.

Sad to say, I need to rewrite my Dissertation at the request of my Chairperson, as well as doing more statistics. This has been an additional stress and burden. (I later discovered that the Dissertation Proposal has the same status as a Legal Agreement and when accepted by the student and Committee, only what is agreed must be carried out during the Dissertation. Asking the student to do additional work, not stipulated in the Proposal, is not allowed.)

On top of this, there have been financial worries over keeping Inner Vision afloat as finances have been slow in coming in. So, there have been many distractions and demands on my time.

Journal - April 8th, 1999 – *The International Remote Viewing Association (IRVA).*

On Thursday, March 18th, 1999, ten professional folk: our financial sponsor, Paul Smith, Russell Targ, Skip Atwater, Hal Puthoff, Lyn Buchanan, John Alexander, Stephan Schwartz, Marcello Truzzi and myself met at the PSI headquarters in Alamogordo, NM to discuss the formation of a new association dedicated to the setting of standards in the remote viewing field. Also present were Victoria Alexander (as observer) and Robert Knight (as official photographer).

Since the early days at SRI and the Fort Mead Unit, the field has become fragmented, with some folk making outrageous claims for remote viewing. So, by lunchtime on the 18th, the group had got to the point of saying "well, if we do nothing, what will happen?" We agreed that the field would continue to fragment, and more outrageous claims would be made in the name of remote viewing. So, we brain-stormed and came up with a name for the association: The International Remote Viewing Association or IRVA, a Mission Statement, decided that our sponsor would be the coordinator of the meeting, Hal Puthoff and Marcello Truzzi would become scientific advisors, and the remainder of the group would become the first Directors. I acted as Interim Secretary for the meeting.

Russell Targ kindly made a gift of his existing non-profit corporation to IRVA. The meeting was a great success. Paul Smith and the sponsor have since drafted a Press Release. It was risky to bring such diverse individuals together under the same roof, as much history has gone down, and many old battles remain unresolved, but the group was exceedingly civil, and a lot was accomplished in one historic day!

The First Members and Directors of IRVA.
Back Row: Hal Puthoff, David (Financial Sponsor), John Alexander, Lyn Buchanan, Paul Smith, Skip Atwater, Angela Thompson Smith and Marcello Truzzi. Seated: Russell Targ and Stephan Schwartz.

Journal - April 8, 1999 – *First RV Conference.*
Following the one-day IRVA meeting on March 18, nine of the meeting folks drove up to Ruidoso to congregate at the Inn of the Mountain Gods to participate in the first remote viewing conference.

Our hosts were Lyn and Linda Buchanan of PSI and the conference lasted from March 19 to the 21. It was another great success.

Most of the IRVA participant gave talks and presentations. I talked about using RV for archaeological work, finding opal, and about receiving news of the St. Exupery project that I participated in eight years ago. Jean-Luc Janisewski, a French remote viewer had sent me a copy of *Paris Match* that contained an article on the St. Exupery plane being found. I was able to share this information with Lyn and Mel Riley and it was very exciting to get feedback after so many years.

Between the meeting and now, Jean-Luc has sent a translation of the *Paris Match* article and I have shared this information with Lyn and Mel who were also viewers on the Saint Exupery project. I hope to present this information as a paper at next year's conference.

The only drawbacks to this year's conference were that some of the technical/audiovisual equipment failed or was not available and there was some confusion over the judging of a remote viewing contest. None of the viewers correctly accessed the target and there was a lot of criticism about the type and level of judging. All in all, though, the conference was a great success and we plan to expand the scope and range of the meeting next year.

Journal - April 8, 1999 – *Intermediate CRV Course.*

After the Conference I rode back to Alamogordo with colleagues and on the 22 March attended Lyn Buchanan's Intermediate CRV Course and it was very helpful. We learned Stages 4 and 5, as well as some Stage 6, plus 4 ½ (ERV). Lyn was sick so he did not monitor personally but came around to supervise, as we took turns being viewer and monitor. I learned how to score my sessions and I went from accessing 50% correct information to 68%.

I am used to doing my sessions solo, rather than with a monitor, so it was detracting to have the session interrupted by a monitor and Lyn as they made suggestions and comments. However, I enjoyed Lyn's more relaxed teaching style and the encouragement of the other students.

Lyn has a plan whereby once you have taken a course, you can return to audit the course. Paul Smith's teaching style is much more formal, and he interacts one-on-one with each student. Yesterday I received a packet of practice targets from Lyn plus a certificate.

Journal - March 8, 1999 – *Remote Perceptions.*

Finally, at the end of November, last year, *Remote Perceptions* was published, and I was able to hold my first book in my hands! It felt great and I still feel the glow of accomplishment! (It is now out of print, but you can still find second-hand copies on Amazon. I hope to republish it at some point). About 1,400 books were sold by the end of the year, which covered my advance and gave me a small royalty check a few weeks ago. Hopefully, the next six months check will be a little larger.

Remote Perceptions is selling well on Amazon and I have advertised it on my website. I am now working on a second book called the *CE4 Enigma*. (Published as *Diary of an Abduction*, now also out of print). I am taking the stand that there is a very real event taking place; that many people are reporting these experiences, but because of its elusiveness, the phenomenon is clothed in myth, superstition and outright fabrication by the authorities. The book will be about my own experiences and how I have searched for answers. I don't think that the book will please the outspoken abductees or the dedicated UFO researchers, or the skeptics, but I hope the ordinary person will read it and be educated about the experience and all the theories and hype surrounding it. I sent some sample chapters to Hampton Roads and they said they might be interested. I need to finish the whole manuscript and send it to them.

Journal - July 19, 1999 – *The 100 Year Flood.*
Summer has arrived quickly and a few weeks ago we experienced a 100 Year Flood that everyone was talking about. It rained about 2" on some parts of the Las Vegas valley and the washes became raging rivers, washing away cars and mobile homes. Luckily, Dave and I were at home, so we were safe and watched the raging waters on TV. By the time John got home from school (his stepdad Jack fetched him) it was almost over. We were on the side of Sunrise Mountain, so we weren't flooded out.

We have been looking after Dave's brother's duck and even he looked drenched at the end of the afternoon. Attitude or Atta for short is a very bad-tempered duck and pecks at everyone who goes near. Dave has built him a "duck palace," a wire enclosure with a pond and a solar cover. When he is out during the day, he has the run of the grassy area in the backyard. The cats give him a wide berth and he also respects them! The boys are a little scared of the duck and stay well away from him.

We have had Daniel all summer and thankfully sharing him with family. His Mom has been having him for her weekends plus Mondays. Dan has been occupying himself building an enormous "ball factory" that takes plastic balls up a huge Konnex construction and the balls then cascade down in one of six ways. It is quite ingenious! He has taken about three weeks to build it and it has kept him out of mischief!

154

Journal - July 19, 1999 – *Little Progress.*

One of the reasons I haven't kept up to date with my journal has been that I have been rewriting my Ph.D. Dissertation. I finally mailed it off to my Committee Chairperson last week. Dave says he would have given up long ago! I completed the second rewrite at New Year and Dave took me away for a few days to the Caliente Hot Springs Motel to soak in the waters. It was a nice break! Then my Chairperson came back requesting a whole bunch of new statistics and rewrites and I lost enthusiasm for a while. Then I got going again and finally got it printed up. I hope that it is accepted this time!

The next step will be to pass it to the other Committee Members: Prof. Stan Krippner and Prof. Bob Jahn. Then it must go to an Outside Reader, and I must defend the work at an Oral Defense. After that it goes back to my Committee and I should be graduated as a Ph.D. I was worried because I thought I would be out of time and money but Saybrook has granted me an extension of time and I am eligible for one more year of school loans.

Another task completed was sending a full copy of the manuscript for the new book *CE4 Enigma* (*Diary of an Abduction*) to Hampton Roads at their request. They asked for a full MS, as I had originally only sent sample chapters. They then suggested some modifications, which I did and mailed it off today! They are excited about the book and it is slated for publication in the fall of 2000!

Now with the Dissertation mailed off and book MS sent off I feel like I am on vacation and about 75% of the stress I was under has fallen away! Dave says I should go on vacation, but I don't have anywhere to go and no money to go anywhere. There is the possibility that Dave will get a few day's work in Santa Barbara, CA and I might go with him. He asked what I would do all day on vacation. Ha! I would read library books, take naps, and walk on the beaches – it would be a wonderful break.

Journal - September 21, 1999 – *Moving Forward.*

Last week I taught my first full-time student in a very long time, there does not seem to be much of an interest now. The student rode down from Canada, fifty-six hours on the bus and another fifty-six to get back home, talk about dedication! The class went very well, and several local people came for part of the training.

My book *Remote Perceptions* did not do as well as I had hoped over the summer, just over a thousand copies were sold. So, my royalty check was a lot less than I anticipated. Hampton Roads said they want to publish my second book, but I might see who else is interested and

HR hasn't given me a contract yet. It is a controversial book, but it has publishing potential.

Journal - October 15, 1999 – *Book Contract.*
Some good news, I received a book contract from Hampton Roads to publish "Diary of an Abduction."

CASE FILES – 1999

Missing Person.
PROJECT: Missing Kindergartner.
METHOD: ERV.
DATE: February 1999.
CLIENT: Private Investigator: Gumshoe.
TYPE: Missing Person.

In February 1999, Gumshoe emailed me a picture of an adorable Kindergarten child, dressed in a pinafore dress. My heart went out to her and helped focus my attention on her location. I first perceived her waiting outside of a school. She was alone and jumping up and down while she waited. I perceived that this was a Catholic elementary school. A car came along, and she got in with people she knew and trusted. I tried a technique that involved "looking through the eyes" of a victim or perpetrator: a form of connection like telepathy but with a visual focus. I saw the scenery, the interior of the car, and where she was headed. Her destination turned out to be a trailer-type house and she was greeted by individuals who I described.

Gumshoe reported that he had located the area, had located the trailer, and had information from someone at a local diner that the child was there. Unfortunately, for whatever reason, he was unable to go and collect her, which was disappointing. He gave several reasons: he developed a migraine, someone at the house said the family had moved, etc. This case got me thinking about parental abduction cases. How can a viewer know who the "bad parent" is, if there is any such thing as a "bad parent?" What if I had found the child and she had been returned to a parent who mistreated or abused her? I have done very few parental abduction cases since the Zoe case.

Binary Sports Betting.
PROJECT: Team Outcomes.
METHOD: Binary RV.

DATE: February 1999. CLIENT:
"Mr. Sports Bar." TYPE: Sports.

Early in 1999, a local businessman contacted me with a project. Much of my work comes from word-of-mouth. Mr. Sports Bar wanted me to see if I could predict the outcome of binary sports teams (Team A versus Team B) in a variety of sports. Rather than using a formal method such as Associative Remote Viewing (ARV), he wanted to supply me with lists of teams named with letters of the alphabet that had nothing to with their actual name i.e. Team Q versus Team K. I tried this for several runs of sessions, but the task became increasingly boring and frustrating and I finally declined any further lists. This brings up an interesting aspect of remote viewing: the subconscious seems to like variety. Doing straight binary choice work bored the mind and did not allow for a flow of remote viewing data.

Intuitive Diagnosis 1.
PROJECT: Green is for Copper.
METHOD: ERV.
DATE: 1999.
CLIENT: Husband and Wife Couple.
TYPE: Medical Remote Viewing.

I got a call at home from a couple who were referred to me from colleagues. This couple, a young husband and wife had been very sick for some time, had seen many doctors, and nothing seemed to help them. As a remote viewer I am not allowed to diagnose or prescribe (by the American Medical Association, AMA) but I can give my opinion. As I talked to the couple, I perceived a deep-green color associated with their problems. I asked them if they had been tested for copper toxicity.

About a week later, they reported that they had their blood tested, as well as the water from their well. The technician thought that his equipment was broken because their samples were off the scale! They did indeed have copper poisoning that they were able to get treated. Very often the subconscious will give information in the form of a color or picture or a song. It is then up to the viewer to understand what this represents, and this comes with experience and practice.

Intuitive Diagnosis 2.
PROJECT: Parasitic Problem.
METHOD: ERV.
DATE: 1999.

CLIENT: Phone Inquiry.
TYPE: Medical Remote Viewing.

On another occasion, I received a call from a man who was having a variety of health problems. This time what I perceived was a load of small, squiggly, biological forms swimming in his bloodstream that I described to him as protozoa. I asked him if he had been tested for Lyme disease. It seems that he had indeed received treatment for the illness and thought he was cured. I advised him to get retested. He still had Lyme disease and was able to continue treatment.

Spiritual Protection.
PROJECT: The Magic Mirror.
METHOD: Out-bounder.
DATE: 1999.
CLIENT: Internet colleague.
TYPE: Psychic Protection.

From time to time, over the past two decades, practitioners of remote viewing have asked me to assist them and participate in practical exercises. One man, needing practice in the Out-Bounder protocol, and asked by email if we could both do five sessions: him sending me five outdoor targets to perceive and me sending him five outdoor targets to perceive. This went well with a limited success. I mentally sent this colleague some local scenes, visited them in person and tried to mentally share some of the qualities of the site. He did the same with his outdoor sites.

Once the ten sessions were complete and we had emailed our results and comments, he sent me another email making an unusual request. He said that he had a theory about telepathy and would like to send some images to me as I was getting ready to sleep. The borderline between being awake and asleep is called the hypnogogic state and is a good way to go Out-of-Body and to receive telepathic images. There is a corresponding situation as we wake up called the hypnopompic state. Many people use these states for metaphysical work.

I declined to work with him on these additional projects, as the times when I am preparing and waking from sleep are my private and exclusive spaces, and I gave him no more thought. A week or so later, as I was lying sleepily in my bed, the most inappropriate images began popping into my mind! I don't usually have these images going through my mind, whatever time of the day it is! Quickly realizing that these images were coming from outside of me I recalled my 'Magic

Mirror", an imaginary device that reflects unwanted images to the sender. It doesn't do any harm; it's like returning an unwanted letter or blocking an email sender. The images stopped and didn't return, and I never heard from this creep again.

Be aware that there are some people who, after getting a little training in esoteric matters, go on a "power trip." They are often men who prey on women or on weaker men who often feel that they are powerless. Never let someone like this intrude into your private mental space. There are many ways to treat such intruders such as the Magic Mirror, imagining a bank vault door slamming shutting, or drawing a metal curtain across your mind. Your mind belongs to you!

RV and the Law.
PROJECT: RV Legal Status.
METHOD: ERV.
DATE: March 1999.
CLIENT: Corporate Lawyer.
TYPE: Legal.

In March 1999 I received a call from a lawyer, a referral from a DOJ contact, requesting a consultation. I was quite willing to work with him and he said that he would send me a written protocol. It turned out that we didn't work together but of interest was a section of the protocol that involved the legal status of remote viewing. As a lawyer, this individual had access to a database of court cases and, in his opinion, not one had ever involved remote viewing. That is, up to that date, nobody had ever sued a remote viewer and there was no record of remote viewing being adversely cited in a court case. This was not unusual as the term remote viewing didn't become publicly known until around 1995. To my knowledge, the only court cases since then have been remote viewers suing (or threatening to sue) other remote viewers!

In another field, I recently asked a psychiatrist colleague, who knew about remote viewing, how the subject was viewed in psychiatric circles. He responded that he had never heard the term, remote viewing, discussed in terms of mental illness, it had never been presented at mental health conferences or written about in medical journals.

Buried Treasure.
PROJECT: Camp Hill, AL.
METHOD: RV using Photo Targets.

159

DATE: February 1999.
CLIENT: John W. Hutcherson.
TYPE: Treasure Hunting.

A request came in from a researcher, John W. Hutcherson and a treasure recovery team that had received permission of an Alabama property owner, Junior Hartley, to look for treasure on his property. Both the property owner, Junior Hartley, and John W. Hutcherson had agreed to work with the recovery team that would be composed of Dowsers Louis J. Matacia, and his colleagues David Gowman, and Dale Wadell. It was believed that there existed one or more treasures on the property.

Camp Hill, Alabama Main Street 1998

According to Louis's conversation with the researcher, John said he "saw" an Indian Princess standing at the treasure site and she was pointing to the spot where the treasure was located. It is assumed that the Indian Princess seen by John may have indicated permission to move the treasures. David Gowman and Louis J. Matacia dowsed Polaroid photos and later sent them to me for my perceptions. John wrote "It is a little difficult to see our red spots marked on the Polaroid photos but both David and Louis received hits on all six of the photos."

The specific location of the property had not been given to Louis. It was anticipated that Louis and his team would travel I-85 south to Dadeville, Alabama to meet up with John Hutcherson. They would then call the property owner, Junior Hartley. They wanted Louis's team to dig for the treasure, recover it and sell the treasure for them, resulting with a 1/3rd split for each party. John went on to say there were three vaults located at the site. I received six Polaroid photos from the team of sites that they were considering searching. I used them for my project and then the Polaroids were returned to the team. Treasure recovery was planned for the time period October-November 1999.

The team asked several heavily front-loaded but non-leading questions about three areas, A, B and C, on the Camp Hill property and I was able to perceive information regarding the locations, the events, time periods and how the specific treasure (if any) could be accessed.

Junior Hartley was excited about the search. However, he had greater expectations about the treasure than the rest of the team, expecting the finds to make him a rich man. Junior Hartley was hoping that the treasures would mean an end to financial hardship, and that the treasures would sell quickly. I perceived that he might get impatient at the slow pace that the treasures are located, their content, and the slow pace at which the selling proceeds. He would need constant reassurance. John W. Hutcherson was also excited, but the actual finds meant more to him than the dollar amounts.

Unfortunately, after providing this information to the group, I heard little more until I eventually initiated a follow-up:

In September 2011, I called the phone number in my files for Junior Hartley to ask his permission to write about this case and had a pleasant conversation. I asked if any treasure was found and they sadly said "No." From my recollection there had been problems with getting equipment to the site, weather troubles and other logistical problems. This emphasizes one of the major problems with treasure hunting using remote viewing. However good the quality of the viewing and extensive the data, if the team cannot excavate and find the treasure the work is basically worthless.

2000

JOURNALS

From 2000 onwards, interesting projects continued to arrive, and I graduated from Saybrook University with my Ph. D in psychology in 2001. In 2002, I relocated to the little town of Boulder City, just to the south-east of Las Vegas, where I continued consulting, researching and teaching remote viewing. In 2003 I worked as Executive Director of the Boulder City Senior Center for a few years but semi-retired to work fulltime in remote viewing: writing, researching and teaching.

Journal - February 1, 2000 – *Mesquite RV Conference.*
Last August, my friend Marilyn Huff and I travelled up to Mesquite, a tourist location, 70 miles north of Las Vegas on the Nevada/Utah

border. We stayed overnight to check out the rooms and conference facilities for our upcoming Year 2000 Remote Viewing Conference, which is taking place at the end of May. Paul Smith, Lyn Buchanan, me, Michael O'Bannon, and Bill Eigles are on the planning committee and we have a good panel of speakers set up. It should be a good function. We are planning for 100 to 150 people attending.

There will be three functions as well as the talks: a Welcome Reception; a Meet the Speakers Buffet; and a Banquet. Jack Houck has agreed to come and so a Spoon-Bending Workshop following one of the evening functions.

We are planning to have an IRVA committee meeting on the Monday following the conference. Sometime in February, Marilyn and I will travel up to Mesquite and try out their cuisine and decide on the food for the buffets and banquet.

Journal - April 26, 2000 – *Mesquite Conference Preparations.*

For the past six months I have been part of the team that has been putting together the Year 2000 Remote Viewing Conference to take place over Memorial weekend in Mesquite, NV. We have been working with the Oasis Resort and putting together a great conference. Paul Smith and I, along with the assistance of a colleague Marilyn Huff, initially launched the beginnings of the conference. "On a wing and a prayer" and with no up-front money, we arranged dates, menus, rooms and other preparations, praying that it would all come together in the end!

We now have a panel of about twenty invited and contributing speakers and about one hundred and fifty attendees signed up and paid already, with still four weeks to go.

There have been one hundred and one things to consider but the preparations haven't taken too much of my time. As well as the speakers, we have Jack Houck giving a spoon-bending Workshop after the Banquet and music events during the Registration and the Meet-the-Speakers reception.

I went with Marilyn, up to Mesquite earlier this year to meet with the Conference organizers and they have been very helpful and accommodating. The Conference will last all day Friday, Saturday and Sunday and I plan to stay over a few days after. A group of us is getting together on May 6 to put together all the Conference materials, such as agendas and programs - should be fun. Lots of preparations.

Journal – April 26, 2000 – *Research Projects.*

In order to keep in practice, I have made it a policy to accept invitations to take part in psi research. The first one this year was offered by Dr. Ed May of the Laboratories for Fundamental research (LFR) located in Palo Alto, CA. The project was RNG-oriented and required 100 computer trials done on a computer program provided by LFR.

A few weeks ago, Paul Smith let me know about a website project run by Marty Rosenblatt. Marty is running P-I-A to generate funds and playing the stock market using Associative Remote Viewing (ARV) protocols. He wants his participants to complete 25 days with 20 targets per day that he uses to generate stock predictions. His pay scale is generous, up to $5,000 for 100% success and ranging down to $250 for 0-30% success. I have put in several days' predictions and, so far, have been ranging from 67% to 78% success.

Journal - June 19, 2000 – *Ph.D. Dissertation.*

The work that has occupied all my time, thoughts and emotions since last year has been to complete my Ph.D. Dissertation. This has been a frustrating experience! Just when I seem to have finished, my chairperson has come back with more work and re-writes! Two of my professors met last month and agreed on what was still needed. I did all the work thinking I would be finished, and then it came back from my chairperson with torrents of changes, argh! It was so disheartening, particularly as my other two committee members said it was a good piece of work!

Eventually, last week, one of the other Committee members, Stanley Krippner, stepped in and said they would send it to the Outside Reader, an important step along the way to its acceptance. What a relief! So, I took a little extra time to get everything completed and sent it off by Fed Ex on Friday, to Dr. Marilyn Schlitz, the Outside Reader.

Today I got a call from the Dean of Students at Saybrook and learned that what I thought was a personal problem, was shared by other students. I was also told that when a Ph.D. Candidate has their Dissertation Proposal accepted, this is like a business agreement, nothing more can be asked of the student, other than what has been agreed to in the Proposal. Anyway, the Dissertation is on its way to the Outside Reader and maybe I can get my Orals completed before the Saybrook Faculty takes a break in August.

Journal - June 19th, 2000 – *Mesquite Conference.*

Memorial weekend saw us all meeting up in Mesquite, NV for the Year 2000 Remote Viewing Conference. It was a great success!

Initially, we were worried that we wouldn't break even with one hundred attendees but, including speakers and volunteers, we had over 300 attendees.

We had about twenty speakers and workshop presenters. The atmosphere of sharing and comparing remote viewing methods and techniques was wonderful and we had representatives from almost all the major teaching and research groups, from here and abroad.

The conference facilities were good despite not laying on enough refreshments and the food at the Oasis was not terrific, but everything ran smoothly. We realized that next year we needed to have a professional timekeeper and not have too many break-out sessions in the side rooms. I was able to get verbal permission from the Psi Tech people to talk about the Saint-Exupery project and presented that to a packed hall. All in all, it was a good conference that people said they would be remembering for years!

Journal – June 19-22, 2000 – *Stargate List.*

For about a year now I have been the Moderator of an online Yahoo email group called the Stargate List. I was standing in for Steve Creitzman when he could no longer moderate. It has been a challenging experience!

The list is an important contribution to the field of RV and acts as a sounding board for ideas, experiences, and calls for answers to many complex problems. (Eventually John Cook took over the list when I was no longer able to run it).

Journal – June 22, 2000 – *ARV Project.*

For several months now I have been participating in an online project using Associative Remote Viewing (ARV) to work targets related to the stock market. The first round of 500 targets resulted in an eventual bust! I was in the throes of finishing up my Ph.D. dissertation. If this teaches me anything, it teaches me that remote viewing performance is affected by those same factors that impact other cognitive functions such as memory and learning. These factors seem to be related to stress, tiredness, illness, as well as a host of psychological and physiological factors.

Marty has set up his company P-I-A online and his website is devoted to his AVM (Animal, Vegetable, Mineral targets) protocol. I am about a third of the way through the second round of sessions. Now that my dissertation is almost done and my book almost edited, I predict that my AVM success rate will continue to improve.

[The remainder of my journal entries for 2000 were family oriented as I took a break from studies, writing and research.]

The River of Gold - 1
PROJECT: The River of Gold 1.
METHOD: ERV.
DATE: 1997 & 2000.
CLIENT: Independent.
TYPE: Geological Exploration.

    Sometimes locations appear, disappear, and then reappear, like the fabled River of Gold on the Nevada/California border. This supposedly subterranean river flows over deep beds of "black sands" that contain large amounts of microscopic gold. There are local tales of treasure hunters being swept to their deaths in the swift current, sometimes being washed out onto the Gulf of Mexico, and that the entrance to the River of Gold was blasted shut by a treasure hunter, perhaps with dead colleagues sealed inside. The location of this legendary River of Gold is wildly speculated and the stuff of historic myth and fable. During a remote viewing class in 1997, the students suggested doing a group session on Halloran Peak, just up the hill from Baker, California. I wrote up my perceptions and put them in my files. Then, in 2000, a client contacted me about the same location, and I shared my earlier perceptions:

    "Further to our conversation on the phone the other day regarding the Underground River of Gold, I found my original notes from the Halloran Peak RV. As I remember, the underground river was somewhere in the vicinity between Baker and the burned area, where I have marked an X. I called the top of the hill coming north out of Baker, Halloran Peak, but I have since learned that Halloran Peak is off to the East. What struck me as unusual was the "breaking wave" formation of rocks in the area. Also, the chasm down to the river appeared man-made and there were bridges across the water. I did not know about the River of Gold at the time but wrote those words under the drawing after I had feedback from the members of the class."

    I never heard back from this client whether he was successful in finding the location or not. However, another group of intrepid treasure hunters have now appeared, and we may try, once again, to locate this mysterious area. Like the fables of the Lost Dutchman Mine in Arizona, the River of Gold captures the imagination, makes men dream of being rich, and adds to the lore surrounding the mountains of the southwest.

Interestingly, they had been out to the area, and reported that they had observed the "breaking wave" effect in the rocks at the location.

They have discovered information that the entrance into the underground section was blocked off with rocks and cement and that there may be deceased persons inside the entrance.

I advised them, before renting a Jeep, mining equipment and heading for the hills, to think of the logistics. Just supposing that the blocked entrance to the mine was found, it would probably take jack hammers and dynamite to blast open the entrance. Once inside, if there were, indeed, dead colleagues sealed within, this discovery would bring in the authorities, and a full-scale inquiry would ensue that might delay any further search for months, or even years.

Imagine a good outcome, the entrance is found and there are no dead bodies inside. It is rumored that the way down to the underground river is treacherous and would probably need the skills of a team of spelunkers: caving enthusiasts, to negotiate the descent. So, having reached the river and set up temporary lighting, how could the gold be accessed?

Remember that the gold is contained in a matrix of black sand, although the gold content is supposed to be very high. The sand would need to be brought to the surface in enough quantities to be worthwhile, it takes specialized equipment to separate the gold from the sand, and it needs a constant source of surface water to operate the equipment. Not an easy task in the desert and it would take some time to leach out appreciable amounts of gold from the black sand.

So, once again, imagine another good outcome. Hard work and ingenuity have brought up enough black sand, which was processed, and a valuable amount of gold dust and nuggets were retrieved. Who owns the gold? In Nevada and many other southern states, the major land owners are the federal government, the Bureau of Land Management, and a small percentage of private land owners. The government has strict laws in place about gold and other minerals being taken from federal land. If the gold recovery site is on Indian tribal lands, there are additional consequences for taking the gold, however far underground it is found. If a private owner owns the land, then permissions and agreements would mean sharing the proceeds. So, locating and recovering treasure from the River of Gold is not as simple as it seems.

I further advised them. Go ahead and look for gold and treasure, it's a good hobby but remember it takes hard work, time, and dedication and "gold fever" has been accountable for many murders

166

among treasure hunters. Gold fever brings out the worst in people: jealousy, distrust, and greed, so keep that in mind when you are searching for the Lost River of Gold.

Promo for the BBC.
PROJECT: BBC Documentary Promotion.
METHOD: ERV.
DATE: 2000.
CLIENT: Tom Kennedy, Kate Simmants.
TYPE: Demonstration Sessions.

Remote viewers often receive requests from the media for information and interviews. These should be carefully evaluated and only agreed to if the publication or radio program have the best outcome in mind. Go to the media's website and check out past interviews and assess the intent of the interviewer and their knowledge of remote viewing. Do they know what they are talking about? If you have any qualms, do not agree to the interview. I have been burned a few times because I did not do my homework!

This was not the case with Tom Kennedy and Jane Simmants, freelance videographers who planned to make a promo video on remote viewing for the British Broadcasting Corporation (BBC). Tom contacted me, very cautiously, before the 2001 IRVA remote viewing conference, to ask if I would consider doing a few demonstration sessions before he committed to a video. I don't usually do demonstrations, but this could get remote viewing some BBC coverage, so I decided to go ahead.

Over a period of a few months, Tom, who had done his homework on remote viewing, sent me the coordinates for three demo projects that I worked sequentially: a sports stadium, a picture of a tiger, and carnival rides at Chessington Park in the UK. Tom was satisfied. He decided to attend the IRVA conference, along with Jane Simmants, to make a pilot piece that he would present to the BBC. Tom hoped it would interest them to do a longer documentary on remote viewing.

Prior to the conference, Tom and Jane visited my home in Las Vegas, filmed a short interview, and gave me a quick remote viewing session to work on-camera. This footage became the lead-in to an excellent short video piece which was completed at the conference. Tom did interviews with the major players in the remote viewing field: Paul Smith, Lyn Buchanan, Bevy Jaegers and Marty Rosenblatt and produced a very nice promo.

Unfortunately, Tom was unable to interest the BBC and the promo languished for about five years before I asked Tom if I could use the

167

footage to show to my students. He agreed and eventually, a decade later, it was generally released for sharing on the IRVA website.

Laboratories for Fundamental Research (LFR).
PROJECT: 100 trials REG study.
METHOD: Micro-PK.
DATE: 2000.
CLIENT: Dr. Edwin May, LFR.
TYPE: Research.

To keep in practice, I have taken part in several uncompensated research projects offered by colleagues. The first one was offered by Dr. Ed May at LFR in Palo Alto, CA. The project was REG oriented (human-computer interaction or micro-PK) and required an initial 100 trials done on a computer program supplied by LFR. I did the 100 trials and the majority went in the high direction which, from past research knowledge, would have equaled a statistically significant effect. There was supposed to be feedback from Dr. May, but none was forthcoming. (About five years later, I asked once more, but Dr. May said that research had been discontinued.)

2001

JOURNALS

In 2001 I graduated from Saybrook University (formerly Saybrook Graduate School) with a Ph.D. in Psychology. During the time I was studying with Saybrook, I had the good fortune to be taught by an expert in the field of consciousness studies; Prof. Stanley Krippner. Saybrook is a unique school in that it allows students to follow unconventional avenues of study. At Saybrook I studied courses such as the psychology of consciousness, the psychology of out-of-body experiences, models of consciousness, and the psychology of shamanism, as well as conventional courses: statistics, research methodology, ethics and critical thinking. My Ph.D. dissertation replicated the human-computer interaction work of the PEAR Laboratory and correlated these with personality variables: creativity, absorption and flow.

Journal - January 9, 2001 – *New Year Update.*
The holidays are past, and the New Year is a good time to update my journal. I am still working from home, having given up the Flamingo office to save money and travel time. My Ph.D. should be
168

granted this month and I will be official! My new book *Diary of an Abduction* will be coming out in March and I should be receiving some advance copies soon. For the past month I have been completing other of P-I-A's ARV projects. It looks as if I am doing only slightly better than chance. My pattern seems to be to do well at the 97% percentile, only to "crash and burn" back to chance level. Marty has also changed the compensation and it does not seem worth the time and effort needed to complete the trials that take more than an hour each.

Journal – April 8, 2001 – *"Dr. Smith."*
I finally got news that my Ph.D. Dissertation was accepted, and I am now officially Dr. Smith! It was a bitter-sweet celebration as the degree took me ten years to complete. Initially, Saybrook did not accept my UK Master's degree so had to take enough credits with them in order to get on the Ph.D. track. Graduation is scheduled for the end of June.

Journal – August 10, 2001 – *Visiting with Ingo.*
I have had some vacation time, partly in Manhattan, and yesterday set up a visit with Ingo Swann. I traveled by subway and found his place quite easily: an old building, over a hundred years old, right in the heart of the Bowery. His place is like an art museum: Ingo being an artist and writer. It's also like a library with shelves of books everywhere. Ingo is reclusive and lives very frugally; painting and writing and having occasional visitors. I feel honored that he lets me visit with him.

Ingo has been called the "Father of Remote Viewing" and, along with Hal Puthoff and Russel Targ, developed all the remote viewing protocols that we now use.

I went over to his place late morning and we went out to lunch at a little Greek pasta place. Ingo was very proud to show me many of his students' remote viewing sessions; including those from Paul Smith, Ed Dames, Jim Schnabel, Bob Durant, and Tom McNear (Ingo's 100% student). Ingo also showed me some of his own sessions that were excellent! I found the clay models of the sessions fascinating.

Journal – September 13, 2001 – *911.*
Here I am in Princeton, NJ and I should have been flying back to Las Vegas today but the horrors of the past few days prevented me from getting home. I arrived safely from a trip to England and have been staying with Dr. Roger Nelson and his wife Leftie in Princeton. Monday, I went to the PEAR Lab and took part in some of their new

experiments including the Robotic Frog and Yantra (a mantra and drum experiment). It was a fun day!

Tuesday was a day of terror as the Twin Towers and the Pentagon were targeted. We watched in horror as the planes crashed into the towers and then the towers collapsed onto each other. We spent the day watching TV in disbelief as the events unfolded. What a terrible day!

It was a warm sunny day in Princeton, but the skies were grey with smoke and debris over New York direction. Many, many people have died and many more injured, the death toll will be in the tens of thousands, we are told.

Yesterday, the firefighters were putting out the fires and even today pulling people from the debris as they try and clear up the mess. The bottom half of Manhattan is under a layer of dust that lies like grey snow over everything. There is talk of retribution and the "doomsayers" are saying this is World War III, but I don't think so, America is hardy and will bounce back.

(What we did not realize at first was that Roger Nelson's experimental Global Consciousness equipment was in the basement as we were watching 911 unfold upstairs. Later, Roger remembered to go and check the output of the EGG, the RNG monitoring global consciousness, and found that it had deviated from the normal output. This deviation had begun two hours before the planes hit.)

Journal – November 12, 2001 – *The London Sunday Times.*
Last week was spent down at Budget Suites teaching a remote viewing class. The class went well, and the students got some good target hits on their picture targets. When I returned home there were phone and email messages from the *London Sunday Times* asking for an interview about the use of remote viewers to "find the terrorists." I told the reporter that I could not name names or departments, but several remote viewers have been asked to help. These viewers had been contacted and approached with RV targets. Consequently, an article appeared in the *London Sunday Times* about the use of remote viewers. Prudence Calabrese has been working with the FBI and many other viewers have been working with other government agencies and departments.

CASE FILES – 2001

"Navy Frank"
PROJECT: Post 9/11 Intelligence Project.

METHOD: CRV.
DATE: October 2001.
CLIENT: "Navy Frank."
TYPE: Applications.

Sometimes viewers don't know their clients until after-the-fact. Such was the case, in October 2001, following the Twin Towers NY disaster, when I received three "blind" sessions via a trusted colleague. The sessions were interesting in that, although I was emotionally frontloaded with 911, this did not seem to affect my viewing. Later, I learned that the client was an individual employed by the Navy, with connections to national security, who sent feedback that my viewings were "helpful."

"It"
PROJECT: "It"
METHOD: ERV.
DATE: 2001.
CLIENT: Independent.
TYPE: Exploration.

A strange question was broadcast on several different TV stations, "What is IT?" The company that was putting out the teaser was an innovative group, owned by inventor Dean Kaman, which was becoming well known for its out-of-the-box ideas and inventions. The new product that was coming out was also being called "Ginger" but what it was remained a mystery. Some people thought IT was a hoax, but I felt there was a reality to the mystery.

I decided to use Extended Remote Viewing (ERV) to look and see what IT was. Eventually, IT turned out to be the Segway, "a self-balancing personal transportation device with two wheels that can operate in any level pedestrian environment" but what I perceived was something else altogether. Even though I didn't perceive IT, I did see something interesting!

Initially, I perceived a group of men standing around a table top. On the table was a round device which, when turned off, looked like a small version of a Lazy Susan: the kind you see on kitchen tables to rotate condiments. It was composed of a black plastic-type material.

There were ports for connections: telephone jack, computer connections, etc. There were also drives for DVD and other computer disks (small computer disks were then being used). When turned on it produced a bluish haze above and to the center of the round disk. What

171

appeared, when it was activated, were sequential three-dimensional, holographic images of cartoon characters: Bugs Bunny and Daffy Duck!

There was the perception of sound with the cartoon characters saying their famous quotes such as "What's up, Doc." There were fits of laughter, with the guys who bent over double with laughter. The device could play images and sound in a three-dimensional format from a computer hard drive, CD and other computer disks. The device could be connected to a DVD/VCR, or to the telephone for face-to-face communication.

I perceived that plans were in the works for a larger version for in-home playing of movies and conference-type presentations. I also perceived the innards of the device. The simplest explanation is that this device was the next step up from computer-generated three-dimensional objects that are normally viewed on a flat computer screen.

I did a second viewing of the innards of the device and in addition to the casing and ports perceived power points and battery housing. Inside were three layers. Viewed from the top, there appeared to be a well in the top, center, within which was located a very bright light source. The top, inside layer consisted of a circle or "bracelet" of light diodes that were capable of projecting pictures. Each projected a slightly different and overlapping picture of the diode on each side. The diodes were aimed at the center light. The projections hit the light source and scattered forming interference patterns which eventually created a 3-D picture.

As more projections were played at a faster rate, they formed a three-dimensional, moving image that could be viewed from 360 degrees around the device. There was a sound system within the device. The 3-D image was best viewed from the side as viewing from the top caused distortions of the image. I felt that this device was the next step up from the 3-D images that are computer generated.

The middle layer of the device was a maze of electronics and circuit boards. The interesting thing was that these circuit boards were circular or donut-shaped rather than rectangular; a new paradigm. The top layer consisted of the projection diodes and the center light. I sent part of the information of to several colleagues and engineers, but nobody showed any interest.

The only person to reply was a UK colleague. Before we knew the true nature of the device, he responded: "I can tell that your remote viewing of this device is very real and from what I've seen and what you've described, I can see how this might work. I think you've nailed it! I also know holographic devices have been a priority for some computer giants for a while now. These require a huge amount of processing power to project the images (which I am told were very real, you could hold a conversation with these holograms apparently. This was last year. Imagine what progress could have been made since then." So, although I did not remote view the Segway, this was not a total loss.

So, even though this was not "IT," the device was certainly interesting and feasible, according to my colleague. The paperwork has sat in my files for years and it is now time to bring "it" out of the closet. I have sketches still. Is there anybody reading this that would like to construct this device? I would love to see it working!

White Paper for the DOJ.
PROJECT: White Paper.
METHOD: Written Work.
DATE: 2001-2002.
CLIENT: Department of Justice.
TYPE: Information.

Around the middle of 2001 to the beginning of 2002, I had contact with a member of staff of the Department of Justice in Washington, DC. For several months we worked on a draft of a White Paper that she could present to the heads of DOJ, to interest them in becoming involved in remote viewing. Unfortunately, this was an exercise in futility and went nowhere. However, I was able to complete several personal projects for her including the Daniel Perl abduction case.

Golden Gate Bridge.
PROJECT: Golden Gate Bridge.
METHOD: ERV.
DATE: 2001.
CLIENT: "Up the Chain."
TYPE: Applications.

I had also been passing on any interesting remote data through members of the military remote viewing community that often made its way "up the chain of command." One piece of information involved the possibility of an attack on the Golden Gate Bridge in San Francisco, CA. Feedback came through the media, that a plot had been "thwarted, based on actionable intelligence" that would have damaged the bridge. I later learned from information that came "down the chain" that my data had been taken seriously.

<u>The Anthrax Scare.</u>
PROJECT: Anthrax Scare.
METHOD: ERV.
DATE: 2001.
CLIENT: DOJ Contact.
TYPE: Forensic.
TEAM: RV Class.

Towards the latter half of 2001, I asked my DOJ contact if there was any way that my group could assist the Department. At that time there was a scare in which letters containing anthrax spores were being sent to media and government offices. A series of questions given to a remote viewing class provided data and leads but I was never able to find out if these leads led to any arrests or inquiries.

2002

JOURNALS

During the summer of 2002, several major events coincided to take my remote viewing path in a very different direction. A good friend and colleague, Prudence Calabrese, had been telling me about a New York client who was offering her some interesting work. Prudence trained with Courtney Brown's Scientific Remote Viewing (SRV) group and had become part of his teaching staff. Professor Courtney Brown had been trained by ex-military remote viewer Ed Dames, who was then head of Psi Tech. Now Prudence was taking her training into applications work. Of interest was the group's work, prior to the Twin Towers collapse, of a project that involved sketches of a plane flying into two tall, thin structures that looked remarkable like the Twin Towers.

For many different reasons Prudence decided to leave the remote viewing field. It is not my place to tell her story, but she basically withdrew from all public RV activity. During 2002 and until Prudence "disappeared" from the field, she tasked me with several paid remote viewing projects. This was very generous of her, as paid remote viewing projects are rare.

<u>"Wild Card" Sessions – 2002.</u>
Prudence Calabrese was a maverick and innovator in the remote viewing community and developed a method she called Wild Card sessions. Normally, remote viewing sessions are carried out in response

174

to a request from a client or group that needs information. Wild Card sessions are remote viewing sessions produced in advance and stored in a file cabinet, ready to be pulled when needed. Each session has a unique coordinate and case name, and this is matched with a new project as it is received. At the beginning of 2002, I completed nineteen Wild Card sessions for Transdimensional Systems. According to Prudence Wild Card sessions are as effective as sessions conducted in real-time. Wild Card sessions have the advantage of being performed "blind," with no up-front information (frontloading) and with no viewer bias.

London – The Field Conference - 2002

At the time that Prudence pulled out of the remote viewing field, she had been deciding to travel to London, England to take part in The Field Conference. Envisioned by researcher and author Lynne McTaggart, the Conference was designed to bring together like-minded individuals and speakers in the combined fields of human consciousness, new physics, distant healing, and alternative energies. Her book *The Field* described her philosophy: rather than being discrete fields of study, such topics were part of something she called a "new, radical paradigm." She proposed that the human mind and body are not separate <u>from</u> but constantly interacting <u>with</u> the energies in its environment.

The Field Conference was amazing: I was tasked with giving two remote viewing workshops of two hours each to over two hundred participants in each workshop! The Conference led to McTaggart developing *The Field Workbook* of monthly informative newsletters and I eventually contributed ten short columns for this publication.

Associative Remote Viewing – 2002.

During the latter half of the 1990s and early part of the Millennium, I participated in studies of a RV methodology called Associative Remote Viewing or ARV. Basically, separate and distinct picture targets are paired with potential outcomes of an event (stock market, sports, or decision-making) and the viewer is directed to remote view the "correct" picture target that is associated with the successful outcome of the event. When the outcome of the event is known, the viewer is shown the winning target picture. There are multiple ways to do this but one that has been promoted as successful has been Marty Rosenblatt's <u>P.I.A.</u> online program.

I participated in Marty's program for several years but kept hitting the same problem. I would be getting good results, in the 97th percentile, and then would "crash and burn" and go into a steep, negative decline. This became so discouraging that I opted out of Marty's program. I asked him why declines were a problem, but he did not know; only acknowledged that they happened, and that the viewer should stick with the program until their performance recovered.

Journal - January 28, 2002 – *The Media.*

After the *London Sunday Times* article there was a flurry of attention from the media, but I took Paul Smith's advice to stay away from the media, as it could "attract the attention of the terrorists." Paul had mentioned that there could be a small but real risk for remote viewers. However, while I heeded his advice, other remote viewers began giving interviews. *Newsweek* was interested but they could not get individuals within government to give their names to be aired in print (if they had contacted and used remote viewers), so they didn't go with the story.

Then the *New York Magazine* wanted to do a story and many of us in the remote viewing community told our side of doing remote viewing for individuals within government regarding the terrorist situation.

A few days ago, Prudence Calabrese of Transdimensional Systems, and Lyn Buchanan of P>S>I, had the opportunity to be on *Good Morning America* but the venue got cancelled because the media could not get confirmation from government sources that remote viewers were being asked to view 911.

I have concluded that any articles written about remote viewing, need to be written by us, the viewers, with our intent and purpose attached to them, rather than let the media run the show.

Journal – January 30, 2002 – *Prediction.*

I have never been a serious follower of astrology or astrological predictions but one this week in an article called Astrocast (I don't remember the publication) by Sydney Omarr prompted me to "Look beyond the immediate. Dare to dream, perceive the future. You could be involved in international humanitarian projects. Don't waver, do it!"

Journal - June 24, 2002 – *White Paper Project.*

At the 2002 Conference I reconnected with an ex-DIA colleague. He and I have been corresponding by email over the past four or five years and I participated in some of his early ARV studies. Recently we talked about getting a proposal together to present to the DIA, to help fund some of his ongoing projects. I also introduced him to Prudence Calabrese, as she has the additional staff and sales ability that we need.

We had several meetings with our colleague and decided that we would present a White Paper and then a Proposal to my colleague's contacts at DIA. The project would focus on five demonstrations of remote viewing:

1. The location and activity of an individual decided on by our customer;
2. Identification of an object in a container;
3. A remote viewing full-body scan and diagnosis of an individual;
4. An aerial overview of a map or installation; and 5. Identification and function of some technology.

When I returned from the conference, I began writing to form the basis of a potential White Paper on remote viewing. This was passed to Prudence to add information about her Group's work, and then back to our colleague who will modify and write it up for the DIA.

(While the viewers described some pertinent data in their sessions, the colleague did not feel it was precise enough for what he and his colleagues needed.)

Journal – June 24, 2002 – *Conference Projects.*

Despite being jetlagged and stressed from helping to run the conference, I had three great "hits" on remote viewing targets. The first one was at Prudence Calabrese's "RV Shoot Out" where viewers from all walks of life and training completed targets. TV4 from the UK was there. They filmed Prudence and her colleague Don hitting a target and my hit was witnessed by a colleague.

Then, I was interviewed by another crew out of LA. I did a live (filmed) target they had hidden in an envelope and I was able to nail the target.

Then, on the Monday morning I took part in Dr. Michael O'Bannon's Electro-Encephalograph (EEG) project, where he was recording the brain waves of remote viewers who were carrying out a "blind" remote viewing picture target. I didn't think I had done well but I got a Hit! The film producers and the EEG study participants promised a copy of my results.

There is so much emphasis on remote viewers having to be in a quiet place to view but this shows that viewing can be done successfully under party conditions with TV cameras recording, for the media while being recorded, and under the stress of being wired-up for an EEG study. I teach my students that a good remote viewer should be able to view anywhere, at any time, regardless of the circumstances.

(Despite being promised the results of this study, especially my own contribution, I eventually contacted Dr. O'Bannon but learned that the study had been "disposed of", which was a great disappointment.)

Journal – June 24, 2002 – *NASDAQ Project.*
Over the past few months I have been corresponding with a young Asian couple who are stock brokers. They proposed a pilot program to predict the movement of the NASDAQ. There would be a series of remote viewings using the Associative Remote Viewing (ARV) Protocol:

- Viewing #1 predicted that the NASDAQ would have a small drop by 73.26 points, it did drop by a small amount. Unfortunately, the couple was expecting me to predict the actual NASDAQ ending score to four digits plus two decimal places! I explained to them that RV was not precise enough to do these four times in a row. So, we settled on an ARV protocol where we would predict the NASDAQ direction at the end of trading: going Up, going Down, or staying the Same, and the degree of movement: Large or Small, within certain parameters. The viewing was to be done on certain days and according to certain moon influences that were being studied by the couple.
- Viewing #2 took place on June 5th and a Small Down movement was predicted. This was correct as the market closed Down at 19.40 points.
- Viewing #3 predicted the market would close at Up, with a Small change. The NASDAQ went Up but within the "Same" parameters.
- Viewing #4 predicted that the NASDAQ would go Up within 1% but this was not correct as the NASDAQ went Down by more than 1%.
- Viewing #5 predicted the NASDAQ would go Up by a Small amount and it did.

Considering the pre-viewing as a Hit, and #4 as a miss, this was five Hits out of six or an 80+% success rate. Unfortunately, despite this success, the couple, while delighted with the result, did not continue with their moon project.

Journal - June 27, 2002 – *Boulder Dam.*
A friend and colleague in the ARV field called saying that he had a dream that terrorists had attacked Hoover Dam. He was quite

interested in setting up a project to look at the situation but when I sent him a contract, he withdrew his interest. I went ahead anyway and tasked some viewers with the Dam at 11.45 p.m., July 4th, 2002 (Coordinate PLHU4920). Viewers came back with indications that the Dam was intact at 11:45 p.m. on that date.

Journal - July 11th, 2002 – *NASA and the Shuttle.*
After I returned from the IRVA conference I received an email from a senior manager who works at the Houston base for NASA payload operations. Initially this was a missing person case and the manager was referred to us by a senior RV colleague. Luckily, the girl was found the next day, so our data wasn't needed. However, an email communication ensued with the manager and we suggested that the Nevada Group (The Nevada Remote Viewing Group or NRVG is a group of trained, volunteer remote viewers) might be able to help NASA in some way. He responded that he liked the idea and suggested several ways that NASA might be able to use remote viewers.

The Manager proposed the following test project that he felt would lay the groundwork for future projects: "If Your Nevada Group could remote view the current Shuttle flow liner crack situation, using whatever protocol you think is best. Any insight regarding the cause of the cracks in the shuttle flow liners, prognosis, or possible effects if no repairs are made, and the Shuttles continue to fly, and repair techniques which could be used now, and how effective they would be, would be interesting and could be a door opener. This kind of detail may be beyond what can be reasonably provided but whatever came through may be helpful."

So, I put together a project tasking with several coordinates for five questions that I tasked ten viewers. Each viewer received only the "blind" five coordinates and the minimal frontloading that this was a project involving a "device."

Hidden Tasking:

- Coordinate #1: H7EO89. Describe the cause of the cracks in the shuttle flow liners.
- Coordinate #2: JK30PC. Describe the prognosis of the cracks in the shuttle flow liners.
- Coordinate #3. LP36IM. Describe possible effects if no repairs were made to the cracks in the shuttle flow liners and the Shuttles continue to fly.

179

- Coordinate #4. GFA593. Describe repair techniques which could be used now for the cracks in the Shuttle flow liners.
- Coordinate #5. QW45V. How effective will these repair techniques be to the cracks in the shuttle flow liners?

When all the data had been received, a Technical Report was put together and emailed to the NASA manager on July 22, 2002. Interestingly, one of the views named the Shuttle as the device in question and the consensus of the viewers was that if the repairs were not carried out this could end in disaster.

(Unfortunately, this prediction came about when, later that year, one of the shuttles exploded on re-entry. I emailed my condolences to the manager.)

Journal - December 8th, 2002 – *Changing Course.*
This past April, I gave the last of a series of Remote Viewing Methods and Techniques courses to a class of six students in the New Mexico Street house. It went very well but I have decided to narrow my focus and concentrate on the Controlled Remote Viewing protocols. After presenting a paper at this year's IRVA conference I had some inquiries from several people who wanted to complete all six stages of the CRV protocol in one course, rather than spreading it out over several years.

So, in the summer, three students, plus my part-time assistant Paul Cook, came to train with me. They did very well and have appreciated my putting the course onto PowerPoint. I have since taught several groups of trainees with great success. I don't have any students for December, so I am able to take a break for the holidays. At the request of some of the students I am adding an additional course, called CRV-Plus, that will cover ERV, RI, and dowsing as application tools. Hopefully 2003 will bring a new batch of trainees, new opportunities to apply these skills and new adventures!

CASE FILES – 2002

On-Camera Viewing.
PROJECT: Missing Footage.
METHOD: CRV Interview.
DATE: 2002.
CLIENT: LA/Australian Film Crew.
TYPE: Filmed Session.

At the IRVA conference in 2002, I was approached by a video company for an interview. I won't name them as they are still holding footage until they can complete their documentary. However, this interview answered the question about why remote viewers don't do live sessions, on-camera.

During the interview, the woman interviewer asked if I would do a session on-camera. This was unscheduled and unexpected, but I agreed. I asked for blank paper and a pen and proceeded to do a live remote viewing session using the Controlled Remote Viewing (CRV) protocol. The session was double-blind as neither I nor the interviewer knew the nature of the picture target. The cameraman had torn a picture out of a magazine and had secretly folded it into his pocket before the interview. When I was finished with the session, the picture was revealed, and I had basically "hit" the target. The picture showed a view from the upper porch of a house looking out over a vista: I had described a location that was partly indoors and partly outdoors, pillars and many other features of the target site.

The interview proceeded with my general perceptions about world events and we talked about the Iraq war that had just started. I stated that I felt it would last much longer than the couple of years that the government was predicting. (Now in 2019, we are still in Iraq.) There were some other predictions that I made during the interview, but I no longer remember them. Perhaps the couple will find the funds to complete the documentary and will eventually release the footage.

[To date, 2019, the footage has never been released. After so many years, it is unlikely it will ever be aired.]

Long Term Stock Market ARV.
PROJECT: Three Month Stock Market Predictions.
METHOD: ARV.
DATE: 2002.
CLIENT: Financial Client.
TYPE: Predictive.

In June 2002, a financial client asked me to conduct a series of three months' ARV sessions focused on the stock market. I decided to give ARV another chance. So, every weekday for three months I contributed an ARV session. When the results were tabulated, it appeared that my results were significant for the first month, began declining in the second month, and dropped off dramatically in the third month. Again, the decline effect became apparent.

Around the same time, a professional couple contacted me to carry out some NASDAQ predictions. This one was a smaller sample of only

5 ARV attempts and was successful in predicting 4 of the outcomes, an 80% success rate. I have concluded that I am an ARV "sprinter," rather than a "long-distance runner."

Trans-Dimensional Systems.
AGUA HEDONIA LAGOON, CA.
PROJECT: Agua Hedionda.
METHOD: CRV.
DATE: 2002.
CLIENT: Trans-dimensional Systems.
TYPE: Applications.

Prudence Calabrese sent me several series of environmental projects including one involving the Agua Hedionda Lagoon (Spanish name means "pestilent water") located in Carlsbad, CA. The sessions were conducted "blind," no up-front information about the location. Feedback later confirmed my remote viewing of an organism that was polluting the lagoon and specific remedies for its clearance. We also worked together on a case involving the disappearance of a missing CA girl, Samantha Runnion (who was later found murdered) and I also took part in a demonstration workshop with Prudence at the 2002 IRVA conference.

Finding "J."
PROJECT: Finding J.
METHOD: CRV/ERV.
DATE: August 6th, 2002.
CLIENT: Family/Friends of J.
TYPE: Missing Person.
TEAM: NRVG.

The following missing-person case was presented by telephone to The Nevada Remote Viewing Group on August 6, 2002. Help was requested in identifying the location of a young adult male, identified as J, who had been abducted in Mexico and the best scenario for his safe recovery. Follow-up information came by email including a photo of the missing individual. It was agreed to carry out this case on a humanitarian basis.

Over a period of a month and a half, J was moved, at least, four times, as his captors played a "shell-game," moving him from location to location. The viewers attempted to locate J at these four locations labeled Locations A, B, C, and D.

It is known in remote viewing that it is almost impossible to locate an individual who is being constantly moved. However, The Nevada Group Team was able to correctly describe relevant aspects of the four locations. Many of the viewers correctly perceived that J was being held in Mexico and perceived Spanish words and places names that were confirmed as known by the client. The client had contact individuals "on the ground" in the vicinity and was able to corroborate many of the viewers' perceptions.

Unfortunately, despite being able to describe the locations and after describing three possible retrieval scenarios, the "ground team" was unable to secure J's release. This was frustrating both to the Nevada Group and to the client and his associates. After a telephone call from the client's sister, about September 17, it was understood that there were many more levels of complexity to this case than were initially known including custody cases, bargains and exchanges, and monetary considerations.

The immediate reactions of the NRVG viewers to this case reflected some of the concerns of Dr. Smith, even though the viewers were not made aware of these concerns prior to being tasked. These concerns relate to the "high strangeness" of the project, and the authenticity of the information provided by the client. There were concerns voiced that this project might be a simulation to either: 1. Test the Nevada Group's remote viewing claims or 2; an effort to discredit The Nevada Group and Dr. Angela T. Smith. However, the client reassured Dr. Smith that this was not a test of her or her RV group but a valid search and rescue project.

Note: Many months after the project ended, an email came into my inbox, obviously meant for someone else, and sent to my mailbox in error. The email related to individuals connected to an air force group in California. The question remains, who were the clients and what was the goal of the project?

2003

JOURNALS

The business client that Prudence Calabrese had been planning to work with in 2002 was now looking for another remote viewer, and Prudence very graciously suggested me. Prudence, at this point, left the remote viewing field. From February 2003 to December 2011 (9 years) I was on a roller-coaster ride with this innovative, interesting and enigmatic client. Over almost a decade, we pushed the envelope of what remote viewing could be used for and it certainly made me a better remote viewer! I am protecting his identify and his company's identity but can disclose that he owned a Fifth Avenue, NY financial company that was influential around the world.

At first, I provided individual data to the client, but we gradually brought in more viewers from a group of trained viewers around the US that we called the Nevada Remote Viewing Group (NRVG). The client provided payments to the viewers for a couple of years then decided to "cherry-pick" viewers that he found productive and he then worked privately with individual viewers, including myself. Eventually, the client provided a monthly retainer for my services.

Among the many topics that were covered were projects related to the running of his business, property ventures, stock market and other financial predictions, legal matters, personnel assessments, and potential world catastrophes that might impact his business such as environmental disasters, epidemics and Earth shifts.

During the latter years of our business arrangement the client provided projects to assess potential buyers for his financial business and many innovative assessment protocols. The client was also very interested in metaphysics and we explored alternative healing, exobiology, longevity, and the spiritual world, as well as my providing an "ear" as a confidant to this busy businessman.

One of the projects proposed by the client was to assess his staff and their reactions to the potential sale of his business. Giving me only the letters, Person A, B, C, D, E etc. my task was to physically describe the member of staff and how they were coping with the impending sale. The method I used for the physical description was to say, "Who does this person remind me of?" For example, Person K might "remind" me of Jon Luc Picard, the TV character. Another would remind me of a tall, burly, red-haired Viking. Using this method, I was able to correctly identify 26 out of 27 staff members and obtain useful information for the client. The one I missed was a "jump": I misidentified the gender and jumped to the next available staff member.

In addition, the client requested predictive remote viewings of future events and the NRVG was able to predict the recession in the financial market as early as the beginning of 2008! The client was reluctant to accept this information at the time but gradually began to accept the recession as a reality. Interestingly, a word that was used in a viewing to report a sudden resurgence; as a "financial tsunami," later started appearing in the media indicating that the client probably included some of our findings in his financial reporting.

Following the sale of his business, his retirement, and his relocation abroad, the client reluctantly decided that he no longer had enough business to retain a remote viewer and we ended our business relationship at the end of 2011. During our years together, I felt appreciated and cards and reviews verified that our work together was helpful. In 2008 he wrote, "How stimulating, exciting, informative, helpful, eye-opening and pleasurable it has been to work together for another year. Our work holds great promise to be widely valuable to many others in the future. With gratitude and sincere wishes for a very good year for you in England." On his retirement and emigration abroad he inscribed in a gift book "As I begin an entirely new life, it is with the greatest gratitude that I thank you for helping me surmount the many challenges I faced this past eight years, and assisting in laying the foundation for our great mission in the future, with enduring appreciation."

Journal - January 28th, 2003 – *New Beginnings.*
It's a New Year and lots of new beginnings, as well as continuities of changes that I made last year. I am really enjoying living in Boulder City in my pretty, little, rental house on 5th Street. Each season I change the theme of the banner that I hang outside the house and plants in the flower bed. (In 2002 I had moved from Las Vegas to live independently in Boulder City, NV. I rented a small house on New Mexico Street before moving to rent the small house on 5th Street).

Things for the New Year: I've developed a new website and continue to give remote viewing courses. George Knapp of KLAS Channel 8, Las Vegas is putting together a documentary about remote viewing and was out here in BC to do some interviews. I have no steady income but enough comes in to keep a roof over my head, food on the table, and I am happy and healthy!

Journal - February 14, 2003 – *Potential Future.*
I just returned from a weekend in California where I have a remote viewing Introduction to three trainees. They did some great work and I enjoyed seeing the ocean and the green hills of Santa Barbara. There were gardens of tropical flowers everywhere! The sponsor suggested that when she received a large cash settlement that she would place some in Boulder City to fund a remote viewing center. However, I am not waiting for this to happen. Similar projects haven't panned out in the past. If it happens, great! If not, it's OK, too. I will email her with a ballpark figure of what it would take to set up such a center. (Unfortunately, this did not happen.)

185

Skinwalker Ranch.
PROJECT: Skinwalker Ranch.
METHOD: ERV/CRV.
DATE: Jan 10th, 2003.
CLIENT: Kelleher & Knapp.
TYPE: Applications.
COORDINATE: SR110202.
TEAM: NRVG.

The following project was originally presented to The Nevada Remote Viewing Group in October 2002 and a request was made for assistance by Mr. George Knapp of Las Vegas. Along with Colm A. Kelleher, Ph.D., George went on to co-write the popular book, '*Hunt for the Skinwalker: Science Confronts the Unexplained at a Remote Ranch in Utah*' in 2005. The work was completed in January 2003 and our remote viewing work was noted in their book.

Help was requested in identifying the nature of activities at a location in eastern Utah, known as the Sherman Ranch, (also known as the Gorman Ranch and later as the Skinwalker Ranch). Tasking focused on the years 1995 and 1996 (Phase One), current activities at the location (Phase Two), and future activities at the site (Phase Three). The work was carried out by the Nevada Remote Viewing Group, an organization I founded consisting of trained remote viewers located around the USA/UK who accept humanitarian projects.

The Viewers:
Two viewers, identified by pseudonyms, initially responded to the project. Later, three additional viewers provided data. The five viewers were tasked with a coordinate, that is, a random series of letters and numbers identifying the project, in this case SR110202. Viewers used a combination of remote viewing methods: Controlled Remote Viewing (CRV) and Extended Remote Viewing (ERV). The viewers were given the following operational front loading: "Describe the location and events at this location as of July 1996." Apart from the coordinate and operational directions, the viewers worked "blind," that is, they did not know the nature of the project nor did they know of the case manager's discussion with the client. Another two viewers contributed data towards current and future perceptions of the ranch. They were tasked with the directions: "The target is a location, describe any current

activity at the location," and "The target is a location, describe activity at the location in five years."

Summary:
The indications, from the first two viewers who completed Phase One, were that this was the site of a military operation, probably conducted by the Navy. There were individuals at the site involved in "target practice" with rifles that involved lying prone on the ground. Men in uniform, such as policemen, firefighters, or soldiers were present. Several oblong devices were described. A sketch and description of a male and identifying injuries or tattoos were described. There was a project ongoing at the site that involves cartographers and maps of the United States. Most of the activity appears to take place outdoors, at night. The three additional viewers perceived gridded and honeycomb surfaces, a flat surface and one that was rounded like a globe. The interior and functioning of the globe were described. Two viewers felt wave-like, seismic vibrations. Current activity at the location indicated a series of installations having been built including a grid-work of wires and small platforms that have been embedded in the ground at the location, a tall, TV-like antenna, and a communications-type building. Future activity, five years on, indicates that a fire, either caused by nature or accidental would have burned the communications-type building and a parcel of land surrounding the tower and building. (Information obtained in 2013 indicated that the communications-type building had been dismantled).

Background Information:
Information about this case was gathered from a newspaper cutting in the *Las Vegas Review Journal,* dated Thursday, October 24, 1996, entitled; "Las Vegas millionaire buys UFO ranch in eastern Utah." The case manager had also heard word-of-mouth accounts of the purchase of the ranch and the local activities. The goal of this project was not to confirm known information but to look for new and unknown information regarding activities at the location.

The Las Vegas Review Journal article, written by Zack Van Eyck, of the *Deseret (Salt Lake City) News,* ran as follows:
"FORT DUCHESNE, Utah – The search for answers to one of science's greatest questions has led Las Vegas millionaire Robert Bigelow to an isolated cattle ranch in the heart of eastern Utah's Uintah Basin. Here, far from the bright lights of his native Las Vegas, the real estate magnate hopes his team of scientists can unearth the roots of UFO folklore prevalent in this region since the 1950s.

Robert Bigelow, easily the most prominent American financier in the paranormal research field, is convinced there is something to the weird stories told by the family of Terry Sherman. Last July, the Shermans broke years of silence and went public with bizarre tails of strange lights and UFOs on their 480-acre ranch. Sherman said he and other members of his family had seen lights emerging from circular "doorways" that seemed to appear in mid-air, had three cows strangely mutilated, and several others disappear. The rancher also reported unusual impressions in the soil and circles of flattened grass in a pasture. The Sherman's story appeared in Salt Lake City's Deseret News and on a national radio broadcast. Several weeks later, Robert Bigelow met with the Shermans and negotiated to buy the ranch for about $200,000. The Sherman family has relocated to a smaller ranch 15 miles away – far removed, they hope, from the disturbing occurrences they endured for 18 months. Robert Bigelow, an apartment developer and philanthropist in Las Vegas, has erected an observation building and moved in a pair of scientists and a veterinarian. He has someone on the property 24 hours a day, recording anything out of the ordinary.

Officially, the research is being conducted by the National Institute for Discovery Science, which Robert Bigelow formed last October. Among the scientists involved is John B. Alexander, former director of nonlethal weapons testing at Los Alamos National Laboratory in New Mexico. 'Our approach is to do good, high-quality research using a standard scientific approach and do what we can to get hard data.' Alexander said from the Institute's Las Vegas offices. 'One of the missions of the institute is to make information widely available.' Robert Bigelow himself declined an interview. Alexander would not provide details of how or why the research is being conducted. Sherman, now employed by Robert Bigelow to maintain the ranch, said he can no longer discuss the activity because of a nondisclosure agreement Robert Bigelow had him sign. Alexander said results of the study would be published in scientific journals and on the Institute's web page. The secretive behavior concerns other UFO researchers, including Ryan Layton of Utah and Chris O'Brien of Crestone, Colorado. Both visited the ranch in July before Robert Bigelow became involved."

Phase One:

Viewer #1 Juice: Used a form of Extended Remote Viewing (ERV: remote viewing conducted in an altered state of consciousness). Her sketches of her perceptions indicated the following scenario: A sketch of a man with dark glasses. "His hair was dark, with that unkempt, spiky, sticking-up look. He appeared to be pushing/pulling another person. I think it was another person. I am unsure because the person seemed to be sagging." A sketch of a man lying face-down on the ground. "This person, I had a very quick look at, but he was lying face down while looking upward. I think he had his hands behind his back." Sketch of a rectangular box. "The rectangular box had many smaller boxes stacked inside. I think the smaller boxes were made of cardboard. The whole thing was sitting on a table with a green and white checkered tablecloth." Sketch of a right hand. "I saw a right hand with these marks on it. These marks were possibly tattoos or injuries." Sketch of a box with a hand taking something out. "A rectangular shape that appeared to have a slot in the front. Something was pulled out. The front had other square-like shapes on it. Sketch of a spring or coil. "This was spring, or coil shaped. It was turning." Other perceptions included her feeling that her hands hurt, especially her left palm and her right pointer finger. She perceived maps of the United States and the concept of something being broken into, such as breaking into a house.

Viewer #2 Dragonfly: Dragonfly used Controlled Remote Viewing (CRV) protocol to carry out her session. She began her session in a state of nervousness and her initial perceptions were of a landmass and a structure. Several life forms were perceived at the site: male and female. As her session proceeded, she continued to feel anxious and perceived images of the Pentagon building, and impressions of the Navy and prison. There was mention made of cartographers and a map. She felt nausea and smelled a fire, as if something was burning. Images persisted of death, a rifle, and military training. There was a visual of a young man lying prone on the ground aiming a rifle at a target. Images of a medical situation with a woman on a gurney. There were fleeting images of firefighters, being on board a Navy ship, and a photographer's dark room with a reddish light. *The viewer felt that the scene resembled a 4th of July celebration and mentioned sparkling lights in a dark sky. Water and wetness were described, and the activity took place, outdoors, on a wet night.* Viewer #2 produced no sketches.

Viewer #3 Scout: Described the location as an institutional area that was mostly gray with weather that was overcast and glum. The main physical building was described as a very large, equal-sided structure with an open, paved, central courtyard, like a quad. The viewer perceived a set of man-made items: An expansive, metallic, honeycombed surface, a man-made open space, and a silvery item, held in the left hand that looks like a pair of ice-tongs. A regiment pattern of motion between the tongs and the honeycombed surface was perceived. There was also a grayish-greenish, "gunky" fluid that runs along the base of the surface. Human-animal interaction perceived several times. At one point, the viewer perceived a quick, human, lateral motion that appeared to be red. The human component of the target site was focused to the point of tunnel-vision on a specific set of criteria or dataset. They are missing some obvious points because they are overly focused on minutiae. Other movements perceived by Scout were patterns like a heartbeat that could be perceived as seismic waves. Other patterns perceived were I-Ching sets of lines and spaces. Viewer perceived that premature conclusions were being made, and decisions being made, too soon, before all the evidence is in. The focus of the intent of the target gave her a headache. Very focused.

Viewer #4: UK - used ERV and perceived a series of shapes and images as follows: A wild shaking such as waves. A sloped, flat wedge shape. A grid-mesh, coated in something, contained behind it is some gelatinous substance with a strange chemical composition. Size of holes is just a bit bigger than necessary to put fingers through to tug on it. Grid with a sphere on top. Sphere has holes in it like the previously mentioned grid. Atop an angular platform, which is itself grid-like. There is energy within the sphere, possibly a power source. There is a large amount of power fed into the grid and is processed by its passage through the substrata of the sphere's contents. Some light – greenish/yellow. The whole assembly (sphere and base) sits amid a wide open, flat area, possibly a room with technical devices around the perimeter, such as an aircraft carrier. The substrate in the sphere is composed of a series of microfibers in a "neural net" looking formation. Embedded in a semi-gelatinous substance. The pattern of microfibers combined with the energy charge to substrate produces results.

Viewer #5: Rocket Man - used ERV to access images and sketches as follows: The feeling of being in a dark place that was stuffy and damp, like a pit. Three humanoid heads bent towards each other and the words "Guard, meeting, talk, day-light." Note, the head to the right has a very thin neck with a large head. Location near water. A wavy line with a triangular shape and a round shape over the wavy line. Flat surface with a rounded shape on it.

Phase Two:

The Nevada Remote Viewing Group viewers were contacted by email and given a new coordinate and the operational directions "The target is a location. Describe the current activities at the location."

Viewer #6: Charles – ERV.
Something reflective in nature, glass perhaps, in an angular object – could be metal or concrete, felt more like a vehicle. Everything was dark. I felt hot. I felt crowded. There was a crowd of people carrying cylindrical, slim objects, crowded close together. A total feeling of confusion.

Viewer #7: Amethyst - Using ERV perceived buildings at the site that had been constructed since Phase One:
A layout of wires or electrical conduction connections, in a grid, connected by small flat plates laid out over a couple of acres of land. A very tall TV or radio tower that extended perhaps more than a hundred feet into the air, composed of interlocking girders in an elongated, triangular formation. Lights and electrical components are seen on the tower. A building the size of an average office building, single story, filled with electronics equipment but too few personnel to man everything.

Phase Three:

Viewer #7: Amethyst - Using ERV, perceived that the activities at the site would be difficult because of a fire that had taken place. It was unclear whether this was a natural fire caused by lightning or other natural causes or was the result of an electrical mishap. The base of the tower and several acres around the tower, as well as the building mentioned in Phase Two, were badly burned and unusable. Very little or occasional activity at the site. Appears, essentially, abandoned five years from now.

Follow-Up:
In Kelleher and Knapp's book, *Hunt for the Skinwalker, Chapter 26: The Military*, they describe input from various remote viewers including The Nevada Remote Viewing Group. The chapter examined the data provided by the remote viewers and concluded that while military involvement could not be ruled out, the unusual incidents at

the Ranch dated back hundreds of years and were tied to Native American legends such as the Skinwalker. Kelleher and Knapp write:

"Though it sounds far-fetched, the idea that some sort of military facility in the underground had surfaced before. Tom Gorman and his family said they often heard heavy machinery or metal equipment coming from under the earth. The fact that the previous owners had warned them to avoid any digging is a curious footnote to this scenario. Why give such a warning?" They also wrote:

"Could the military be responsible for the phenomena observed at the ranch? The fact that military personnel were seen on several different occasions in the vicinity strongly suggests that the property became, at some point, a topic of interest for intelligence services. Whether they were attempting to monitor an unknown phenomenon or were gauging reactions to their own secret endeavors is not known and may never be known."

Recent news from a colleague about the Ranch indicates that it is securely "locked-up" and inaccessible to outsiders. Inquiries about a possible visit to the Ranch go unanswered.

Wired for Science!
PROJECT: Wired for Science.
METHOD: Research.
DATE: July 2003.
CLIENT: O'Bannon.
TYPE: EEG/RV Research.

In 2002, the IRVA Remote Viewing Conference moved from its venue in Las Vegas to Austin, TX (in later years it was to return to Las Vegas.) I had an opportunity to do my "bit for science," to get wired up to an electro-encephalograph (EEG: measures brain waves) and do a couple of remote viewing sessions! A colleague's husband was completing his doctoral research in psychology and needed to assess what was happening, in terms of brain function, during remote viewing sessions.

The research took place in three parts: once the viewer was wired up to the EEG recording, they were asked (a) to look at a picture visually and to complete a mock remote viewing session (usually the picture feedback is hidden from the viewer), (b) To imagine a scene and to do a session from memory, and then (c) to do an actual Controlled Remote Viewing (CRV) session with a hidden feedback picture.

My "c" session began by my stating on my paper that I was "Wired! Anxious, tense and nervous." Both of my first ideograms and gestalts I declared as a "structure," there were also indications of land, and my session summary stated" Initial perception of a definite structure in a flat landscape. White, curved structure with striations. Surroundings are cherry or pinkish colors, green, black and white. An aesthetic impact of a stately and dignified nature. Rounded structure with pillars and striations. Purpose: seeing far away like a radio telescope or observatory. Not biological. Big white structure. Massive. Composed of concrete, glass and metal. Purpose: seeing or looking."

The picture feedback showed a structure, a country church with a metallic pointed tower among fields containing stripes or striations from plowing. Stately and dignified. Not a total hit but close enough. Unfortunately, even though feedback was promised, regarding my EEG results, it was never received, despite several requests. Later follow up revealed that the researchers did not feel that the study was productive and that they had destroyed the data!

Amy Lynn Bradley.
PROJECT: Amy Lynn Bradley.
METHOD: CRV/ERV.
DATE: November 13, 2003.
CLIENT: Bradley Family.
TYPE: Missing Person.
TEAM: NRVG.

In July of 2003, I received a request from a friend who was in contact with the mother of a missing girl, Amy Lynn Bradley. Amy's mother was requesting help in finding her kidnapped daughter. I immediately tasked the NRVG group with a humanitarian project. The FBI had some leads on the case but there was no further information where Amy could be found.

Background:
The story was that the family was on a cruise. During the time they were docked at a port, Amy disappeared, only taking her cigarettes and lighter. She had been seen drinking in the ship's bar, earlier in the evening, with several young men who were locals from the docked location. There was no sign of a struggle, but Amy was gone. Several viewers returned data from directive questions regarding the disappearance of Amy Lynn Bradley.

The first directive of this "open search" project was: Go to the moment in time that Amy was last seen by her family. (Open search means that the viewers have at least minimal frontloading and are using more spontaneous remote viewing methods.)

Remote Viewing Data (Amalgamation from several viewers):
There is a person and a small machine in my ideogram – the machine is a telephone.

Directive: Follow her to her destination the night she disappeared.
I get free and easy – a puffy cloud – a bird flying through a puffy cloud.

Directive: Get the story of Amy's disappearance by the entity of Amy herself.
My first ideogram begins easy and ends up violent. What I see is like a 'film noir' with the only colors being black and white with blue and blue green. I see a person – a large ship in the distance. In my next ideogram there is water, waves, ocean-like, flat-line. As I concentrate on the ending of the line. I get a sea-sick motion to it. My ideogram is strange – unusually long and getting longer each time I go back.
Directive: What are the circumstances behind why she is missing?
Female – crying – hysterical – can't tell if she's old or young – not very pleased with what's going on – misses her dad. I look at her and say – poor kid. She's crying because, 'I lost my daddy.'

Directive: Describe Amy.
I told Amy that her mother was looking for her and loved her. I told her to call in her guardian angels for comfort. There didn't seem much else to do. I would not be surprised that she has died. Her light is very dim. This is a real tangible target. The target is alive. I saw a young girl with long blonde hair, I would guess the age at about 14-18. She was walking on the beach, there were dogs running around near her. I think she is blonde and about 7. Woman in white – This is a female that is wearing either a nurse's uniform, or something similar. She is also wearing soft shoes like a nurse. She is the missing daughter. She has been missing for more than six months. She was taken by force.

Directive: Identify Amy.
Flower – white or off-white, reminds me of a lily. What is important to me about the lily is that it is a hard-petal flower that floats on water.

Directive: How is Amy's health now?

I tuned into Amy who does not look in good shape. I think her mind is altered, certainly by fear, but probably by drugs. I got that she's alive, but in bad shape. Also, that she wants to be found. I also got a sense of a girl with blunt, blond bangs, but wonder if that's an analytical overlay.

Directive: Where is Amy now?

I see her often in the trunk of a car. I moved back to the target (Amy) and found her lying down. Resting? My impression is that Amy is kept on the move in an area where there are pine trees and water. She is being kept in a smaller home or vehicle like a motor home. I got the impression of a man and child in a small room. Road through front window – possibly a motor home.

Does the vehicle they are traveling need to be pumped like a motor home?

I see Yosemite Park. Going by that park. Stopping in it or driving through it. There is some reason why the car stopped. I see an old Plymouth, with fins on the back like a Ford Fairlane. Metallic blue Plymouth Fury, 1960, early, seats four people; 2-door. Starts with F, possibly a Plymouth Fury hard top, same color top; blue on blue. At one point I saw blue and white. There is nervousness about the car being pulled over.

They are driving east without a destination. I cannot get a take on the car except maybe it is old and dark blue. Sometimes it is white and light blue. Maybe they are stealing cars. They stay in tacky cheap motels. Next impression was a strangely shaped vehicle that morphed into a car. The shape was like a canoe. Next impressions were of large cylinder objects, gray, like silo's you might see near train tracks, or a farm. There were more than one. More terrain images came in including a hill with homes on it with a road towards the bottom. There's moisture in the distance. Not sure if it's a lake, river or bay. Hilly treed area - evergreen trees. There is an arched section; possibly a tunnel with cars driving through. Impression of eastern Washington/Northern Idaho, but the moisture reminded me of the Great Lakes area. The trees remind me of the Pacific Northwest.

I picked up that she is in an apartment, obviously held against her will and tied up much of the day. The apartment is in an old, tall building in a seedy area, perhaps New York City. The windows are blacked or blocked out, except one that her captors can look from. She is on at least the 4th floor, perhaps the 8th or 9th. There is a sign that

195

the elevator is broken. She was moved there at night. Don't expect her to be there more than a week to 10 days; they move her, as they are very watchful and tense. There is something that reminds me of a pavilion with pillars – open spaces and something that reminds me of a school or a neat little building with steps up to the door. There is a room which has a metal table or lab table – chemistry. It reminds me of the tables I saw sharks on at the shark's board. There are chairs, a trunk that's empty but not dirty or squalid.

Directive: Location of the missing daughter by dowsing methodology.

The daughter seems to have been or is now in a great deal of danger. The location of the missing daughter by my dowsing method seems to be in southern Louisiana – between Baton Rouge and New Orleans. I come up with north of Tallahassee, near the panhandle of Florida. I got that they were in the Kansas panhandle. I ran my hand over a map of Kansas with my eyes closed and that seemed the warmest spot. The child may also be dehydrated. I dowsed a map of the US looking for Amy. I got a 'Yes' only in Central Kansas in the area of McPherson and Hutchinson - not Wichita and not Topeka.

Directive: Describe the terrain.

I saw like a river with a bridge going over it. Next impression didn't make any sense. I saw clear bubbles, so I wrote bubble wrap, because it was like in a sheet. I then saw white bags placed on the roadside like someone had put out laundry or white trash bags. Became an area with green grassy hill, white house, like you would find in the country. Some trees; flat leaf, not pine.

Possibly related to the sighting in April 2003 as per the FBI files. First impression was in a crowd of people. They were outdoors, looking, searching, and wearing black, overcoats. (The FBI is seeking information regarding the identity of these two individuals. They may have information about the disappearance of Amy Bradley.

- The first Unknown Male (#1) has been described as White; in his late 30's or early 40's; between 5'11" and 6'1"; balding; with red hair and a red beard.
- The second Unknown Male (#2) has been described as in his early 30's; approximately 5'11"; with dark, wavy, shoulder length hair.

Viewer Data (prior to the pictures of the two men being released) I saw a male, dark short hair, beard, heavy set, 30-45 years in age. Main character, male, chain smokes, dark hair, dark eyes, olive complexion, tallish (5'10 or so), 30-45 years of age, lean to medium build, severe personality, perhaps noticeable scar on his left cheek. His eye on the same side of his face is droopy, some sort of muscle damage.

She has been taken by a man and woman who are not married. They both have dark hair, the man thin on top, the woman shoulder length - about 40ish. He is calling the shots and she is following out of her need to belong to him and her fear. Maybe his initials are D (Dennis) or DD. A man with large eyes is driving. He has dark hair, balding, and smokes Marlboros. He has a tattoo on his upper left forearm – blue – Reminds me of shape of an anchor. Can't tell what it is. There are at least four people in the car.

I saw the ocean again, it was the ocean with rough waves crashing onto a low, rocky cliff. The word "wharf," various people drinking from glasses.

I keep getting a picture of the curly headed woman which may or may not be a woman. This person is small framed and effeminate or feminine. He/she seems kind but calculating, and capable of telling lies which are believable. I can see this person's background: a person who is an outcast – a loner. In school this person was shunned because of sexual orientation. A word comes to mind: "mousy" a name this person was called that many times; timid yet angry inside. I can also see that 'curly' has tried hard to befriend the missing daughter by 'putting on' the female persona and acting as a girlfriend and/or family member. There are lies and deceit here. I see 'curly' rubbing hands together in a nervous and deceitful fashion. I see a danger in 'curly.' 'Curly' is ready to do anything to conceal this action including the death of the daughter. That would hurt 'curly' because he feels that the kidnapped daughter has come a long way in becoming a friend – or so it is perceived by 'curly.' I get at least three months prior to this October for this scene.

This is how I read it. I am putting my own bias tilt towards this summary. I see two males, ("Nate" - Angry male person "dober" (doper?) curly?), ("Michael"?) and one female, outdoors, possibly camping in an area with mountains (with a lighthouse and trees) around. Someone is or has made a trip from Phoenix (Near Sedona, Arizona?) to Oakland. Located near a lodge, which may be near a post office (ranger station or someplace a uniform is worn?). The reason I'm suggesting the ranger station is because of the mention of a "Park" in my session. The pumping station, is interesting? Take great caution in approaching the malicious (perpetrator) is a pale skin (white or similar) male in his mid-40's, brown hair, blue eyes. There was an older female presence. I got the word like "Omni–ance."

Directive: Show me how perpetrator makes money?
Underneath vehicle. Bottles, Alcohol. Squarish, possibly a Mechanic. Sounds like "Ladero."

Additional Information:

This man was seated, it looked like he was at a computer screen or TV. He was young, early 20's I'd say. He had brown hair in a typical man's cut, but it was straight and a little longer right over his forehead, it fanned out a bit. He seemed to be annoyed, looking at the screen, then it looked like he threw a pencil down and got up.

This I believe was another young man, 20's also. He had blonde hair, a short cut, blue eyes, a narrow face; I think he had a hat on. Golf and country club. Very rich and very refined people, not newer money, but old money. Bush league with money – reminds me of Texas with older man playing golf. I can see him only from the back, white shirt, beige pants, shoes, and hat. Man is thinking, 'I can never win at this game.' He swings at the ball and misses. He hits it 350 feet down the fairway. Golf guy has health problems, feels like a heart problem. There is a yacht near the golf course – a two story ship. There is a lot of money flying around.

Directive: Is there anything else to bring forward of importance?
I have a song in my head, '...one toke over the line – sweet Jesus - one toke over the line. Sitting downtown in a railway station – one toke over the line." We are dealing with a drugged person who is being transported from one sight to the next. They are headed northwest. 560 miles northwest of starting point, whatever that means.

Feedback:
All this data was passed onto the colleague to give to the family and the FBI. To date the whereabouts of Amy Lynn Bradley are unknown. A few years ago, Dr. Phil McGraw (of the Dr. Phil Show) carried out an investigation, following up leads on the disappearance of Amy Lynn Bradley and a photograph was obtained that showed a woman who could be Amy, a few years older, looking obviously drugged and working as a prostitute or something similar. Nothing was confirmed and the photo was just that - a photo. Amy's story is a possible example of many others: young women being kidnapped, drugged, made reliant on their captors and forced into prostitution. It is hoped that, eventually, her story will have closure for her and her family.

Home Security Device.
PROJECT: Home Security Product.
METHOD: ERV.
DATE: 2003.
CLIENT: Aerospace Engineer.
TYPE: Potential Business Opportunity.

Clients often approach me with requests for information about potential business opportunities. For example, in 2003, clients requested a project regarding a home security product that was being developed in New Mexico. They needed to know: would the product be financially successful, would the company be successful, would they, as investors, get their money back and when, what would the company be like five and ten years-time, what was the intention of the founders of the company, how many rounds of investors would there be, should customers invest and what was the best time to invest?

As is usual with this type of project, I used Extended Remote Viewing (ERV), sometimes called Spontaneous Remote Viewing, with minimal up-front information (non-leading questions) to access new information for the client. For various reasons, which were perceived during the remote viewing, the customer was advised not to invest in this company. It was later discovered that the company did not do well financially, and the customer saved money by not investing.

Oregon Murder Cases.
PROJECT: Oregon Murder Cases.
METHOD: Coordinate RV.
DATE: August 2002 to June 2003.
CLIENT: Mad-Dog Group: Burton, Oregon.
TYPE: Criminal Investigation.
COORDINATE: 0068

Between August 2002 and June 2003, I received a request from Ralph Burton and his Oregon 'Mad-Dog' remote viewing group for assistance with a humanitarian project. The group had been following a case involving the disappearance of two Oregon school friends, Miranda Gaddis and Ashley Pond of Oregon City, Oregon.

Background:
Ashley Marie Pond was born in 1989 and grew up in Oregon City, Oregon. In August of 2001 she accused a local man, Ward Weaver, the

father of her friend, of trying to rape her. Then, on January 9, 2002, Ashley disappeared on her way to school.

On March 8th, 2 months later, Ashley's close friend, Miranda Diane Gaddis, a year younger than Ashley, also vanished. Ralph's group had been working with the FBI on the case but needed more information. Ralph gave me the names of the girls as coordinates but, as is my policy in such cases, I didn't look up any details. I prefer to do the viewing before I get feedback and I had not heard of the case until I received Ralph's assignment. Using a "stream of consciousness" method of remote viewing called Extended Remote Viewing or ERV; I perceived Miranda standing on the side of the road waiting for the school bus. A modern, black sports-type car, like a Camaro, came by and the window rolled down. A man talked to Miranda and I perceived that he wanted to talk to her. He persuaded her to get in the car and promised to drop her off at school. Instead he took her to a deserted culvert where he strangled her. Ralph sent me feedback that a possible suspect in the murder case drove a black Camaro-type car and was this like what I saw? I confirmed that it was.

Over the next few months up to around September 25th, 2003 I carried out several additional viewings for Ralph including information about the man in the car. I perceived that he lived close to both girls, in the same neighborhood, and I drew Ralph's attention to a shed at the back of the man's residence. There was a box there that was important with a blue-ribbon design on it. When Ralph asked what the most important feature of my viewing was, I stressed the shed and the box.

On August 13th, 2002, Ward Weaver III, a middle-age neighbor of Miranda and Ashley, was arrested for raping his son's girlfriend. The son informed police that his father had confessed to killing both girls! Weaver had, apparently, dug a hole in his back yard and covered it with concrete (saying it was the slab for a hot tub). FBI agents found the remains of Ashley Pond beneath the concrete slab in a 55-gallon drum. Then they found the remains of Miranda Gaddis in a microwave box in the storage shed at the back of Weaver's property.

On October 2, 2002 Weaver was charged with the murders of the two girls (including rape and sexual abuse) and in September 2004, he pleaded guilty and was sentenced to two life sentences without parole. We didn't solve the case; that was done by the FBI and the local police acting on tips from Weaver's colleagues and family, but I like to think that our data helped bring closure to the case and justice for Ashley and Miranda.

2004

JOURNALS

During 2004, my main work was carrying out projects for my major financial client. I have not included those projects here as they were proprietary. As I mentioned, this forward-thinking businessman helped "push the envelope of remote viewing" and introduced me to many new topics including assisting him with RV projects related to his financial business, as well as investigating anomalous topics such as the location of Atlantis, the origins of the Sphinx, and ET topics.

You can read more on these projects in my book *Tactical Remote Viewing.*

2005

JOURNALS

Journal – January 27, 2005 – *RV Update.*
For the past year my volunteer group, the Nevada Remote Viewing Group has been meeting the client's remote viewing projects. However, there hasn't been any profit after the viewers have been paid and any other money put back into keeping the company running.

Last month I closed out the corporation but will keep the name going. I have been working at the Senior Center of Boulder City in Boulder City to bring in additional income, but this has taken most of my time. So, I've put RV teaching on a "back burner" until summer except for a 5-day class that I am conducting at Loch Lomond, Scotland in April.

I have also begun to let the client task the viewers directly, as he prefers to pick and choose the viewers for each project. He is giving the tasking duties to one of his assistants and I will assist her when necessary. The client will still task me personally on projects that involve him, his company and his farm. I was pleasantly surprised that many of the viewers agreed to work directly with the client.

Journal – May 29, 2005 – *Update.*
As I start this new phase in my life, I am looking forward to working from home again! I have really enjoyed the year and a half working at the Senior Center, but the time has come to return to full-

time RV teaching, writing and remote viewing consulting. My working-vacation, teaching at Loch Lomond last month helped me realize how much I enjoy teaching and traveling. I have already arranged a CRV Advanced course for the end of June and one student for a regular CRV course mid-July. In the meantime, I have been getting ready for my new venture. I've bought new business cards, brochures and letterhead and have been busy printing these up for distribution. I also plan on continuing the Non-Profit Certification course and to apply what I learn to remote viewing.

Journal – May 29, 2005 – *Loch Lomond, Scotland.*
It is about six weeks since my trip to Scotland, but all the wonderful memories remain with me – the view out over the Loch from the Old House, the dozen wonderful and eager students, and Mike and Stella Webster's gracious hospitality.

The students did very well even though it was incredibly hard work for me and them. I had planned on eight students at the most but there were so many more that were interested. Over five days all the students went through the 6 stages of Controlled Remote Viewing (CRV) and finished up constructing 3D models of their Stage 6 picture targets.

Mike Webster wants to make the Loch Lomond site the UK base for the Nevada Remote Viewing Group and I agreed. I have a standing invitation to go back to teach whenever there are enough students available. 2005 is proving to be an interesting year.

Journal - July 19th, 2005 – *Up and Running.*
At the end of May, my major NY business client came through with about seven new projects plus the NRVG carried out a "cold" case police project that we haven't had feedback on yet. A large group of NRVG viewers worked on the police case and we got a good deal of matching data!

Journal - August 15, 2005 – *Completing Cycles.*
It's mid-August already and my days alternate between "working hard" and "hardly working!" This has been a wonderful summer of reassessment and replenishment. Every day brings new activities and I feel that I have completed many cycles and activities that remained uncompleted.

CASE FILES – 2005

Rings of Saturn Feedback Project:

METHOD: ERV.
DATE: 1994 & 2005.
CLIENT: Intuition Services.
TYPE: Exploration.

Remote viewers may often have to wait many years before receiving feedback on their sessions. This one took 11 years! In my 1998 book *Remote Perceptions*, I documented an RV project, undertaken in 1994, for Intuition Services of California. The project focused on the rings of Saturn and anomalies within the rings. It was front-loaded, used Extended Remote Viewing (ERV), sought unknown information, and had only me as the viewer. The project fit the requirements for a valid prediction in that it was carried out prior to the information becoming known, there was a verified chain of custody of the data, and documentation of the data prior to the event.

In 2005, the magazine *Science News* (Nov. 19, 2005, Vol. 168, pp. 328-29) published an article entitled "Groovy Science: Cassini gets the skinny on Saturn's rings" that provided feedback for the Rings of Saturn project. Also, a recent internet search located information about the Cassini venture: "On July 1, 2004, the Cassini-Huygens spacecraft performed the SOI (Saturn Orbit Insertion) maneuver and entry into orbit around Saturn. The primary mission ends in 2008, when the spacecraft has completed 74 orbits around the planet."

Ron Cowen, a Science News writer, recently wrote, "Now, the Cassini spacecraft, which entered orbit around Saturn last year, has completed the most thorough examination ever of the rings. Until last May, the craft has spent most of its time orbiting Saturn's equator. That orientation is great for close-up studies of the planet's moons, but provided only an obscured, edge view of the intricate ring system. Then, Cassini got a ringside seat. Just as scientists had planned, the craft rose out of the equatorial plane and for the next 5 months viewed the rings from above and below the planet's equator. From those perches, it has studied the full breadth of the rings in unprecedented detail. With the flood of new data, astronomers may be on the verge of answering some centuries-old questions about the rings." Cassini scientist Joshua Colwell of the University of Colorado has said that, "It's amazing to me that something as prominent in the solar system as the rings, still has so many fundamental unanswered questions."

Following are excerpts from *Remote Perceptions* concerning the Rings of Saturn prediction, with the related verifications from Cowen's article.

"In the early 1990s, at least two separate groups were formed: Intuition Services was formed in California. I was commissioned by

Intuition Services to undertake a remote viewing of the rings of Saturn. After two unsuccessful attempts to approach Saturn through the rings, I approached the planet from a vantage point a few thousand miles above its 'north pole,' and viewed the rings as a flat circular area. From this vantage point I was able to view the various elements of Saturn, its rings and planets."

Feedback: The Cassini craft also took up this orientation to view the rings.

Intuition Services provided a set of questions for guidelines, as follows:

1.   Are there natural phenomena that would account for bright luminous light sources in the rings, or in the vicinity of Saturn?
Data: There are some very bright "hot rocks" circulating in the outer rings that have been attracted by the intense gravitational pull of Saturn. These rocks are both thermally and atomically "hot." They circulate in the outer rings for varying periods of time while their constituent elements are broken down and distributed according to their degree of breakdown, between the rings.

Feedback: "Cassini has identified a new moon in the outer rings of Saturn, provisionally named S/2005 S1; the tiny, newfound moon has a diameter of about 7 km and reflects about half the sunlight that falls on it, like the brightness of the neighboring ring particles. Some of Saturn's moons are particularly effective in sculpting the rings because they have a special relationship, called a resonance with the ring's particles." "The whole (F ring) region is probably just a chaotic bumper car zone of moonlets that are getting scattered,' suggests Jeff Cuzzi of NASA's Ames Research Center in Moffett Field, California."

2.   Are there rings that are incomplete? If so, how did the missing ring segment disappear?
Data: The main factor that describes Saturn is "cyclic." Due to its intense electromagnetic pull, space debris is constantly, but erratically, attracted to the planet. This debris initially rotates in the outer rings and undergoes a process of degradation, then the various elements are distributed among the rings according to the degree of molecular "weight." Much like a gas spectrometer, which distributes elements in a banded strip, except, in the case of Saturn, the strip becomes circular. Because of the random and irregular nature of the space debris that is pulled into the gravitational field, the rings fluctuate in their

completeness and cycle from open to closed along both their length and width-the rings are not uniform in their density. This cyclic nature of the rings is dictated solely by the nature and amount of debris that enters the gravitational field.

Feedback: Carl D. Murray and his collaborators at Queen Mary University in London have performed simulations that suggest that "Saturn's moon Prometheus approaches and recedes from the F ring every 14.7 hours," confirming the cyclic nature. The team's simulations indicate that "each time that the moon begins receding, it pulls out strands of particles from the narrow, twisted ring. One orbit later. . . Saturn's tug distends the region from which the strands were stolen, creating the channels seen in the Cassini images."

3.   Describe the nature and origin of the planet Saturn. How will the planet evolve and eventually die?
Data: Saturn evolved from a collection of electrically charged rocks that became attracted to each other and formed a nucleus. Gradually, as the mass became more magnetically powerful, it attracted an increasingly greater number of similar elements. These initial, charged rocks may have come from an earlier Saturn-like planet that became too "overcharged" and disintegrated. This may possibly be the future fate of the planet we now know as Saturn. We tend to think of Saturn as static, but it has a decidedly cyclic and dynamic nature.

Feedback. "There's an enormous time variability in the rings," says (Jeff) Cuzzi. 'New clumps of material have appeared in rings since July 2004, when Cassini began orbiting the system. 'Rubble-pile moonlets' small, loosely bound collections of icy particles appear to be continually assembling and breaking apart in the rings,' adds Colorado's Colwell." "Astronomers have proposed that the rings formed when an icy saturnine moon got smashed to bits by a meteoroid or when a comet or moon that came too close to its parent planet was torn apart by gravitational stresses."

4.   Are the gaps in the rings natural or created by extraterrestrial intelligence?
Data: No. The gaps in the rings are the effect of the cyclic nature of the rings themselves and the debris that they attract. Gaps will continue to occur and close in the rings at cyclic periods.

Feedback: Recent Cassini observations are providing new clues about the past and future evolution of Saturn's rings. Cassini images released by NASA in September 2005 reveal changes in Saturn's D ring, the innermost ring, over the 25 years since the Voyager craft looked at the system. One of the strands, or ringlets that make up the D ring, is now only one-tenth as bright as it appeared in 1981, and has migrated towards Saturn by 200 km."

Ingo Swann has stated that one of the requirements for remote viewing is the availability of feedback. This can sometimes be a problem for viewers who attempt planetary viewings, such as the Rings of Saturn. Feedback may not be immediately available and may take many years to become available. Waiting for feedback requires patience but receiving the feedback can be both validating and rewarding.

Himalaya Rescue Attempt.
PROJECT: Himalaya Rescue Attempt.
METHOD: CRV/ERV.
DATE: July 27th, 2005.
CLIENT: FS.
TYPE: Missing Person.
TEAM: NRVG.

On July 27, 2005 I received an email from a colleague asking if the group had time to do an urgent humanitarian project. After confirming that we did, he sent the following information and tasking: "Missing male, six days out, in the Himalayas. Describe the target, is the target alive, locate the target and are rescuers on track or in the right area?" The missing individual was a young man named Trevor Sokol.

A request went out to the Nevada Remote Viewing Group the same day. Eleven viewers responded to the project. My colleague also put me in touch with a friend of the missing young man's family, FS. A map was sent out to viewers for dowsing and other perceptions on July 28. However, viewers noted various locations on the maps and there did not seem to be any consensus. All maps were forwarded to our contact and others who could forward them to the search team.

The following feedback came from FS. "Today (7/28) six more Sherpa were hired and now twelve are still searching. Other RVers, whom the family contacted yesterday a.m. have confirmed a reading so incredibly closely. We are getting pretty much the same info from everyone. Still alive; broken leg and head injury and out of view, also the exact circumstances of the interaction/split with his hiking partner. Please continue to pray with us that they find him." Phone call on 7/30 indicated that he had not yet been found but a helicopter team had been brought into the search.

The following data was received from the remote viewers:

Analysis of the viewer data indicated that he possibly started out with a companion, either a female (correct) or an Oriental male. Stature is smaller, maybe wearing yellow outer garment. There was sexual tension and some anger. The other person may have left him alone out of pique and at some level is ambivalent about the event. (Correct) This person may be able to give a motive for the target's wandering off, but they do not know where he is. He or she is not really holding back information. This may just have been a relationship the target was brooding over when he lost concentration.

Feedback:

Unfortunately, after many weeks of searching the family and Sherpa team gave up. They had not found the missing young man. My final perception was that he would be found in the future by another team that was unconnected to this one and the finding would be accidental. Sadly, to date he has not been found.

This case report shows how disappointing and frustrating searches, such as this one, can be. Not all remote viewing sessions result in finding the missing person, locating the lost object or apprehending the criminal. Remote viewers need to accept that their work may or may not help a case, but it is important that they continue to help. Remote viewing rarely solves cases alone but can add vital information, the "missing piece of the puzzle" to the case.

Missing Reno NV – Cold case.
PROJECT: Missing Reno NV Woman.
METHOD: Coordinate Remote Viewing.
DATE: June 5th, 2005.
CLIENT: Violent Crimes Department.
TYPE: Cold Case: Missing Person.
Coordinate: Alpha060605
Team: Nevada Remote Viewing Group.

The following cold case, Alpha060605, was received on Sunday, June 5, 2005 from an anonymous detective with the Violent Crimes Department at an anonymous police department. The case involved the disappearance of a 36-year-old woman near Reno, NV in June 1985. After 7 years of her disappearance not being resolved, she was declared legally dead by the Medical Examiner's Office. The police department decided that it would like some closure regarding the location of this woman's body.

A general call went out to viewers who have worked with the Nevada Remote Viewing Group in the past. Twenty viewers volunteered to take on this project, as an unpaid, humanitarian effort, and were individually tasked as follows on June 6, 2005 under Coordinate Alpha060605.

"Target is a location, describe the location. Something can be perceived at this location. Do not describe the event or persons related to this case. Describe the location where the focus of this case may be found in current time. Both aerial and below-ground movement exercises might be helpful. Please provide landmarks and anything else that will pinpoint a location, in current time, where the focus of this project might be located and found. Please provide any other information that is perceived that might help this case come to resolution. Please scan and email or fax your full sessions by the end of this week to the contact information below."

All the data and analysis, including the perceived location, were given to the relevant police department that acknowledged its receipt. However, we heard nothing more. There was talk of getting a private team together to go out to the area and search.

Receiving feedback on a project is desirable but not always available. Remote viewers need to understand that feedback is optional in practical remote viewing cases, such as this one. It can be disappointing and discouraging but "comes with the territory." The viewer's only hope is that the data was useable. Remote viewing data is never used alone but in conjunction with other known information and can give police departments "an edge" in helping to solve cases.

2006

JOURNALS

Journal - April 30, 2006 – *Publishing.*
Today is my 60th birthday, a new decade and the beginning of a new era. 2006 so far has been interesting. I've continued to live on 5th Street in Boulder City: writing, researching, teaching and enjoying life. In March two of my current books *Shire* and *River of Passion* were accepted for publication by Publish America. The contracts were signed and sent off last week. I am excited as it is unusual for one publisher to take two books at once. I must complete *Shire* by July 1st and *River* by August 1st, so most of my summer will be spent writing! *Shire* is a

collection of small vignettes about growing up in Bristol during the 1950s. *River of Passion* is a historical novel about the village of Shirehampton over the ages.

<u>Journal - April 30th, 2006 – *Scotland.*</u>
I just got back from Scotland this past Tuesday after three weeks at Loch Lomond. The Highlands were wonderful: snow and sleet when I arrived, daffodils everywhere and twin lambs in the fields. The students for the basic and advanced classes were beyond my expectations! Loch Lomond was as beautiful as always and I managed, with Mike and Stella Webster's help, to visit some interesting places: the 300 yr old Drovers Arms Pub, Kilmarten Standing Stones and burial cairns, Stirling Castle, and Edinburgh, which included the Castle and Holyrood Palace. Mike and Stella were wonderful hosts and were very generous of their time and energy, even showing me how to see auras. I managed to see light blue auras around Mike and Stella but that was all. Their group, Waveform, is based on shiatsu energy, and Mike and Stella now teach others to perceive this energy and to carry out healing. Now I am eager to get back to remote viewing applications work and writing.

<u>Journal - May 29th, 2006 – *Who's calling?*</u>
A few months ago, while I was sitting at my computer, I heard a woman's voice ask "Angela?" I didn't recognize the voice at the time and thought it was someone at the door. I opened the front door but there was nobody there. I went to the back door and nobody was there either. The voice sounded very real. I thought, maybe that it was my friend Phyllis, trying to contact me, as she was in Sedona, taking a course in energy healing. When she got back, I asked her, but she said it wasn't her.

At the next book club meeting, here in Boulder City, one of the "Young Moms" mentioned that every time she passed my house in her car, she mentally called my name and asked me to come to the door or window to let her know I had heard her! I had told one of my close friends about hearing the voice calling my name and she was able to confirm to the "Young Mom" that I had heard her. I then asked her to say my name in a questioning way and it did sound like the voice that I heard. However, I haven't heard her since. The "Young Mom" is pregnant and, sometimes, pregnant women have heightened psi abilities. She is intrigued with the concept of remote viewing but is very religious which has become a barrier to her exploring her natural abilities.

Journal - May 29th, 2006 – *Text Targets and Videos.*

I've decided to add several new concepts to my remote viewing training. The first being text-only targets that I have already tried in Scotland and with the Advanced students last week here in Boulder City. All the students were able to correctly describe their target, getting the gist of the subject and even able to get actual (and relevant) words from the text. There has been a misconception that viewers cannot perceive text, but these students have proved that wrong!

There is research from Ganzfeld studies that dynamic, moving targets are better perceived than static, 2-dimensional picture targets. So, over the summer I plan to record and store small files of active targets for the students to view. I may do some type of research but haven't yet decided how to do this. Students do well with static targets, and it would be interesting to see if they do any better with dynamic targets.

Journal - May 29th, 2006 – *Psi Research.*

Before I went to Scotland, Dr. Dean Radin contacted me looking for trained remote viewers to take part in a psi test that he has developed. From what I understood; viewers would carry out 50 trials describing a picture target that the computer would pick from four possible targets. I completed the first 50 trials and felt that I had done reasonably well. Later, I got an email from Dean saying that I had done "quite well" and would I like to do another 50 trials. I treat tests like this as an educational game and usually do well. I heard nothing more from Dean until I met him at the IRVA conference, and he told me that, out of the people who had participated, that I was the "winner!" Well, I am not sure what that means in terms of scores, but he said he would ask me to do another 50 trials later. I had an opportunity to ask Paul Smith about Dean's study and he said it was research to show some "higher-ups" actual RV/Psi data. If it advances the future of RV, then I'm happy.

Journal - May 29th, 2006 – *Missing Girl, Salt Lake City.*

When I was teaching in Scotland, I received a "life or death" tasking from a colleague in Las Vegas regarding a girl who had been missing for 36 hours. No other information was available. I "blind tasked" the four Advanced viewers, with no frontloading, then when they came back with some data, gave them some limited frontloading that had been provided (missing 36 hours, missing girl).

The target coordinates were 1911/2006 with the tasking to describe the missing person in detail, the target's current location, current activities and health." I sent off the students' data from Scotland to Las Vegas. Our colleague provided some feedback that "the young lady was

210

15 and the location was Salt Lake City, UT. Her case had been changed from a missing person to a runaway."

Feedback came from Las Vegas that many of our viewers' descriptions were "very close": two members of the Advanced class had identified the sex, height, weight, and stature and her attitude. Others in the class got her location that was "consistent with the area." Our colleague later reported that our data "enabled the parents to recognize where she was and who she was with and to go and get her and bring her home!"

He wrote "The family and friends of the missing girl are eternally grateful for the fast and professional and thorough way we conducted our activities. I am happy to announce that the young lady was found last night, in good health, and returned home to her family. A large amount of the data collected by this RV group was consistent with all aspects of the focus questions. Great job everybody!"

Journal - May 29th, 2006 – *The Murdered DJ.*

While I was at the IRVA Conference this year, Robert Knight, a photographer, told me that he had a project for me. He later tasked me with a humanitarian project that I worked "blind" from the CRV coordinates 8314/7902. I perceived a lot of data indicating a sense of injury to a body, the presence of water, and something "perforated." My ERV data then revealed "long, snake-like reticulated shapes, structure with a red tile roof seen from a helicopter, and a workman's bench with a screw-vice device."

Robert said he would send minimal frontloading: this was a case of a missing friend of his. He wrote "A very long-term friend of mine has gone missing 14 days ago. Last known movement was to take a short boat trip with a business partner who he was falling out with over a large sum of money. We cannot find him and the man he was unhappy with claims he does not know where he has gone. Both parties were living on a boat in San Pedro, CA, in a boat club."

My ERV perceptions (at that time) were that the man in question had been stabbed in the gut and would be "found in the water." I didn't perceive this as seawater but "water with a greenish-tinge like a backwater or inlet that mixes with fresh water. There are long streamers of weed in the water. There is land and a large town nearby. I perceive this as a "crime of passion" – not just about money but about relationships and fidelity issues."

Robert went to LA with his wife Maryanne and saw a news item by which he knew that this was his friend who had gone missing. The TV news flash reported that the Coroner's Office determined Monday that a "man found floating in the ocean off Avalon in Catalina Island died from a gunshot wound."

"The man's body was found by the captain of a passing boat last Thursday, floating in the water, six miles off the Avalon Isthmus" reported Deputy Dana Camarillo of the LA Sheriff's Office.

Robert contacted the Coroner's Office and was finally able to get confirmation that the dead man was indeed his friend, partly because of three missing fingers on one hand.

The NRVG team was also tasked within 36 hours of the initial tasking and all indicated death, murder, and details related to pain, nausea etc. Robert also had a dream, during this time, and was awakened to three "bangs" beneath his couch. Possibly his friend? There was news that the police had searched the partner's boat and house and the partner had been taken in for questioning but, as of that time, nobody was in custody.

The detective on the case asked for further information on a possible accomplice and three further viewers perceived a stocky, Hispanic male. Robert is currently out in LA and will let us know of any further progress with this case. We hope that justice will be done, and Stephen's murderer will get caught and captured, as well as any accomplices. This is what remote viewing is all about: actual, practical work that has some social value!

(Further work was done on this case, a location where the murder may have gone and possible accomplices. The murderer was later apprehended in Montana and returned to California for trial. The trial lasted until 2012 when we could talk and write about the case.)

Journal - May 29th, 2006 – *Stolen and Recovered Items.*
Prior to the IRVA Conference, my main client called to say he was very upset about the loss of a very expensive pair of sunglasses. He had looked everywhere and could not find them. He was concerned about poltergeist activity. I told him that he would find them at the new house, (where he was in the process of moving). I told him they would be sitting by the kitchen sink on the counter. He doubted me but when he got to the new house, the sunglasses were sitting on the counter in the kitchen, next to the sink. He was very happy to have them back!

At the IRVA Conference, one of the volunteers had some jewelry stolen. It was wrapped in a red silk pouch and, she thought, had been stolen from a friend's hotel room. She asked for anybody who had taken photographs of her at the conference to send them to her. She also reported the theft to the hotel and the LV police.

I wrote to her: I would like to try something that I have done for other folks, sometimes I am able to "place" missing objects back into

212

the possession of the original owner, when they have been stolen or lost." I don't know how it works but I'll give it a try. Look for it in a week or so, in a place where you have looked before."

By this time, she was back in Colorado. She reported that after the conference before she unpacked, she had searched everything three times. She had also gone through the briefcase (where the pouch was eventually found), several times but the pouch and jewelry had not been there. (The night before the jewelry was found, she had a dream that she should look once more in the briefcase pocket and that was where she found the red satin pouch and the jewelry)!

Journal - May 29, 2006 – *Media.*
The media seems to be taking a renewed interest in remote viewing. In March, the *Readers Digest* excerpted passages from Paul Smith's book *Reading the Enemies Mind* for an article that was read by millions and brought a new interest to the field. Several local people commented on the article.

Then, before the IRVA Conference, a local reporter, Joe Schoenmann from *Las Vegas Life Magazine* came for a short class, with a buddy, Scott. Joe wrote an article called "The Mind's Eye Spy: One Reporters Staggering Trip through the Wormhole of Remote Viewing." The article was a good review of remote viewing and detailed Joe's amazement as he took the training. It was good publicity for the IRVA Conference, too and many others in the RV community.

All the interest from the media is interesting but I need to remember that their goal is entertainment, not education of the public. It is very flattering to be interviewed but it can get "heady" and can waste a lot of time. The *Las Vegas Life Magazine* generated some interest, but the public's interest is fickle and short lived, but the experience did have an impact on Joe. (However, I always say "Today's news, tomorrow's fish and chip paper!")

Journal - May 29, 2006 – *Exobiology Project.*
For the past two years my NY financial client has been providing me with paid projects ranging from very practical business sessions to more esoteric projects. The client has become very interested in Earth's "neighbors" and the ability of some people to communicate telepathically. He has put this together into a project that we have been carrying out since January of 2006.

Called the Exobiology project, we have been contacting our cosmic "neighbors" and the races that have been contacted and that have communicated so far have been fascinating. The client was worried that there would be too much overlay and imagination in the sessions.

However, I feel that there has been some very real communication and each of the races has had a distinct "personality." The client has talked about writing a book in a few years.

I approach each session with an open, non-judgmental mind and see what transpires. None of the races, so far, have declined to participate. The races have ranged from the angelic Whites to the almost demonic Dark Ones.

Journal - May 29, 2006 – *IRVA and Classes.*

Since the end of April, I have held two remote viewing classes and attended the IRVA Conference. Four students came to the CRV Stages 16 course, the first week. All of them completed the class and did very well on the targets. They were happy with their Stage 6 models. The class ran from Sunday through Thursday as the IRVA conference ran from the Thursday through Sunday. The conference rooms were full of orbs which we were able to photograph. The Advanced Class, after the conference, became a week of exploration and by Day 4, the students were remote viewing "text only" targets. The viewers were able to perceive words and the gist of the new articles that had been downloaded from BBC.com that morning. One involved Bush's decision to direct 6,000 guards to the US/Mexico border and other news stories. Both viewers got lots of details even though they were monitoring each other. Both classes were a great success.

Journal - September 17, 2006 – *Publications.*

What a busy summer! I wrote most of the summer while the client's projects kept me afloat financially. We have continued with the Exobiology projects and it has been an interesting summer. Publish America needed my book *Shire* completed by July 1st and *River of Passion* by August 1st! Some days I was either writing one long chapter or two short chapters a day! I was burned out on writing by the end of August and sick of the books.

Shire got published earlier this month and *River of Passion* is going through the editing process and will be ready for publication in November or December. At the end of September, I have a book review and signing at the Boulder Dam Hotel and another one on October 7th at the Treasured Times Tea House. When *River* is published, I will venture farther afield with some book store signings. However, I know from experience with *Remote Perceptions* that book signings can be a washout and a disappointment.

I am very happy with my first experience with Publish America and they did a great job with *Shire*. They offered me the opportunity to edit the book myself, but it looks as if they are editing *River of Passion* themselves. Which is OK, as it is a lot of work. On Wednesday I will take copies down to the Writers Roundtable and I will be presenting a copy to the Boulder City Library.

Journal - November 5th, 2006 – *Dowsing Course.*

2006 has been an enigmatic year: on the one hand it seems to have lasted forever and on the other hand it has proceeded in quick bursts of activity. I am writing this in Austin, TX, having just completed Paul Smith's Dowsing Course that he is filming for a DVD series. It was a fun class and I learned a lot about dowsing that I didn't know about before. (But concluded that I am not a great instrument dowser).

This year I completed writing my two new books and one has already been published, the other will be out next spring. *Shire*, my little book of reminiscences about growing up in England during the 1950s was completed by July 1st and came out in August. I was very happy with it: it's a fun little book with stories, recipes of the era and black and white photographs. My second book: *River of Passion*, was completed by August 1st but won't be available for editing and publishing until next spring. I am happy with it. By the time I was finished with *River of Passion* I was burned-out and was glad to see it off to the publishers. During July I was either writing one large chapter or several small chapters every day!

I obtained the historical background for *River* from textbooks and online but remote viewed the stories contained in each chapter. The stories took on a life of their own, as they never turned out exactly as I had planned at the beginning. For example, the story of the Rag and Bone Man's Horse became a story told by the horse herself. She had a horrible real life but, in my story, she imagines herself to be a unicorn with a flowing mane.

Journal - November 5th, 2006 – *Main Client.*

Since the spring of 2003, I have been working with a financial client who has provided me and my remote viewing team with projects ranging from the mundane to the esoteric. All the projects have been a challenge and a learning opportunity!

Initially, the client had no idea what remote viewing was about, so he and his wife came for a week's training in Boulder City. They both did well and had a better understanding of the protocols and some of the limitations of the process. Recently, the client has been pushing the boundaries of the process by doing series of sessions focusing on off-planet topics. These have been quite successful but, like many esoteric topics, does not have enough feedback to make great claims. I complete the projects with an open, non-judgmental mind and I am often surprised by the data. Eventually the sessions may be made into a book but that's a way down the line. Personally, the projects have opened my eyes to many new possibilities.

(The Exobiology Project became part of a book I co-wrote with C. B. Scott Jones in 2014 entitled *Voices from the Cosmos*)

Journal – November 5, 2006 – *Dowsing Class.*

There is much to catch up on including my writing, courses, classes, new ventures and old ventures. 2006 has been an enigmatic year; on the one hand it seems to have lasted forever and on the other hand it has proceeded in quick bursts of activity. I am writing this in Austin, TX, having just completed Paul Smith's Dowsing Class that was videotaped for eventual release as a Learn Dowsing course that will be sold online. It was a great class and I learned a lot about dowsing that I didn't know before. Especially the role of dowsing in the history of remote viewing.

CASE FILES – 2006

International Predictions.
PROJECT: International Predictions.
METHOD: ERV.
DATE: 2006.
CLIENT: Predictive.
TYPE: Business.

A colleague requested that the Nevada Remote Viewing Group access information using the following tasking, followed by frontloading and a further session with additional questions.

The initial tasking asked: "Please give an overview of events for a designated country (Israel: the name of the country was not given to the viewers) for the next ten years from December 2006, through December 2016. Please give timelines for any perceptions." This was an ambitious future-looking project and it was doubted by the client that this could be done. All the data for this session and the follow-up session were passed "up the chain" of individuals known to the Nevada Remote Viewing Group.

Analysis:

It must be remembered that "blind" sessions are often "noisy" in nature. That is, a lot of personal expectations, extraneous data, telepathic overlay, and other intruding information may be reported including symbolic or figurative wording. Given that the analysis time was short, there were a few interesting correspondences in the data. However, the bulk of this preliminary "blind" tasking is quite dissimilar. Remote viewing experts have noted that the further a date is from the actual occurrence, i.e. doing a viewing of 2016 in 2006, the less accurate it will be. The converse is truer, the closer the viewing to the actual date of an event, the more accurate it will be.

What was perceived from this first session was that 2007 marks a time of upheaval that intensifies by the middle of the year and peaks towards the end of 2007. In 2008, activity quiets down but by the early summer events again begin to escalate. 2009 is a year of very little activity, the economy is good, and this is a "boom" year. However, this is the "calm before the storm." 2010 is marked by disruptions in communications caused by electromagnetic attacks and disruptions in the distribution of food and other resources. There is political upheaval. The year 2011 is a year of anger as the public seeks answers from investors and politicians. By 2012 the people are still angry; there are further disruptions to the food supply; and an introduced disease of crops. In 2013 talks take place to ally the country with other countries for strength and stability. These talks may have something to do with space exploration as a joint effort. In 2014 the public develop their own militias as they feel great mistrust of the government and the military. Russia offers assistance in 2015 and this is accepted despite continued disruptions. Events quiet down in 2016 with fewer disruptions. However, the rest of the world is in turmoil regarding the Middle East.

When this data was given to a political analyst, he reported that the initial data sounded correct and that the potential future data was feasible!

Missing Salt Lake City Teenager.
PROJECT: Missing Salt Lake City Teenager Missing.
METHOD: Controlled Remote Viewing.
DATE: April 2006.
CLIENT: Las Vegas RV Group.
TYPE: Missing Person.
Coordinate: Alpha060605
Team: Advanced Remote Viewing Class/Scotland.

217

In the spring of 2006, Dr. Smith was teaching an Advanced course in Scotland. An urgent email from a colleague in Las Vegas alerted the group to a missing girl. The only information given that she had been missing 36 hours and the case was urgent.

The students were "blind tasked" then given minimal information in order to carry out the project. Their results were emailed to the colleague who passed them on to the parents of the missing girl. Other viewers from different RV groups in different locations also provided data. The viewers provided enough information for the parents to know where their daughter was and who she was with. They were able to collect her and take her home. The viewers had correctly described the location and surroundings, the girl herself and her current location.

Mind's Eye Spy.
PROJECT: Media Outreach.
METHOD: CRV Training.
DATE: May 2006.
CLIENT: Joe Schoenmann, Las Vegas Life.
TYPE: Media.

Public outreach through TV, radio, magazines and newspapers can be a curse or a blessing to remote viewers. Occasionally a reporter will come along that renews our faith in the media. In May 2006, a Las Vegas reporter, Joe Schoenmann, then writing for *Las Vegas Life*, developed an assignment to cover the weird and wonderful world of remote viewing. The outcome of this was a fantastic article titled '*Mind's Eye Spy: One Reporter's Staggering Trip through the Wormhole of Remote Viewing.*'

Joe had done his homework, interviewed many of the key players in the remote viewing field, developed a "Brief Timeline of Remote Viewing History" for his article, and then decided that he might like to try RV training for himself. He writes: If remote viewing is real, then can't a skeptic like myself learn? I call Angela Thompson Smith. A well-known remote-viewing teacher in Boulder City. Maybe she can help me "see" what remote viewing is all about."

Joe Schoenmann relates how he decided to bring a skeptical friend along with him to his first session; the friend Scott thinks that "remote viewing might be excellent fodder for the comic book stories" he is always writing! This comedy continues when Joe and Scott cannot find my house in Boulder City and I must wave them in!

Joe and Scott are surprised at how ordinary my house is: no walls draped in black, no crystal balls, and the fact that I am not wearing any "wizard-like clothing!" Joe adds: "She seems normal, almost motherly. She does one unusual thing, however; she listens."

After an extensive interview by Joe and Scott on the topic of remote viewing we proceeded to the training section of their visit. Working with a photo in a manila folder, bearing the coordinate S23JS032106, I walked Joe through the first stage of Controlled Remote Viewing. Scott waited in the living room outside my office. Joe describes the process: "The process is taxing. I could almost feel the smoke coming out my ears." The target was a building and Joe mentioned "structures," which was a Stage 1 "hit" in CRV terms." Scott "nailed" his third session. Joe reported how Scott felt about this "...He was trying to deny it, trying to rationalize it, trying to think of some other way it could have happened."

On the way back to Las Vegas, Joe kept going over their results in his head, "How could I have done that, where did it come from?" He ruled out coincidence or accident, were the photos pre-planned? He added "None of that was true. I did this thing, well enough, to be convinced that something was happening. Not easy to admit for someone like me, a hard-wired journalist who has spent more than two decades looking at everything with a critical eye for the absolute truth. To admit as much almost seems a negation of not just my career, but, in some ways, who I am." Six years later Joe was to return to interview me about the Denver DJ murder case for the *Las Vegas Sun* newspaper. Missing Actor: Joe Pilcher.

PROJECT: Joe Pilcher.
METHOD: Controlled Remote Viewing.
DATE: June 2006.
CLIENT: RV Referral.
TYPE: Missing Person.
COORDINATE: 060620KP1

Over the years, the Nevada Remote Viewing Group had received requests for assistance with missing person's cases. An example was the case of missing actor Joe Pilcher who disappeared in the northwest. The case was a referral from another remote viewer with the coordinate 060620KPI. Unfortunately, Joe has never been located and may have drowned in Peugeot Sound, according to authorities. He may also have gone to Mexico.

Such is the case with many projects referred to remote viewers. When viewing helps locate and recover an individual, alive and well, that is fantastic! However, much of the time the person is never found or is found dead. This can be especially disturbing when the missing person is an infant or small child. While always keeping hope, the most that viewers can aim for is helping to bring closure to a case.

My background training as a registered nurse and social worker has been a great help when handling missing person's cases, especially when viewing deceased individuals. My advice to viewers wanting to work missing person cases is, expect to be disturbed, frustrated and disappointed. Occasionally, the person is found alive and well, as in the case of a Salt Lake City teenager, this is a cause for celebration but is more it is often the exception. Unfortunately, to date, Joe Pilcher has not been located.

Devil's Hole.
PROJECT: Devil's Hole Crash Site.
METHOD: CRV, ERV, and Site Visit.
DATE: June 21st, 2006.
CLIENT: Wood & Wood Enterprises.
TYPE: Anomalies.
COORDINATE: FSAM.

This interesting case involved a remote project followed by a site visit. A tasking and map were received June 21, 2006 from Wood and Wood Enterprises requesting assistance with a remote viewing project. The target was designated RV Target: FSAM. A remote viewing session and a follow-up assessment of pictures of the site revealed that there had been a crash of a "tangible" at the site and that the tangible was still available to be discovered. Frontloading indicated that a 1949 prospector had witnessed the crash and described the impact. A site visit on Monday and Tuesday, August 21 and 22, 2006 resulted in the discovery of background information related to the prospector, who reported the crash to a newspaper reporter, but no tangible evidence was located at the site.

Himalayan Climbers.
PROJECT: Himalaya Climbers.
METHOD: Controlled Remote Viewing.
DATE: October 2006.
CLIENT: Mexico City Client.
TYPE: Missing Climbers.
COORDINATE: ADR103106
TEAM: Nevada Remote Viewing Group.

A request was received via members of The Monroe Institute discussion list and a client in Mexico City, Mexico in October 2006. The tasking involved two climbers who had gone missing in October in Northern India. The following tasking was given by email to a group of the NRVG remote viewers.

"This is an urgent humanitarian case that we need to turn around quickly as possible. I would like to get as much information back to the client as possible by tomorrow evening, Wednesday, November 1st. We know information about the event but now need information about the location, landmarks etc. So, this is purely a location remote viewing. "Coordinate ADR103106: The target is a location at the current time and date. Please describe the location, landmarks, and any other information that is perceived that might be relevant to this project."

Follow-up Tasking (after initial viewing received):

Four viewers who had responded by Tuesday evening with sessions were sent frontloading as follows, in order to access additional information about the missing climbers.

"Here is some follow-up to the humanitarian project and a request for further information. If you could return this by Wednesday evening, November 1st, 6 p.m. PST, it would be appreciated. The target is the location of two men, climbers, who went missing in Northern India back in mid-October. Our first attempt looked at the location, if you could now check with the men themselves and report any perceptions."

Analysis:

Five viewers responded with data. Several viewers agreed on the following: that the target site was outdoors in a rocky area which tallied with the initial tasking but which the viewers were unaware of. Viewers described a lake, a boating area (possibly now unused) a wooded area, and rocks, a road, and a gas station. Specific landmarks were described: Two of the viewers perceived one or both men having suffered a bloody wound, possibly of an ankle, with one or both experiencing shortness of breath and extreme nausea. One viewer saw both men down in a ravine with one man injured and the other unable to help. It is possible that one or both men succumbed to altitude sickness: shortness of breath and extreme nausea, with one man injured during a spell of bad weather that came through the area. It is the analyst's opinion that at least one of the climbers had perished, possibly both, from altitude sickness after experiencing chest pain, shortness of breath and extreme nausea. This occurred during bad weather. To date, the climbers have not been found.

Being Neighborly.
PROJECT: Being Neighborly.
METHOD: ERV.
DATE: December 2006.
CLIENT: Neighbor Friends.
TYPE: Business.

From time to time, remote viewers can be of assistance to their colleagues and to their friends and neighbors. During 2006, at the beginning of the housing bubble collapse, a close friend and neighbor in Boulder City, NV was considering selling a house in California. She and her husband were beginning to be worried by news of the potential collapse of the housing market and asked for my assistance. When I heard about the potential sale and that my neighbors were prepared to wait until things got better, I had deep-gut feeling that they should sell immediately! They contacted their realtor and were able to make a sale almost immediately – the day following the sale, the house devalued by $100,000!

Later, I was able to assist the husband land his "dream job." In December of 2006 he planned to travel to a very large information services company for an extended interview. There would be a day of interviews with 7 senior managers within the company and my neighbor was very worried about these interviews. Writing down the numbers 1 through 7 on a notepad, I visualized each interview and each interviewer: their gender, their personality and how my neighbor could best handle the interview with each person.

When he returned from his trip, he gave me feedback. It seems that as he went through the interviews, each of the managers matched the information I gave him. The interviews progressed in the order I had written them down and he was able to use my advice to work with each personality and their interview strategy. He got the position!

Sandy Macauley - Engineer
PROJECT: Scottish Missing Person
METHOD: CRV.
DATE: Fall, 2006.
CLIENT: Friend of Family
TYPE: Missing Person.
Coordinate: Unknown
Team: NRVG.

Sandy Macauley's picture shows a laid back, friendly-faced, perhaps a little quiet, and a shy guy. Mr. Macauley was last seen alive on October 1st, 2006 when he went to work at his office at the PURE Energy Center in Unst, in the Shetland Isles. *The Shetland Times*, a year later, Friday 5th October 2007 writes how he went in late and his computer was again accessed at 5 a.m. the following morning on October 2nd, when he then disappeared. There had been no leads on his disappearance.

Sandy Macauley's wife, Jane, wrote how much she missed her husband and how difficult the previous year had been. She believed that he was still alive somewhere. "He's not afraid to say what he believes, and he refuses to accept injustice on either a very small or a very large scale. His humanity and fervent beliefs have touched the lives of many who have known him." Sandy had recently attended an alternative energy conference in Europe. It was reported that the Coastguard and volunteers had searched "unstintingly, the length and breadth" of the isle of Unst but Sandy had not been found.

The Macauley project came via a colleague in the remote viewing field and was first conducted "blind" by three viewers, followed by sessions conducted with minimal frontloading.

The client, a friend of Sandy's wife, gave the group feedback that this project involved a male and was perceived to be a missing person. The client asked "what had happened with this person two months ago on the night of October 1st and the following Monday morning of October 2nd. Was he still alive and what was his current location?"

One of the viewers perceived that the missing male had fallen over a cliff and had died and this was eventually found to be correct. Body parts were eventually dredged up off shore, by a clam boat, and it was deduced that the man's body had been washed out to sea. A thigh bone was subjected to DNA analysis that confirmed the body belonged to Sandy Macauley. Police said that there were no suspicious circumstances leading to the death although Jane Macauley stated to a friend that Sandy knew the cliffs well and could not have fallen over. So, the actual cause of death remains an enigma.

2007

JOURNALS

Journal - April 1, 2007 – *Publishing.*
River of Passion, my new book with Publish America has got to the publishing stage. In mid-February I began the editing process, opting to do it myself rather than leaving it to the publishing house. The first

editing came back with many errors. When the book was type-set all the apostrophes and quotation marks got deleted from the text and these all had to be replaced, by hand. Local friends and colleagues helped proofread and edit the books.

River is now finished with an end of May publications date. Publish America produced a lovely cover which I approved. It combines Stonehenge at sunrise with the River Avon in the foreground. *Shire* hasn't sold well, only 50 copies in the first couple of months of publication. I thought it would be more. I am hoping that, with the publication of *River* that *Shire* will piggy-back and do better.

Journal - April 1, 2007 - *Colombian Children.*

Over the past few years something wonderful has been happening. During the years 1972-1974 I worked as a nurse at the Paraiso Infantil orphanage in Villavicencio, Colombia. During that time over fifty babies and children made their way through the orphanage nursery. Most spent between six months and up to a year there before being adopted by American and European families. I kept in touch with some of the families but, eventually, lost touch with many of them. During the past few years, wonder of wonders, the children, now grown into young adulthood, have been seeking me out. Being a bit of a paper "packrat": journals, letters, and photos from that time, I have been able to provide them with requested information about their time at the orphanage.

Two recent requests are remarkable. The first was young Andrew (orphanage names used) who is now a US soldier, just back from Iraq. I was able to provide him with baby photographs from the orphanage plus other information. He said that he had no photographs of himself as an infant except for his passport photo, and he said he cried when he received the photos and information that I sent to him.

Another is Leah, who arrived at the orphanage after I left. Her mother had been shot in the marketplace and Leah and her two brothers were eventually taken to the orphanage. One of the brothers was adopted by a European family and Leah and her other brother were adopted in the US. Through a series of adventures Leah was re-adopted and found her older brother. This week, Leah, her brothers, and adoptive mother are returning to Villavicencio to find their birth family and to see if the orphanage is still standing. It will be interesting to see what they find and what pictures they will take. They have promised to send copies!

(I received a wonderful photo CD with pictures of the orphanage which is now being used as a Christian school in Villavicencio, Meta,

Colombia. The photo CD and my journals formed the basis for my book Colombia Quest.))

Journal - April 1, 2007 - *Visit to NY 1.*

Over the past year and a half, I have continued to provide consulting services to our financial company sponsor in Manhattan. Most of the projects were "exobiology-communications" related. Also, during this time, we did some work on historical events and monuments including the history of the Sphinx. All these projects kept me financially afloat and the client has indicated that he wants to continue to work with me. We have now gone back to working business-related projects and these will be ongoing for the next few months as the client prepares to sell his business this fall.

The client also has a strong interest in alternative health and is bringing over three practitioners to NY next weekend. He has invited me to participate with them and is flying me out and putting me up in a hotel in NY for the weekend. It will be interesting to see how they work, and I hope to learn from them. The client wants me to work with the German nutritionists on Friday morning and the Hawaiian anatomist on Friday afternoon.

Journal - April 15, 2007 - *NY Visit 2.*

I returned on Saturday to Boulder City after a very interesting trip to NY. The city was very cold as it was still in the grip of winter. We had flurries of snow on Friday morning! I arrived on Thursday evening and met my client and his wife when we went to a beautiful Japanese restaurant for dinner. The food was exquisite: it looked like pieces of oriental art and almost too beautiful to eat!

On Thursday morning I got up early and walked over to the Hotel San Carlos to meet the two German nutritionist/healers: Sabina and Gerlinda. We had a lengthy two-hour consultation about diet and healing which was very helpful. They pronounced that I needed to go off all gluten foods i.e. wheat, rye and oats and to also go off all dairy for three months. I will try this for a few months. When I came home, I switched to goat's milk, cheese, and yogurt (that they recommended) and threw out all my cereals, cow's milk and cheese.

In NY, I also met with the Hawaiian dancer/anatomist Billy May who gave me a series of exercises to do at home involving weights. He was very positive and energetic. The last evening the client, his wife and I went to a great Greek fish restaurant in Manhattan. All the fish was fresh, on display and had been flown in that day from Greece. The food was delicious, and I began my gluten/dairy free lifestyle. I felt energized in New York and had no problems with jet lag or tiredness.

Journal April 15, 2007 - *New York 3.*

On Saturday morning, I met with the client and we traveled over to the Bowery to meet up with Ingo Swann at his residence. Ingo had been reluctant to meet my client, but he was very gracious, and we spent most of the morning with him. The client had extended an invitation to Ingo to meet the German nutritionists, but Ingo declined.

During our visit in Ingo's basement, amid his luminous artworks, Ingo smoked his cheroots and blew smoke everywhere, while we chatted – typical Ingo. My client had taken his copies of Ingo's books over to be signed by Ingo and Ingo gave me two new signed books: *Psychic Sexuality* and *Reality Boxes* that I am looking forward to reading.

Ingo at 74 years old is not a well man. But he keeps going, writing and painting. He told us about a personal problem he was having, and I offered to do a remote viewing for him when I got home. He said he would probably not go to the IRVA Conference this October. The past two years he has been bothered by people who feel that they have a claim to his attention and who follow him around everywhere at the conference. It would be a pity if he didn't attend as has so much wisdom to share. Ingo is still a "crusty curmudgeon" with very decided views of people and society, including the RV and parapsychology fields. He is still alive and kicking!

Journal - Sunday, April 15, 2007 - *Monroe Institute.*

At the beginning of April, a colleague emailed me a copy of a request from the Monroe Institute, searching for a new Executive Director. Many of the skills and training that they are asking about are ones that I have, such as computer knowledge, experience, and knowledge of parapsychology and human consciousness. Many of the additional skills such as public relations, program development etc., I covered at the Senior Center in the UNLV non-profit certification course.

I have asked several professional colleagues for references and plan to work on my application today. I love the east coast, especially Virginia, and don't want to stay in the desert forever. So, I think I will apply and see what happens. If I don't get through the first cut, it will be good experience.

Journal - May 13th, 2007 - *Dr. Ed May's Visit.*

Last weekend, Thursday, Friday, and Saturday, Dr. Ed May was here to conduct a study. He has been collecting subjects from around the southwest and we ran twenty subjects over the three days he was here. Basically, his study is examining the theory that the nervous system can pick up on an unexpected "startle" noise – before the noise is heard.

Subjects were wired up for heart rate and listened to "white noise" over a headset. At random intervals a loud sound was heard over the headset that was designed to create a "startle" response. In some of the previous subjects a slight increase was seen in the heart rate prior to hearing the startle sounds.

It was an interesting three days and I talked at length to Ed about all sorts of things. Ed was manager at SRI's RV group towards the end of its program, then became the manager of SAIC's RV program. Now he has a private laboratory, Laboratories for Fundamental Research (LFR), located in Palo Alto, CA. His colleague Talia Shafir, was also here, but did not come to assist Ed with the study. We had lunch together the day before Ed got here and discovered that we know a lot of people in common.

I think Ed had a good time here and really enjoyed my cats and the local restaurants. It will be interesting to see what his research shows. He has promised to send feedback and charts when he has done his analysis.

(Interestingly, when I asked about this research a year or so ago, I was informed that Ed cut the study short and it was not completed.)

Journal - May 13th, 2007 – *Monroe Institute.*

This past Wednesday I had a telephone interview with the Monroe Institute for the position of Executive Director. The interviewer said he would be putting my name forward to the Board who would be calling people for a telephone interview after the middle of June. This would be a fantastic opportunity and it would be wonderful to live and work with the Monroe group.

Journal - August 2nd, 2007 – *Rancho La Puerta.*

Where did the spring and summer go? It's August already and we are over the halfway mark through the summer. The south-west has been in a drought but now we are in the monsoon period with rain and thunderstorms most afternoons.

The position at the Monroe Institute is still in the works. After a successful telephone interview and a request for more written information I was told that my name had been forwarded to the Board. On the grapevine I have been told that the job won't be filled until September and the top five candidates will be called for an interview prior to that. I had been putting off taking a vacation but finally decided in June to travel for a week to Rancho La Puerta in Mexico from the 4-11 August. This will be my first vacation in several years and I am looking forward to it.

My major client has continued to give me more projects, but we are now doing mainly business-related work rather than the anomalies investigations. He has continued to challenge my RV skills and abilities with some fascinating projects.

Journal - August 29th, 2007 – *Mexico.*

It is almost the end of August and this month has gone quite quickly. The highlight of the month was a trip south of the border to Rancho La Puerta in Tecate, Mexico. It was a wonderful week of organic meals, birds and flowers, lovely weather, meeting interesting people, meditation, hikes, water exercise, drumming, massages, writing classes, evening lectures and many other activities. I had a little house in Los Arboles: "The Woods," which was very private and secure. Although I was quite active, I didn't lose any weight, but I did lose inches and gained muscle. It was a wonderful experience.

I still haven't heard anything from the Monroe Institute regarding a follow-up interview and it will be almost four months since I first inquired. I will wait until September 1st, then will contact the TMI recruiter to see what is happening.

Journal – November 21, 2007 – *Thanksgiving.*

I have been making plans to move back to England: probably for a short six-months stay, possibly for longer. I have had this question in my mind, where do I want to retire? I am already getting a small monthly pension from England and, next spring, I will be eligible for Social Security. This will not be a lot to live on, but my client wants to continue working with me for a couple more years.

CASE FILES – 2007

Location of Daniel Perl.
PROJECT: Location of Daniel Perl.
METHOD: ERV.

DATE: September 27th, 2007.
CLIENT: DOJ   Contact.
TYPE: Missing Person.

Daniel Perl was an American journalist who had been kidnapped while working as the South Asia Bureau Chief of the Wall Street Journal and based in Mumbai, India. He was abducted in Pakistan where he had gone to investigate possible links between Richard Reid (the "shoe lace bomber") and Al-Qaeda. Unfortunately, he was killed by his capturers before he could be located and rescued. The remote viewing of this event produced sketches that matched the location where Pearl was being held captive before his death.

Lost at Sea.
PROJECT: Lost at Sea.
METHOD: Controlled Remote Viewing.
DATE: 2007.
CLIENT: Colleague.
TYPE: Missing Person.
COORDINATE: NAW7/1/07
TEAM: Nevada Remote Viewing Group.

The following case was received from a colleague who was coordinating work on this unsolved case. It was hoped that new data might shed some light on the matter.

The following tasking was first given "blind" to a small group of remote viewers, under coordinate NAE 7/1/07, and then followed with frontloading as follows: "This cold case involves the disappearance of two men and the teenage son of one of the men. They went fishing off the coast of Florida. The boat was found capsized on the coast of Florida with many unusual features regarding its eventual location and circumstances. One man was found dead in a small cabin while the other man and his son are still missing. The family of the missing man and son are seeking closure regarding the event and their whereabouts, particularly of the son. Any remote viewed information would be appreciated."

All the data plus the viewers' sketches were forwarded, first to the colleague and then on to the family. To date, the case remains open and unsolved. The family contacts me from time to time desperately asking for additional information. I must tell them that nothing more has been perceived. It is presumed that the father and son were lost at sea.

JOURNALS

Letter send out to clients, students, friends and colleagues.

2008 saw the relocation of Dr. Angela Thompson Smith and the Nevada Remote Viewing Group (NRVG) to the United Kingdom and the temporary renaming of the organization to The Wessex Remote Viewing Group (WRVG). After 27 years living and working in the United States and many years carrying out remote viewing in the US, it was time to "come home." The WRVG is currently located in the south of England and continues to carry out remote viewing consulting, research and writing.

Dr. Smith also continues to carry out consulting work for our long-term financial client and this coming spring marks the 6th year of our collaboration. We continue to thank our patron for his continued interest in remote viewing applications and research. Working with him has inspired a renewed interest in longevity, healthy living, and an understanding of metabolism, nutrition and exercise which prompted a summer of water aerobics, water Tai Chi and swim.

One of the highlights of the year was receiving feedback on the finding of Steve Fossett's light aircraft which sadly crashed after taking off from Reno, NV. Last year several remote viewers participated in a real-time Google Earth TURK session to scan segments of the southwest desert for signs of the downed plane. Using intuitive methods several of us scanned around and provided coordinates for locations which we perceived as the location of the downed plane. (I felt that Fossett had a heart attack or stroke in the air and this is what caused his plane to crash). His body was found with the plane debris and his personal papers had scattered and were found by hikers. The coordinates of the crash site and the coordinates provided by me and other viewer were within 50 miles of the crash. While not on-target, if the search had been extended to these farther coordinates, there remains the possibility that the plane and Fossett's body could have been found sooner.

January was the beginning of sorting belongings and packing boxes for storage prior to shipping in August and this process was nostalgic but very freeing as many items were given away, sold, shredded, or given to charity. At the end of April, I paid a preliminary visit to the UK to look at potential places to relocate and settled on the market town of Wimborne, Dorset in the south of England. I lived there in my teens and twenties and trained as a nurse at nearby Poole Hospital, so I know and feel comfortable with the location. There is also a strong interest in remote viewing and similar interests here in the south. This area was once the great Kingdom of Wessex and this inspired the change of name to the Wessex Remote Viewing Group (WRVG).

While I was visiting the UK in the spring, I located the Bucklewell (a sacred cave and spring) in my home village of Shirehampton, Bristol and paid a visit. I wrote about this sacred spring in my novel *River of Passion*. During 2007, I continued to attend the Boulder City Writers Round Table and found a similar writing group in Wimborne, Dorset called the Cotton Spinners.

The NRVG carried out a couple of remote viewing courses in the US over the past year: CRV in Houston, TX and Boulder City, NV, and the RV Advanced Course in Boulder City and at Loch Lomond in Scotland. November saw a class meeting in Wimborne for a CRV course at the Allendale Center however CRV training courses have been put on hold over the winter.

In 2008 I began putting together materials for a new book which goes beyond *The Secret* and *Intention*, adding new factors and dimensions needed to create our desired lives. We go through life allowing other people, groups and events to shape our lives instead of creating our own reality. I will be working on this over the coming year.

In February, I traveled to Molokai, HI with Elder Hostel to learn about the culture, food, dance, customs, language and many other aspects of Hawaiian life. While on Molokai we visited Father Damien's leper colony (now Hansen's disease) which was both tragic and beautiful. Several of us experienced intuitive "flashbacks" to life as it was in those hard, early days.

Remote viewing projects over the year included: business, real estate evaluations, crypto-history, anomalies, and continued projects for our main client.

Talks were given for podcasts and radio: for a New York Arts Magazine program in July, for the BBC's Radio Bristol program in October, and for the Salisbury, UK TAG folk in November.

New projects for the coming year include the possibility of participating in a TV series of how intuitives solve real-life problems with innovative tools such as remote viewing. There is also the possibility of taking part in parapsychology research and becoming involved with remote viewing groups already established in the UK, such as the Loch Lomond group.

The Ark of the Covenant – 2.
PROJECT: The Ark of the Covenant 2.
METHOD: CRV/ERV.
DATE: February 15th, 2008.
CLIENT: Colleague.
TYPE: Historical Enigma.
COORDINATE: NAW7/1/07
TEAM: Nevada Remote Viewing Group.

A project was requested from a senior colleague on February 15th, 2008. The Nevada Remote Viewing Group was polled and 5 viewers, including myself took part in this project. The tasking was the "Current Location of the Ark of the Covenant per coordinates" – No analysis has been performed on these sessions to date. Viewers were tasked "blind" on an event and a location. There did not seem to be any concordance between the viewers on this project except that the target felt like a remote location, very much like a desert.

The Bucklewell.
PROJECT: Search for the Bucklewell.
METHOD: ERV & Physical Search.
DATE: 2008.
CLIENT: Independent.
TYPE: Archaeological.

The Bucklewell is an ancient cave and sacred spring located in the village of Shirehampton in Bristol, England. Bubbling up from the dirt floor the spring has flowed within the limestone overhang for thousands of years. Perhaps it was there in Neolithic times and served as a freshwater source for the local people. It was there, when the Romans occupied Britain as the remains of a Roman altar are reported to be located nearby. Over the centuries the spring gained a reputation as a source of healing waters, specifically for maladies of the eyes. Excavations of the land on the top of the cave revealed small holes or pits in the rock, maybe for offerings, and a small owl statue, gazing out over the River Avon flowing below the cave.

Growing up in Shirehampton, I had heard about the Bucklewell, but nobody knew where it was. Some villagers remembered that there were several natural springs around the village. One in the vicarage grounds was said to be a warm spring causing the horse chestnut trees nearest the Tithe Barn to burst into leaf well before its neighbors. There was another spring, a cold one that flowed through the basement of the Life Boat, a local pub, and kept the beer cold before refrigeration. There were rumors that the Bucklewell spring flowed under Station Road and could be accessed through a manhole. On Shirehampton Golf Course, another spring would fill up a small pond where kids fished for tadpoles and stickleback, small colorful fish. The pond was eventually filled in when locals started dumping trash into the waters. However, as a child and young person growing up in Shire, I never knew where the actual Bucklewell was, but it always intrigued me.

A childhood friend told me how her father would take a clean pillowcase and collect watercress that grew in the waters flowing out of the cave. She said that the cave was situated overlooking the river, below an allotment: land rented from the local Council for growing fruits and vegetables. During WWII, locals dug out the cave to increase the flow of water that was used to water the gardens above. So, the cave was a reality and I wanted to see it.

Finally, in the mid-1990s, I visited England for an extended vacation and began seriously looking for the Bucklewell. After a few false starts and disappointments, I heard about a Bristol historian who had built a replica of an ancient Round House on a small meadow near the allotments and had been excavating the site. Paul Worrilow is a pleasant, knowledgeable fellow and my guide to the Bucklewell – and, wow, I finally got to visit!

Interestingly, I had written about the Bucklewell in my historical novel, *River of Passion*, and even though I had never seen it, it was just as I had visualized it! *River of Passion* was based on the actual history of the village of Shirehampton, but the stories were mostly remote viewed. Climbing down the dirt bank to the well I had a great sense of déjà vu and touching the stone of the cave was a thrill.

Paul brought his sheepdog, Lucky, down to the well and Lucky began digging in the soft, wet dirt at the mouth of the cave. Lucky unearthed a small glass bottle that Paul told me might have been used to hold the sacred waters. My ancestors can be traced back, at least five hundred years in the area, and I wondered if one of them had once owned the bottle. When I returned to the States, I got on the Internet and learned that such bottles were often called "witch bottles": they contained wishes and prayers and often small items such as human hair and nail clippings. My bottle only contained mud but was greatly treasured. Such a magical visit!

While I was visiting the well, I learned that, in the past, the waters were said to having healing abilities, especially for eye maladies. I have had severe myopia and astigmatism since childhood, and I took the opportunity to splash some of the water on my eyes. Before I returned to England the following year, I needed my eyeglasses replaced. Whether as a result of the spring water or not, my vision had improved by one diopter, a fair improvement!

Bucklewell Field.
PROJECT: Bucklewell Field.
METHOD: CRV/ERV.
DATE: 2008.
CLIENT: Paul Worrilow.
TYPE: Archaeological Exploration.
COORDINATE: 051008JP.
TEAM: Nevada Remote Viewing Group.

Another field at the side of the Bucklewell excavations looked interesting and Paul Worrilow speculated that it might contain something interesting (when he gets around to digging there). He suggested that some remote viewers take a "look" at the field and what lies beneath. So, I tasked several viewers as well as taking a "look" myself, even though I was fully front-loaded, that is, I had knowledge of the field already, its location and top appearance. What I was looking for lay under the surface.

The viewers were minimally frontloaded: "If you would like to try your hand at an archaeological project i.e. a piece of land that has remained undisturbed for many hundreds of years, here is your chance to look at something "hidden." Feedback may take a couple of years to unfold or it may never happen, but it's worth trying. Attached is a picture for those of you who prefer frontloading. If you do not want frontloading do not scroll down and do not click on the attached picture."

"The best way to tackle this project would be to divide a landscape-oriented 8x10 piece of paper into a grid i.e. 10 x 8 one-inch squares and look at what lies underneath, looking at layers under the surface. There will be some limited feedback regarding what is currently known about the location, but other feedback will have to wait until there is an archaeological dig at the site. This is purely a humanitarian project and done as a donation to the young archaeologist working the site. Please let me know if you are undertaking this project. The coordinate is 051008JP"

As I already knew what was located underneath the adjoining piece of land i.e. the Buckle Well, and what the top looked like, I focused on what might be found directly under the top layer of grass and dirt in

234

the adjoining field. I perceived light-colored, oblong stones with an unusual design. These were seen to have several bands of lines circling the squared ends, with longer lines connecting the encircling bands of lines, on several sides. These were perceived to be Roman in origin. Also stacks of rounded rocks on top of each other were perceived to be under the grass. Also perceived were lines or rows of rounded, boulder-type rocks, extending from the river inland. I also perceived a lower jaw but probably of a dog, ox, or other animal, rather than human. Then, over in the center right of the field, evidence of habitation was perceived with carbon from round fires and pottery shards. Also, a round circle of rounded stones was perceived in this area. Probably river rocks rather than from inland. The pottery shards in this area were perceived to have very faint patterns of bands and circles.

The team perceived other information about the site. One viewer, a man who had trained with me wrote: "The target is perceived to be a landscape, unused now but prior multiple inhabitants. Target site feels very old. Target is perceived to be a landscape containing multiple manmade structures located underground ranging in depths of 3 ½ feet to more than 40 feet. Target is perceived to have been inhabited numerous times. Six distinct habitation periods are perceived: 1700 AD, 1500 AD, 900 and 500 AD, 400 BCE, and 900 BCE (Dates are approximate +- 50 years)."

Another of my viewer students wrote that she perceived activities at the site in its historical past: women working, they had dowries and there was silver hidden near the river bank under a structure. There was evidence of bead making and other crafts. She reported that the group of women who lived at the site were small and smart and self-sufficient (maybe the men were away fighting); they had secrets and pretended to be something they were not. They were doing trades that women didn't usually do. They were prepared, educated and wealthy. They had trades such as tanning, metalwork and weaving. They kept to themselves, being distrusting of others and raised animals: chickens and oxen. The women pretended to be poor (probably to avoid robbery and pillage) and took care of their own.

She also reported that she perceived a structure with rafters which sounded like an Anglo-Saxon or earlier architecture, but she may have perceived Paul's Round House nearby. Inside the structure were iron hooks for cooking pots, a fire pit and dirt floor. She perceived land, irrigation and crops grown in rows but, again, she may have perceived the nearby allotments or much earlier strips of land farmed by serfs.

JOURNALS

Written for clients, students, friends and colleagues.

2009 was a year of change, of turmoil, of moving and eventual resettlement almost back to the point where I started in September of 2008. The early part of 2009 I was still in the UK and deciding if I wanted to ride out the very cold winter in the south of England or return to the warmth of Boulder City, Nevada (or indeed what to do with the rest of my life)! I had many adventures during my six months in the UK visiting historic towns, sacred sites, the ocean, the countryside and I met some wonderful new friends. I gave some local talks and an interview for the BBC on remote viewing, conducted an ERV course at Loch Lomond, Scotland, and continued doing consulting work for my private and corporate clients.

I eventually decided to move back to the US, had my belongings shipped and I arrived back in Nevada in the middle of February. Once I arrived there were a series of moves: a friend's guesthouse for a few nights, a small sublet on Avenue C for a few weeks, a duplex with a pool for almost a year on Avenue B, then I was offered the tenancy of my old cottage on 5th Street and I moved back there the beginning of December, 09. I feel as if I have come "home."

In the UK I attended a weekly creative writing group, The Cotton Spinners, and learned a great deal about many different writing genres that I decided to share with my US colleagues by starting up a creative writing group at the Boulder City library. I've learned so much, too, in preparing the weekly topics. In November I attended writing workshops at Rancho La Puerta in Tecate, Mexico and came back with many ideas for a new novel based on my early years in Colombia, South America. (Currently published as *Colombia Quest.*)

When I returned to the US, I found that there were some restrictions on holding classes at my home office and I decided to rent a small office in Boulder City. At the same time, I realized that, because of the faltering economy, I needed a way to put my education and experience to professional use and began training as a life coach. My new business Mindwise Consulting, in the Hyde Business Center, offers consultation on a wide range including remote viewing training.

Some of the consulting and research highlights for the year have been participation in a remote viewing project for a Virology Laboratory in Colorado (assessing sick from healthy plants) and a DARPA Balloon Challenge (perceiving the location of ten large balloons across the continental US). The virology project was a success, but I did dismally on the balloon challenge. I have concluded that I am a pretty decent remote viewer but do not do well with dowsing!"

CASE FILES - 2009

Plant Virology Study.
PROJECT: Plant Virology.
METHOD: Binary RV.
DATE: 2009.
CLIENT: Morse/Van Atta.
TYPE: Research.

A research study entitled *A Triple Blind Study of the Non-Local Perception of Plants Infected with the Tobacco Mosaic Virus* was recently written up by Dr. Melvin Morse and his colleagues. In the study remote viewers attempted to identify sick plants from healthy plants. Project Manager, Mike Van Atta emailed tasking sessions, consisting of groups of coordinates. Some of the plants were later found to be healthy, some sick, and the viewers perceptions were compared to the plant findings.

As the protocols became more refined and controlled, it was found that viewers could indeed correctly identify sick plants from healthy plants. I volunteered to participate in this study and was able to correctly identify 80% of the sick plants in one trial and 100% in another trial.

An innovative approach was taken towards the end of the trials. The researchers provided two extra coordinates (case numbers) connected to two plants: one known to be sick and one known to be healthy, for the viewers to get a "feel" for the plants' health. (These plants were not in the actual study.) I feel that this really helped the viewers get "on signal line" to correctly identify the sick plants.

Rather than use Associative Remote Viewing (ARV) or some other complex viewing method, I decided to use the Ideogram feature from the Controlled Remote Viewing (CRV) protocol, where the viewer makes a short doodle or drawing after writing the coordinate. If the Ideogram went up at the end, I judged the plant healthy, if it went down, it indicated a sick plant. This seemed to work as well as ARV. Interestingly, it was reported that the plants that had been identified as sick were found to begin to recover after being given attention during the study!

Time for a Swim.
PROJECT: Time for a Swim.
METHOD: Remote Action.
DATE: 2009.
CLIENT: Independent.
TYPE: Independent.

Between 2002 and 2009 I continued to give occasional classes in remote viewing to interested individuals and groups. One class included a couple of very-reserved, older ladies who were excited about learning intuitive ways of accessing information. As well as covering many of the straightforward aspects of remote perception we explored topics of time and space and energy – they had curious minds!

At the end of a successful training week, the ladies invited me to their motel, overlooking the Lake Mead-side of Boulder City to spend the evening and to swim. We arrived about five o'clock and from their balcony we saw that the pool was occupied by a group of very rowdy teenage boys. The ladies were upset and said that, no way, could they go down to swim with the boys there. I felt that there must be some way to change the situation and figured there was enough justification to use remote influence.

The boys' noisy and boisterous behavior was causing other families to avoid using the pool and several groups turned away from enjoying the water. I told the ladies that I would sit on their balcony for a while and let them know when it was OK to go down to swim. Then, I thought about what teenage boys wanted: fast food like pizza and hamburgers, beer and girls. Following this line of thought I then started repeating a mental mantra which went somewhat like this: "Boy, it's so boring here, I could just eat a slice of pizza, washed down with a can of cold beer, bet there would be girls there too, I'm so hungry, or a hamburger with all the fixings, would be just right, that would be great." Gradually, over the next few minutes, the boys started packing up their towels and putting on their shoes and leaving the pool area.

One young man stayed behind, lying on a lounger and was not making any effort to leave. So, I focused on him and repeated mentally "It's so boring now they have left, bet they're having a good time. I'm so hungry, I bet they are having hamburgers, pizza, beer, meeting girls" and after a few minutes he got up and left, too. I called to the ladies that the pool was empty, and we could swim!

Mind-to-mind communication is a little understood area of human consciousness and denied by conventional psychology. Remote influence (RI) has been given a little attention in the parapsychology literature but only barely touched on.

2010

JOURNALS

Shamanic Ordination.

In 2010, I decided to become a shamanic minister in order to create a fusion of all my experience and training under one organization. After much paperwork and waiting, I was ordained as a shamanic minister with *The Circle of the Sacred Earth* located in Massachusetts. Until I began looking back at my personal understanding and education in shamanism, I had not fully realized what a wonderful path I had taken. It is often in retrospect that we see the wholeness of our experience. While I had already been sharing my skills with my community, I wanted to take things to the next level and become a more effective practitioner of shamanism.

Background.

I am an Englishwoman, born and raised in the Avalon counties of Somerset and Gloucester and aware, from a very young age, of the mysteries of nearby ancient sites such as Stonehenge and Avebury. From early childhood I felt a deep connection to the Earth, to the countryside, the stones and rocks, springs, caves, trees, the seasons, herbs, wildlife and ancient traditions. In my childhood I had a wonderful teacher who taught me the names and uses of British wildflowers and herbs and I knew that the Earth was a living entity.

My life has been a continuous spiritual quest, exploring Buddhism and Christianity, but always coming back to the ways of the Earth. As a young child I had Out-of-Body Experiences (OBEs) which my family dismissed as imagination, but which have continued to the present. At first my spiritual journeys were spontaneous, but I learned to direct them to specific places. In my twenties I learned that not everyone has these experiences and I sought to understand them through study and exploration. Now I teach these abilities to others.

What is Shamanism?

Shamanism is a term referring to a range of beliefs and practices regarding communication with the spirit world. A practitioner of shamanism is known as a shaman and the practices most often promoted by shamans are; drumming/rattling and dancing to facilitate healing and journeying, interpretation of dreams, and the practice of divination. Shamanism encompasses the belief that shamans are intermediaries or messengers between the human world and the spirit worlds. Shamans are said to treat ailments/illness by "mending" the soul: alleviating traumas affecting the soul/spirit restores the physical body of the individual to balance and wholeness. The shaman also enters supernatural realms or dimensions to obtain solutions to problems afflicting the community. Shamans may visit other worlds/dimensions to bring guidance to misguided souls and to ameliorate illnesses of the human soul. The shaman operates primarily within the spirit world, which in turn affects the human world.

What is a Shamanic Minister?

A shamanic minister provides "direct spiritual revelation" through shamanic journeying and ritual and offers spiritual healing, counseling and training. Ministers can officiate at weddings, funerals, rites of passage and adoption ceremonies after registering with the state. Additional duties can include cleansing, clearing and dedicating homes, land and work spaces. Most shamanic ministers are also registered with non-profit training organizations. Many have primary training in conventional caring professions such as doctors and nurses, social workers, physiotherapists, and psychologists.

A shamanic minister has the same responsibilities, rights and duties as a minister of any other belief system except that the shamanic minister has access to many different resources and practices. Shamanic ministers accept and respect other religions and often incorporate spiritual leaders of these belief systems into their rituals: for example, Jesus of Nazareth, the Holy Spirit, and Buddha. A shamanic minister relies on an array of spiritual animal guides and other helpers to help provide healing, mediation, leadership, and assistance with preserving traditions and ceremonies within their community.

Community.

Community has always been important to me, from my teens onwards: training as a nurse and social worker, a psychologist and as director of a senior center has allowed me to be in contact and of service to others. Since childhood, I have always been a seer: having the ability to discern, empathize and understand others on a spiritual level. I now use this ability in humanitarian work: for example, in missing persons work, disasters, and conflict resolution.

Healing.

As a nurse and social worker, the ability to heal has always been important to me. During training as a registered nurse, I would quietly use my healing abilities to augment those of the medical profession, especially when they had given up on a patient and especially if that patient was a child. Early on, I learned that not everyone could perceive as I did, and I understood the ethics and responsibilities of such abilities.

Divination.

Rune casting has been an important part of my spiritual path. I encountered the runes in 1980, in England, and first learned a Saxon futhark or alphabet. Five years later I encountered the writings of Rune Master Ralph Blum. Several years of practice assured me of the benevolent and guiding qualities of the runes when used as a divination and decision-making instrument. A few years later, in 1986, I learned the Goddess runes from Dr. P. M. H. Atwater and began making personal runes from special stones that I collected from all parts of the world. It is a privilege to carry on the craft of rune casting and to pass these teachings on to others.

How did it all start?

My training in animism and shamanic practice began, at first unofficially, in New Jersey where I joined local drumming and spirit journeying groups. In 1990 my studies took me to Saybrook Graduate School, and I was very fortunate to have the opportunity to study with incredible teachers. Courses relevant to shamanism included: dream analysis work with Dr. Stanley Krippner and drumming workshops with Ruth-Inge Heinze, interviews with folk mystic Vasily Vasilyevech Nalimov in Moscow, Russia, as well as graduate-level credit courses in healing touch, the psychology of shamanism and the psychology of Out Of-Body-Experiences. I attended Dr. Hank Wesselmann and Jill Kuykendall's *Spirit Medicine: Vision Seeker* workshops at Esalen Institute and Westerbeke Ranch in CA and plan to continue my training with them.

Experiencing Journeying.

One of the most amazing journeys occurred during a drumming workshop with shamanic teacher Ruth-Inge Heinze in California. (Ruth-Inge has since transitioned to the spirit world.) During the workshop, Ruth-Inge beat a small copper bowl in a 4-per-second beat designed to create an altered state conducive to journeying. As she walked around the group, we relaxed on the floor with cushions and blankets and entered our journeys. At first, nothing seemed to happen – it takes about 10 to 15 minutes to enter an altered state – then I became an Eagle! Flying over wooded forests I followed a river until it poured over a huge waterfall. Swooping down over the falls I felt the spray, the wind through my feathers and heard the roaring of the waterfall. Tiring, I settled on a branch and ruffled my feathers, feeling my talons gripping the tree, and rearranging every feather right down to my tail. At that point the copper bowl beat slowed, and we were brought back to full consciousness. I had become an eagle in every aspect. It was awesome!

On another journey, led by Ruth-Inge, I found myself sitting cross-legged, a young boy Initiate in an ashram. I was probably around 9 or 10 years old and I understood that I could not move, speak or cough until the session was over. As I sat cross-legged in meditation, a fly landed on the young initiate's nose! There was no way that I could brush the fly away, I was not allowed to move a muscle. So, I tolerated the fly, letting it crawl around my face until it flew away to bother someone else. I was so happy for this small comfort of not having a fly on my face that I felt completely at peace.

What Next?

Being a modern shaman in our scientific, skeptical, and religious society is not an easy path to take. To the scientists I offer my academic credentials, to the skeptics I offer my lab results, and to the religious I offer 1 Corinthians 12: 1-11 – from the Holy Bible: The Gifts of the Spirit. It is a path I have taken with joy, conviction and enthusiasm. In keeping with modern practice, I offer my shamanic training and experience under the category of spiritual/transformational coaching within the umbrella of my life coaching business Mindwise Consulting. I make no secret of my shamanic training which has been readily accepted by my clients. Life is a great adventure and I am excited to see where the path next takes me.

CASE FILES – 2010

Hotel Montana, Haiti.
PROJECT: Hotel Montana, Haiti.
METHOD: CRV/ERV.
DATE: January 12, 2010.
CLIENT: Las Vegas RV Group/DH.

TYPE: Missing Persons.
TEAM: NRVG.

January 2010 saw a tremendously destructive earthquake in Portau-Prince, Haiti. Caught in the ruins were two humanitarian workers who were visiting the Hotel Montana. The hotel collapsed around them and their families were desperate for news, especially the family of Walt Ratterman.

Walt's family contacted remote viewers in Las Vegas who then contacted viewers all over the United States. Our group provided information that led the family to believe that Walt had been in the middle of the hotel, descending a concrete staircase, when the quake hit. The viewers pinpointed the location as well as significant landmarks such as helicopter landing pads (large red Xs) and a large tree in the middle of the hotel grounds.

There was also information describing the second humanitarian worker and the belief that they had both succumbed to their injuries. Their bodies were later found in the general area pinpointed by the viewers. At the IRVA Conference 2012 it was a pleasure to meet Walt's widow, Jean Ratterman, who had come to the venue to thank the viewers.

Feedback.

At the 2012 IRVA Conference at Green Valley Ranch Resort, NV, I was approached by two delightful ladies; one of them introduced herself as Jean Ratterman, the widow of Walt Ratterman. She had read the introduction to my IRVA talk that mentioned the Haiti Earthquake. She had come to the conference specifically to thank us! I explained that not all the viewers were at the conference, but I would share her thanks. I was deeply touched that she should travel across the country to talk to us.

I asked her several questions during lunch. The first being "Was our assistance helpful?" She confirmed that not only was our work useful, but it gave her and her family assurance that there were people supporting them: physically, emotionally, and spiritually.

Mrs. Ratterman asked why we had suddenly stopped sending data later in the search? I explained that we had been asked to "stand down," at the request of the family. "This was not so," she said, and the request probably came from the search organizers. The viewer data was especially needed, she added, towards the latter part of the search. Every remote viewing project is a learning experience.

2011

JOURNALS

<u>Journal - January 1, 2011 – *New Year Resolutions.*</u>
Today is the first day of a new year and another new beginning. I don't like to make New Year Resolutions but plan on continuing my daily goals:
- Learn something new every day.
- Do something new every day.
- Help at least one person every day.

I also brought in a new credo this past year that I try to live by: "I see you, I hear you, I understand you, and I love you!"

This credo does not mean we have to be involved in everyone's lives. We can choose the people in our lives and can also exclude those who are detrimental to our growth and development. Being raised a Christian I was taught to include everyone and subsume any feelings of dislike for some people. I now know that I can feel compassion and caring without sacrificing my own values, ideas and spiritual

244

development. At age 64, I have finally accepted that I do not have to allow family to manipulate me and make me feel bad if I didn't do what they wanted or felt was their due as family members. I can choose people in my life who contribute love, caring, light and sharing.

Journal - January 11, 2011 – *Spring.*
I walked to town and noticed that small daffodils, called narcissus, are already in bloom, even though the nights have been dipping into the 30s and we have had bitter winds blowing down from the Sierra Mountains. There is snow on the mountain tops and flowers in the town! My friend, Barbara, told me yesterday that despite the cold weather, her lavender is still blooming and being visited by humming birds. Where do these tiny birds roost at night and how do they survive the freezing nights?

During August and September 2011, several work opportunities materialized but, just as quickly, disappeared. One of my late summer students wanted to arrange several remote viewing courses on the Australian Gold Coast for October of this year. We put an ad in the Australian magazine, Nexus, and put a deposit on rooms at the Magic Mountain, a Gold Coast resort but we didn't get enough students to cover the expenses, so sadly we had to cancel the event.

Then, I was put in touch with a paramilitary training group in Las Vegas that offers training to police, the military and the public. We worked on developing and presenting a course on tactical remote viewing. The organizer put together a dramatic video for his website but, once again, there were too few students signed up for the course.

Unfortunately, one of the military leaders of the original remote viewing projects called up the paramilitary training group and convinced them that remote viewing could not be used for tactical work. This created a situation where it was impossible to move forward with this project, even if we had students ready to sign up!

At the end of November, I heard from my longtime business client that he was finishing up our business arrangement and closing out the retainer that he had graciously sent for several years. So, 2012 will be a year of searching for new job prospects.

Aesthetic Impact Webinars.
In 2011, Teresa Frisch, ER Nurse and Remote Viewing Manager, initiated a series of Webinars through WebEx and asked if I would contribute several series. Between July 15th, 2011 and November 18th, 2011, I gave PowerPoint presentations and answered questions on the following topics: Out-of-Body Experiences (OBEs); History and

Evolution of the Study of Parapsychology; Cultural Series I: Reading the Rune Stones; Symbology as a Language; Cultural Series II: Shamanism – The Respected Practitioner; Psychokinesis (PK) and Anomalous Perturbation; Telepathy: Uncommonly Common Experiences; Human Consciousness; and Meditation Methods. The talks have gained interest from a wide audience and are available on Teresa's Aesthetic Impact website and YouTube.

CASE FILES – 2011

Predictive Notes.
PROJECT: 2011 to 2017.
METHOD: ERV.
DATE: 2010-2011.
CLIENT: Business Client.
TYPE: Predictive.

We are living in difficult times: worldwide financial crisis, chaotic weather patterns that cause displacement and poverty, rumors and fears that paralyze action, repression of independent thought, and a lowering of expectations and aspirations. What can we look forward to? Will society, worldwide, continue to deteriorate or is there some hope for the future.

The major problem that the world (and particularly the US) will have to face is the "denial of entitlement." Over the past fifty or so years the US has been a leader in a certain type of lifestyle that has practically been guaranteed to even poor families. This "entitlement" has assumed that the comfortable lifestyle that has been enjoyed by many will continue indefinitely, even in the face of impending change. This expectation of a certain lifestyle has been copied around the world, particularly among the younger generations. This has led to whole generations now facing hard times that have no idea how to be adaptive or resilient.

The words "imaginative, inspired, inventive, resourceful, ingenious, and innovative" have no meaning for whole groups of young people. If you asked them what these words meant they would give you examples of inventors and pioneers from the past, rather than current examples. There has been a steady decline in innovative thinking, discovery and invention with many people thinking "by rote" rather than with their whole brain/mind. Unless this changes, the country and the world are weakened and will continue to decline.

So, what can we do now to cope? When I first came to the States in 1981, I quickly realized that Americans are free to say, do and be whoever they want as long as they have a permit, a license, an authorization, a certificate, or other endorsement which has been granted by some governing body for which a fee has been paid. In fact, I soon realized that local, city, state and national economies relied greatly on these permissions and regularly update and modify these sanctions of public behavior and belief.

I also realized that it did not matter what kind of person you were, you could usually obtain an authorization for some activity or behavior through filling out the necessary forms and paying the fee. Personal integrity, intelligence or reliability are not usually factors in the granting of permission.

As we go through the changes brought about by natural and civic events over the next decade, there will need to be a rise in innovative thinking to deal with new situations. How this will happen is unclear but will probably occur through the appearance of speakers and thinkers who will, at first, be decried and denied but who will later be New Thinkers for a New Era.

Following are some predictions that I generated for my client around 2011:

2011

Nothing much changes, there continues to be a steady negative decline in the economy, loss of homes and loss of jobs. The future is anybody's guess, and nobody seems to take responsibility or want to make any changes. There is the potential for change but there is an ennui and lack of interest in change.

2012

There is a feeling that the country is defenseless yet strong which seems a contradiction in terms but brings about some major changes. Local, city and state governments are given greater leeway to govern and most people are happy about these changes. Central government does not seem to have as much authority as it has in the past.

2013

There is a greater cooperation between local, city and state governments across the country resulting in a net-like governing pattern rather than the tree branch-like pattern of the past. There seems to be greater communication across the country and more involvement by individuals in the running of the country.

2014

Despite some major problems with mass communications and travel most people view these changes as necessary to bring about change and reform. Most people are willing to put up with a certain amount of disruption for things to change.

2015

A feeling of strength, the country is stronger yet not richer, as resources are poured into rebuilding and refinancing what has been broken down. It is perceived that the average individual and family have less than they had five years ago but are stronger and happier than they had been. There is a sense of hope for the future and a rebuilding of the country.

2016

There is a rebuilding taking place with individuals adapting to new conditions with new ideas. There is reform in the air despite a lack of resources and leadership. Centralized education seems to have changed to smaller groups spread out over communities with everyone giving time and effort to rebuilding.

2017

Many projects are coming to fulfillment and completion and new initiatives are being taken. There is more personal responsibility and less reliance on centralized government. There is a sense of hope for the future.

Possible Human Trafficking Case.
PROJECT: Missing Girl from Highway I8o.
METHOD: CRV and ERV.
DATE: September 10, 2011.
CLIENT: RK.
TYPE: Missing Persons.
TEAM: NRVG.
COORDINATE: 111011-BN

An urgent request was received from a colleague, RK. He gave a coordinate 111011-BN and requested that this case be handled as soon as possible. The coordinate was sent out to the NRVG as a "blind" humanitarian tasking. There was no frontloading and there might be follow-up tasking. The viewers were requested to complete a remote viewing session up to Stage 4 or perceptions, plus sketches, from any other method were OK. A rapid turnaround was requested. The actual case involved a young lady who was taken from her car on the I-80; the family was "going nuts" not knowing where she was or what had happened to her.

ATS – ERV Perceptions.

As I didn't know the abducted girl's name, I called her "Honey" and went searching for her.

I found her, to my surprise, in a motel room. I don't know what time period; i.e. date I was able to contact her. She was locked in by key, so this is not a card-locked door. I asked her several times to talk to me, I asked her *"Honey, please talk to me."* She asked *"Mom, is that you?"* I told her "no", but she could talk to me.

Over a short period, she gave me the following information. By my time 10 a.m., she thought it was early evening her time, by the sun in the sky, sun was behind the motel so had already passed over-head. So, her room possibly faces easterly. There were no landmarks: mountains or tall buildings on the horizon. She doesn't know exactly where she is but thinks it is along the Gulf Coast/Florida coast. I perceived that stretch of the coastline in my minds-eye.

When she can look out of the window, she sees trucks in a parking lot. She is not permitted to look out the window and the curtains and a plastic solar curtain are kept closed. She was afraid to look out the window.

The location is a third-rate motel that is used by truckers. She hears crying coming from another room. She does not seem to be sick but locked into this room for long periods. There is no phone, to check the location, it was taken out. No identifying newspapers or other papers to identify the location or address.

I asked her to describe her captor: He is Puerto Rican, about 5' 10", wears regular clothes, jeans and black T-shirts. He has a gold stud in one ear (R?) and a glint of a gold tooth. He is slightly overweight but not obese. He does not speak much English. He smokes but not in the room, outside. He has a loose cough.

He often has another younger man with him who looks up to the older man. The younger man does not speak any English when he is in the room. She is not supposed to get off the bed except to go to the bathroom, when he is not there. She is not allowed to make any noise. I left her with a "virtual hug" and said I would try and locate her again.

I perceived that one male was no longer alive and perceived the following. Perceive it to be a male, young, 20s, dark hair, dressed casually. "Left behind." Lying on back. Nobody else around. However, don't see any blood on surface. "It was quick." "Hole in the head." He is dead or alive?

RK responded that it has been several months since the abduction. Also, that there had been "serial killers or killers that have hit 85 times in the past few years along the I-80." RK passed on the information to the authorities and there were some matches with the viewers' perceptions.

2012

JOURNALS

RV Contribution to the APA.

Around the same time Teresa Frisch decided to carry out a project for presentation to the American Psychological Association (APA). She first initiated a pilot project, sending out a coordinate to volunteers. I decided to participate as this was probably the first time that remote viewing had been presented to the APA. The first target was the Navy Pier in Chicago and I perceived quite a few correct elements. The target for the APA session was the Grand Hotel on Mackinac Island in Michigan and Teresa's work was presented at a poster session at the APA meeting. 2012

Journal - April 14, 2012 – *RV and Reiki.*

A couple of months ago I heard from Dr, Melvin Morse who had inherited a non-profit organization from Dr. Charles Tart: The Institute for the Scientific Study of Consciousness (ISSC). Dr. Morse had been working on a pilot project that incorporated Boyosan Reiki Ho, an original form of Reiki healing practice originated by Usui Sensei with Controlled Remote Viewing (CRV).

Dr. Morse invited me out to Delaware at the beginning of April to participate in a week of CRV combined with healing practices. Using a heuristic, exploratory process, the group got up to speed with the CRV protocols, up to Stage 6+ and then used Stage 4 to create a dialogue between the viewer and the "spirit" of several different patents' diseases and disorders.

The viewers worked "blind," having no prior contact with the patients or their medical records or diagnoses. The dialogues were discussed between the viewers and these were used as the basis for healing efforts which followed the viewings. Some of the patients were then available for hands-on-healing: polarity therapy, Reiki, and shamanic energy work, while others were worked on remotely.

250

In between, we had Skype contact with Mike Van Atta in Colorado who gave us a historic background on Reiki Ho – that asks that you see inside the patient before healing them. The patients who had received remote healing were then contacted by Skype, following the healing, for feedback, by remote viewers and patients.

During the week, we worked as a team: Dr. Melvin Morse, his organizer who is a polarity therapist; the site organizer and owner who is a healing oil practitioner; and a Reiki healer, a retired NASA engineer (who became the group's historian, recording the sessions).

We spent the week at a beach house at Rehoboth Beach, Delaware and we had a chance to take a few trips to see the nearby ocean, boardwalk, Gerar Lake behind the house, and an evening ride around Delaware's small towns and light houses. I felt very bonded with the group and made several long-term friendships. Also, part of the group was Dr. Morse's wife and their two delightful young daughters!

I really felt that I was living the shamanic life: "seeing" and healing using CRV and drumming, calling on my power animals, and other spirit helpers for assistance including Usui Sensei, who came to help. All the wonderful results occurred during that week following the CRV/healing interventions.

Journal - April 15, 2012 – *Gold Prospecting.*

Earlier in March 2012, I had a client who was interesting in utilizing remote viewing to locate gold in Nevada. While the client was out "in the field" prospecting, grid dowsing was completed in Boulder City to locate specific areas that he could search. Later, when he was "on site" I was able to correctly identify two locations using Extended Remote Viewing (ERV) over the phone. ERV is a stream of consciousness method of remote viewing.

At the first location I perceived some land formations that the client was directly looking at, that resembled the shape of two butt-cheeks, with a wash or ravine between them, which turned out to be correct. Also, at another location, I perceived a tall, peaked mountain that was seen at his 2 p.m. direction. That is, if noon was directly in front of him, 2 p.m. would have been at a small angle to his right. He confirmed that this was also correct and that there was a verified gold mine on this mountain.

The client wanted me to go out with him into the desert to prospect for gold, using remote viewing "on site" but I have learned from experience that this does not work for me: there are too many distractions.

Journal - May 8, 2012 – *U. of Delaware Study.*

Recently I did a day of remote viewing research for Dr. Melvin Morse's group and the University of Delaware. (I later found out that this was not a formal request from the University but an inquiry from two grad students.) The grad students were working on a research project involving iron-rich cells which tended to either, die and clump together or to clump in long chains that clogged up waterways and water systems. Results of the research would be known in two years. This information was not given to the viewers until after the research was completed.

The viewers were given "blind" random coordinates, knowing nothing beforehand about the research and they completed three consecutive sessions focusing on the research and on potential research outcomes. I did my three sessions and felt I had good contact with the task.

The evening of the research, Dr. Morse called with some good news that the researchers felt the viewers had made good contact and related some potentially useful outcomes for their research. This was exciting! I was tired at the end of the research day but felt good that I had contributed to the research. (Eventually, Dr. Morse gave a talk about the research saying that the researchers would not let the results of the viewing be known, it was so accurate that other researchers could "jump the gun" and carry out similar research.)

Journal - May 8, 2012 – *Las Vegas Sun Magazine.*

About a week ago, I was contacted by Joe Schoenmann of the *Las Vegas Sun Magazine – City Life,* about doing an interview about the upcoming IRVA conference and my RV work. He was particularly interested in the *DJ Murder Case* that was published in the *Las Vegas Sun* and will be presented at the upcoming conference.

Joe had come out to Boulder City in 2006 and had written a very nice article about IRVA and the history of RV. He had decided, at that earlier time, to try remote viewing himself and did well! He included a write-up of his experiences in his *City Life* article. So, when Joe contacted me again, I agreed to the interview.

During the timing of the interview (he also interviewed Robert Knight, who's story is also intertwined with the story), the then current editor of *City Life,* tried to stop the story. Robert reported that someone outside the magazine also tried to kill the story – twice! However, leaders within the remote viewing community and others, including the LA detective on the DJ Case, stepped in and their interviews were included, and the article published. It turned out to be a very favorable and well-written article.

Journal - July 10, 2012 – *Colorado Fires Rain Dance.*

At the end of June, Colorado was having devastating wild fires particularly around the Colorado Springs area. They have been in a drought which has affected the wild fires. An anthropologist friend from Bristol, England posted a Facebook message to "shake your bones and dance to the Rain Gawds (Gods)" Soon there were thousands of people dancing and drumming for rain, around the world, at sunset, wherever they were!

The next day, the fires were still raging but someone posted a weather map that showed a small cloud circle over the Colorado Springs area, that deepened and extended and, a few days later, there was a rain storm, then the weather turned monsoonal and deluged Colorado!

I believe the group energy had an effect: our intention, intention, and ritual activity coupled with the emotion generated by the dancing and drumming. It shows how the intention and attention of thousands of people can have an effect. (This is not so far-fetched: researcher Dr. Roger Nelson once published a scientific paper showing that the intention of thousands of returning Princeton alumni, wanting a rain-free parade (the P-rade) created multiple dry days despite rain in nearby towns.)

Journal - September 12, 2012 – *Forecasting Stocks.*

Doing some financial forecasting work for a new client using a Google Data Sheets feature, six monthly forecasts for three dates for up to 63 different stocks. Frontloading is via ticker (stock) abbreviations but as I don't know stocks this does not contaminate my data. Realized that some days I am "working hard" and others "hardly working" but this works for me!

Journal - September 14, 2012 – *What is Time?*

I began the day, as I often do, logging onto a group of websites that feature 24-hour observation of African watering holes, where animals come to drink. Early morning, I watched an elephant herd at Djuma, located at Kruger National Park in South Africa. African time is nine hours ahead of Pacific-time, so I was watching the elephants at my local time, but it was afternoon already in Africa! The elephants were ahead of us in time and the question that crossed my mind was, *"What is time?"* I watched as some of the younger elephants at Djuma negotiated a climb over the earth dam wall, using various tactics: some sliding down; some sidling, all made it. It was raining at Djuma and the dam, that failed earlier this year and rebuilt, is gradually filling up. Such an amazing way to start the day!

Journal - September 17, 2012 – *UK Searches.*

Worked with a client over Skype for three, one-hour targets today to access the location of three UK targets: frontloading: ancient treasure, a Viking battlefield, and another area where a hoard of silver was potentially buried. The process was one that we had worked on before, the client accessing locations on Google Maps of the area of interest and creating a grid corresponding to the selected map portion. The client then scanned and emailed these grids to me. I would then use RV to assess the portion of the map, using the grid, for further investigation. I didn't get to see the maps and I did not know the locations, all I had to work with were the blank grids.

When the client received each grid, he would create a new grid that he would scan and send to me by email. We were going down to ground level, to narrow down the field. The client was pleased with my work and said that I had successfully located areas of interest. In fact, one of the maps overlapped the ocean and I was able to somehow avoid the ocean on the grid. I found the process interesting, but it was very labor and time intensive.

November 12, 2012 – *Sub-Atomic Particles.*

When my consulting income from my long-term client came to an end last December, I decided to accept any projects that came across my desk that weren't illegal, immoral or unethical! Consequently, I have had an amazing year! My income did not increase greatly but I participated in many interesting projects such as remote viewing the form and function of sub-atomic particles for a group of physicists.

December 8, 2012 – *End of Year Update.*

As we get nearer to the end of the year, I give thanks that I have survived another year. My policy of accepting new projects that came across my desk has proven interesting. I have had to turn down a couple of borderline unethical projects, but it has been an interesting year.

The highlight of the year was being able to complete and write-up the *Denver DJ* project as the case went through the courts. During the six years the case was in litigation, our group, the NRVG, was unable to talk about the details. The case has now been written up by the *Las Vegas Sun* and I appeared with Robert Knight, (the friend of the murdered man who initiated the case) on Coast-to-Coast. Since then, I have also presented the case at the International Remote Viewing Association (IRVA) conference.

Now, the NRVG has been working on the Amelia Earhart-Fred Noonan project and I hope to present this at next year's IRVA conference. Recently, a colleague gifted me with a two-night stay at the Green Valley Ranch Hotel and I used the time to present the Amelia results to a group. Our guest of honor was Mr. Al Letcher, who was the first to task me with the Amelia project back in 1998.

CASE FILES - 2012

ISSC.
PROJECT: Healing Study.
METHOD: Shamanism/CRV.
DATE: April 14th, 2012.
CLIENT: ISSC.
TYPE: Medical Intuitive.

Dr. Melvin Morse in Delaware inherited a non-profit organization from Dr. Charles Tart: The Institute for the Scientific Study of Consciousness (ISSC). Dr. Morse had been working on a pilot project that involved Boyosan Reiki Ho, an original form of Reiki healing practice, developed by Usui Sensei, along with Controlled Remote Viewing.

Dr Morse invited me out to Delaware at the beginning of April to participate in a week of CRV combined with healing practices. Using a heuristic, exploratory process I got the group "up to speed" with the CRV protocol, to Stage 6 Plus, and then used Stage 4 to create a dialog between the viewer and the "spirit" of several different patients' diseases and disorders. Viewers worked "blind": having no prior contact with the patient. Dr. Morse was the only one with knowledge of the patients and their medical records.

These dialogs were then discussed between the viewers and were then used as a basis for healing efforts that followed. For example: one healer offered polarity therapy, another hands-on Reiki, others various types of distant healing, including shamanic drumming and healing.

Keith Goldberg Murder Case.
PROJECT: Keith Goldberg.
METHOD: ERV.
DATE: July 3rd, 2012.
CLIENT: National Center for Missing Loved Ones.
TYPE: Missing Person.
TEAM: NRVG.

Keith Goldberg was a Las Vegas cab driver who was murdered in a "love triangle." Following the murder, his body was missing. A local group, The National Center for Missing Loved Ones contacted me, and seven viewers provided information to the organization. The consensus was that the body was hidden somewhere behind Sunrise Mountain and towards the Lake Mead National Park.

Unfortunately, the organization thought we would also be going out into the desert to look for the body, which we were not able (or authorized) to do and we had to educate the group on the logistics and limitations of remote viewing. The Group saw the body in a drainage ditch in standing water, covered with a blue tarp.

The body was eventually located about a year later. The National Park Service was reluctant to let a search organization go into the park to search for the body, making them buy insurance first which they couldn't afford, but they did eventually find the body and brought closure to the case. To date we have not been able to find information about the exact location of the body.

Electron Study.
PROJECT: Geography of an Electron.
METHOD: CRV/ERV.
DATE: July 5th, 2012.
CLIENT: Private Physics Lab
TYPE: Physics Exploration.

I never know what new projects are coming across my desk: missing people, business matters, or treasure hunting, but the one from a physics lab was fascinating. I had read how early remote viewers had successfully "looked" at the cell structures of plants. The current project was to remote view the geography inside and outside of an atom and how all the parts worked together!

The researcher was happy with my work. He wrote: "As far as feedback; I'd rate this session a 10 on a scale of 1 to 10. 100% of the information correlates to what we intuit and is helpful."

2013

JOURNALS

Since completing my contract with our major, long-term client at the end of 2011, the past two years have been an exciting time – going it alone and generating new interest in the RV community. After receiving a monthly retainer from our patron, bringing in enough funds to maintain Mindwise Consulting has been a challenge!

At the beginning of 2012, I made a commitment that whatever remote viewing projects came across my desk, if they were ethical and legal, I would accept them. I made the same commitment at the beginning of 2013 and will do the same for 2014 and onwards.

However, I haven't done it alone: far from it, I have had the support and backing of the RV community, particularly members of the Nevada Remote Viewing Group (NRVG). These dedicated, volunteer remote viewers, who ask for no publicity, who give of their time and abilities (even though most have demanding day jobs) must receive my thanks! When I send out a call for volunteers, not all this unstructured group responds, but those that can, do. They know that, whenever possible, the cases will be relevant, provide closure for the people involved, and may even save lives. They are like a volunteer firefighting team: they have the wish to help the community, have trained and practiced for these events and, afterwards, move back into society to their regular day jobs. They receive feedback whenever possible, even if it is bad news, and they grow as operational remote viewers.

2012 and 2013 have seen the expansion of my remote viewing explorations: looking back into the past with cases such as the search for Amelia Earhart; predictive work into the future, looking at what might be in store for us over the coming decades; down to the basest elements of matter, beyond the subatomic level; and out into the deepest reaches of space. There are no limits to where remote viewing can be applied. I am excited to see what comes across my desk in 2014 and beyond!

Journal January 4, 2013 – *New Year Update.*
2012 has come and gone with some interesting new clients and projects from across the country. When my long-term retainer stopped,

I knew I had to bring in some additional income. I had considered moving to Delaware, but this is not on the books for 2013. Last year was a fascinating time of trying new projects and, hopefully, 2013 will bring in more of the same.

Journal February 12, 2013 - *Wow, Time Flies!*

Last year was a time of "belt-tightening," "hunkering down" with less income and work coming in than previous years but 2013 seems a lot brighter.

Last summer, I decided to post some of the Exobiology Interviews that I had completed for my long-term client and looked around for a suitable venue. The Exobiology Interviews were ET interviews that were commissioned by my client back in 2006. Over a period of a year we interviewed (via a form of remote viewing protocol that included telepathy) many different races. The project was dropped at the end of 2006 to return to business-related remote viewing. The client and I had planned on writing a book together.

After several fruitless inquiries, I finally had the good fortune to hear from Donald Ware, who decided to post the Interviews out to his 600+ email list. I posted the Interviews incognito, at first, to see what the response would be. The Interviews were posted weekly until all had been posted and the response from Don's group was very positive. Among this group was an old friend, C. B. Scott Jones Ph.D., and he suggested that we write a book together that would include the Interviews! So, for the remainder of 2013 and into 2014, Scott and I have been writing, editing, and creating a book together; *Voices from the Cosmos*.

POSTSCRIPT

This book is entitled *30 Years of Remote Viewing ...and Counting*, for a reason. There is more! Now in 2019, the potential to continue working in the remote viewing field is increasing. One of the reasons for writing this book was to answer a question that is often asked by my remote viewing students: "What is there to do after training?"

What indeed! I hope this book answers that question. Students must remain aware of potential projects, clients, and customers need to become educated to just what remote viewing can and cannot do; researchers need to step outside the lab and recognize that, at some point, research needs to be augmented by applications work. I believe it is with applications that the true strength of remote viewing will be shown.

In my spiritual practice, I am expected to be "of service to my community" and that community can be worldwide. This is the concept of Kuleana – "being of service". However, it does not mean taking every case, every project, or taking on the responsibility that others need to take for themselves.

While I was re-editing this book for publication, I was encouraged to continue it up to 2019. That will have to wait for a later edition! For now, I have just made some editing changes to the current edition.

As remote viewers we often "do the impossible" yet need to remain professional and centered. Being a remote viewer is a great privilege and responsibility; undertake it with joy, with energy and with compassion.

About the Author.

ANGELA THOMPSON SMITH, PhD.

Angela Smith has worked in the US as a medical researcher, research coordinator. As an instructor for the University of Nevada. A remote viewing trainer and as a research contractor for individuals, businesses and organizations around the United States and abroad. Angela Smith describes her life as taking place in three parts: first working as a nurse, social worker, and medical researcher in the U.K. and the U.S.; the second part of her career focused on human psychology when she worked at the PEAR Lab at Princeton University. NJ and studied for a graduate degree in psychology at Saybrook University, CA; and in the third part of her life, after decades of study and experience, Dr. Smith was ordained as a shamanic practitioner. She is an author with multiple published books. Currently Angela works as a remote viewing trainer and consultant, life coach and writer in Boulder City, NV.

Contact Information: mindwiseconsulting@gmail.com
www.mindwiseconsulting.com

Printed in Great Britain
by Amazon

32156967R00145